HIGHER

ENGLISH

SECOND EDITION

Jane Cooper

DYNAMIC LEARNING

HODDER
GIBSON
AN HACHETTE UK COMPANY

With thanks to the staff and pupils of Firrhill High School, especially Cara Pullar and Keri Millar.

The Publishers would like to thank the following for permission to reproduce copyright material:

Photo credits p.49 © The National Trust Photolibrary/Alamy; **p.62** © jeremyculpdesign/Fotolia **p.75** © STAN HONDA/AFP/Getty Images; **p.78** (top) © Everett Collection Historical/Alamy; (bottom) © Allstar Picture Library/Alamy; **p.112** (left) © Facebook; (middle) © Twitter' (right) © Pinterest 2018; **p.118** © GL Portrait/Alamy; **p.125** © Martin Godwin/The Guardian; **p.160** © TSPL/Writer Pictures; **p.170** (top) © Marcel Schauer/stock.adobe.com; (bottom) © Arthur Schatz/Life Magazine/The LIFE Picture Collection/Getty Images

Acknowledgements pp.21–2 Extract from *Mortal Causes* © 1994 Ian Rankin, reproduced with the permission of Orion Publishing Group and Rogers, Coleridge & White, literary agency; **pp.22–3** Extract from *The Big Over Easy: A Nursery Crime* by Jasper Fforde © Jasper Fforde 2005, reproduced by permission of Hodder and Stoughton Limited and Viking Books, an imprint of Penguin Publishing Group, a division of Penguin Random House LLC. All rights reserved.; **pp.38, 39, 40, 47** Extracts from *Touching the Void* by Joe Simpson, published by Jonathan Cape, reprinted by permission of The Random House Group Limited © 1988 and HarperCollins US; **pp.41–2** Extract from *The Reading Promise: My Father and the Books We Shared* by Alice Ozma, copyright © 2011, 2012. Reprinted by permission of John Murray Press, a division of Hodder and Stoughton Limited, and Grand Central Publishing, an imprint of Hachette Book Group, Inc.; **pp.68–70** 'Vegetarians With Teeth' from *Hugh Fearlessly Eats It All*, by Hugh Fearnley-Whittingstall, reproduced with kind permission of Bloomsbury Publishing plc; **pp.82, 86, 88** Extracts from Sandi Toksvig: 'Today we can all celebrate whom we choose to love' © Guardian News & Media Ltd 2014 and Rogers, Coleridge & White, literary agency; **pp.104–7** Extract adapted from 'Skype and cheap calls give an illusion of closeness, but homesickness is still real' by Ian Jack © Guardian News & Media Ltd 2013; **pp.111–14** Extract adapted from 'Conscious computing: how to take control of your life online' by Oliver Burkeman © Guardian News & Media Ltd 2013; **pp.118–20, 128** Extract from 'Textual healing', Sunday Herald, 2013, reproduced by permission of Liz Lochhead; **pp.124–6** Extract adapted from 'Dry bars — is England sobering up?' by John Harris © Guardian News & Media Ltd 2014; **pp.129–31** Extract adapted from 'The new boom in home tuition' by Daniel H. Cohen © Guardian News & Media Ltd 2013; **pp.134–5** Extract from 'Recline and fall: if you tilt your seat back, I'll steal your dessert' by Alex Hern © Guardian News & Media Ltd 2013; **pp.137–9** Extract from 'What's happened to home cooking?' by Genevieve Fox © Guardian News & Media Ltd 2013; **pp.vii, 142–4** Extracts adapted from 'Why I can no longer face tutoring the progeny of the rich and aspirational' © Guardian News & Media Ltd 2013; **pp.148–9** Extract from 'Swedish cinemas take aim at gender bias with Bechdel test rating' © Associated Press 2013/Wright's Media; **pp.150–1** Extract from 'Cinema programmers beware: feminist films can flunk the Bechdel test' © Guardian News & Media Ltd 2013; **pp.153–5** Extract from 'Do you work more than 39 hours a week? Your job could be killing you' by Peter Fleming © Guardian News & Media Ltd 2013, **p.155–7** Extract from '"Heck it was productive": New Zealand employees try four-day week' by Eleanor Ainge-Roy © Guardian News & Media 2013; **p.161** 'Brooklyn Cop' from *The Many Days: Selected Poems of Norman MacCaig* by Norman MacCaig, Birlinn, 2010. Reproduced with permission of the Licensor through PLSclear; **p.168** 'Hotel Room, 12th Floor' from *The Many Days: Selected Poems of Norman MacCaig* by Norman MacCaig, Birlinn, 2010. Reproduced with permission of the Licensor through PLSclear.

SQA material is reproduced by permission, copyright © Scottish Qualifications Authority.

Every effort has been made to trace all copyright holders, but if any have been inadvertently overlooked, the Publishers will be pleased to make the necessary arrangements at the first opportunity.

Although every effort has been made to ensure that website addresses are correct at the time of going to press, Hodder Gibson cannot be held responsible for the content of any website mentioned in this book. It is sometimes possible to find a relocated web page by typing in the address of the home page for a website in the URL window of your browser.

Hachette UK's policy is to use papers that are natural, renewable and recyclable products made from wood grown in well-managed forests and other controlled sources. The logging and manufacturing processes are expected to conform to the environmental regulations of the country of origin.

Orders: please contact Bookpoint Ltd, 130 Park Drive, Milton Park, Abingdon, Oxon OX14 4SE.
Telephone: (44) 01235 827827. Fax: (44) 01235 400454. Lines are open 9.00–5.00, Monday to Saturday, with a 24-hour message answering service. Visit our website at www.hoddereducation.co.uk. Hodder Gibson can be contacted directly at: hoddergibson@hodder.co.uk

© Jane Cooper 2019

First published in 2015 © Jane Cooper
This second edition published in 2019 by
Hodder Gibson, an imprint of Hodder Education
An Hachette UK company
211 St Vincent Street
Glasgow G2 5QY

Impression number	5	4	3	2	1
Year	2023	2022	2021	2020	2019

Cover photo © Andrea Izzotti stock.adobe.com

Illustrations by Barking Dog Art

Typeset in 13/15 pt Bembo Regular by Integra Software Services Pvt. Ltd., Pondicherry, India

Printed in Italy

A catalogue record for this title is available from the British Library

ISBN 978 1 5104 5772 0

MIX
Paper from responsible sources
FSC
www.fsc.org
FSC™ C104740

Contents

Introduction

The Higher course gives you many opportunities to display your English skills. Your spoken English will be assessed in class; you will also send away a portfolio of your writing and you will sit an exam at the end of the course.

All these different assessments give you an opportunity to become more skilled in the four key areas of English: *reading, writing, talking* and *listening*. As you progress through the course, you will have chances to work with literature, with language and perhaps also with media.

You might be in a class where some pupils are working towards Higher while other pupils in the same class are working towards National 5. Some pupils might start off aiming for Higher but realise that it is a better idea to sit National 5 this year. The courses have the same structure, allowing pupils to change to National 5 if they need to.

One part of the course is **internally** assessed. You will be assessed on your use of spoken language, either through group discussion or by giving a presentation.

This will be assessed in school by your teacher. Your spoken work will not be graded, but you will know if you have achieved the standard or not.

Some parts of the course are **externally** assessed:

- You will send away a **portfolio** of two pieces of writing to be marked by someone outside of your own school.
- You will also sit an **exam** (sometimes called the **Question Paper**) that assesses different aspects of your reading skills. One of the tasks will test your ability to read a piece of non-fiction you have never seen before, under exam conditions, and answer questions on it. You will also answer questions on a set Scottish text that you have studied in class, and you will write a critical essay about a different text you have studied in class.

Planning your time

Your Higher exam will probably be in early May and your school is likely to give you some time off for study before and during the exams. But, if you only start revising then, you're leaving it far too late.

You'll have about two weeks off school for Easter, a month or so before the exam. But, if you only start revising then, you're still leaving it a bit too late.

The most effective way to get all your knowledge and learning fixed in your head is to do a little tiny bit of revision every single day, all the way through your Higher course.

When you get home each afternoon, review what you've done in class. Read any notes you've taken or answers you've written, and re-read any notes or handouts your teacher has given you. If your teacher has given you back any assessed work, look at how he or she has marked it and at any comments written on it.

Doing all this will help to fix the learning in your brain. Also, if there's something there you don't understand, or if you seem to have missed something out, you can go back to your teacher the next day and ask about it.

At the weekend you should do something similar. Read over everything new that you've done that week. It should feel more familiar now.

If you get in the habit of working like this, not only will you be painlessly filling your brain with knowledge, but the exam, and the revision for it, will feel much less daunting. This advice, of course, works for every subject, not just English.

To help you to see as clearly as possible that you are covering all the skills and tasks you are meant to tackle, this book is arranged in chapters that go with each key element of Higher English. Don't panic if that's not quite how your teacher tackles your course. Because English is often about gradually improving skills rather than acquiring chunks of knowledge, your teacher may teach you something, or give you an activity, or get you to complete a task or challenge, in such a way that you are acquiring or improving a skill and then showing that you've done so.

So, here are some questions that you should be able to answer about any piece of work you do in English this year:

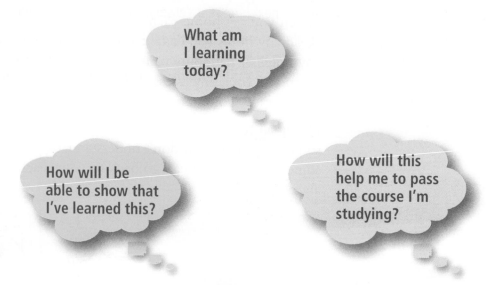

If you don't understand what you are doing, or why you are doing it, (very politely!) ask your teacher.

How to use this book

Every chapter of the book covers something you will be assessed on and will make clear what is being assessed. Each chapter will help you learn how to pass these assessments.

One phrase comes up very often. It is mentioned in almost all of the tasks and assessments. We are going to look at this now.

Detailed and complex language

At Higher level, you are expected to be able to understand, and use, 'detailed and complex language'. You need to know what this means.

Active learning

Work with a partner. Together, read over the following passage. It is written in detailed and complex language.

> Working as a private tutor nowadays is a bit like being a confiseur for Marie Antoinette: no matter how much you spin the sugar into a confection about feeding society, you're really just making life sweeter for the rich. And I should know, having taught a predominantly wealthy elite for over a decade.
>
> A decade into the most thorough economic malaise since the Great Depression, and amid more cuts than you'd find on a straight-to-DVD movie, it should come as scant wonder that one of the few boom industries is private education. In the strata of the recession-proof uber-rich, the private tutor can often appear as simply the next human accessory, summoned before the court to perform.
>
> Yet in a society plagued by the disease of aspiration, it's no longer just about the very rich. Salaried and striving parents are queuing up to fuel the boom in a market valued in excess of £6bn a year, hyperventilating that their kids are being left behind as an already unequal form of education plunges into something that would make the feudal system look like the dictatorship of the proletariat.

You might need to read the extract more than once. When you are ready, answer these questions to show you understand the idea of detailed and complex language:

- What do you notice about the lengths of sentences?
- What do you notice about the number of sentences?
- What do you notice about the vocabulary?
- What do you notice about the writer's ideas?
- What did you notice about the writer's style and techniques?

Try to get used to spotting detailed and complex language. You will find it in newspapers like the *Guardian*, *The Times*, the *Herald* and the *Scotsman*. You will hear it in some television programmes (such as *Newsnight*) and in some programmes on BBC Radio 4.

CHAPTER 1 The Writing Portfolio

You have already learned that much of your Higher English is externally assessed — marked by someone outside your school. You will sit an exam. The different parts of this are covered in Chapters 3, 4 and 5. You will also submit a writing portfolio, which you will learn about in this chapter.

Your **writing portfolio** is worth 30 marks, which also makes it 30% of your total mark for Higher. You will produce **two** pieces of writing, each marked out of 15. These pieces will come from different genres. The portfolio will then be sent away to the SQA to be marked.

You will complete your portfolio by building on skills you have already developed earlier in school, particularly in the National 5 course where you produced a similar portfolio.

It may take you most of your Higher year to get the portfolio together. You may wish to try the different sorts of writing taught here at different times, and to produce a number of different first drafts before you decide, with help from your teacher, which two are best and should be redrafted for the portfolio. You cannot produce multiple redrafts of the same piece; each piece can be written once, marked, and then redrafted for final submission. That's it!

Here's an idea that you may not have thought about:

YOU CAN'T BE A WRITER IF YOU AREN'T A READER.

Pupils, even Higher English pupils, sometimes say, 'I don't like reading.' English teachers really can't understand that sentence. To an English teacher, saying 'I don't like reading' is as bizarre as saying 'I don't like people' or 'I don't like food.' The world is so full of things to read, there must be *something* out there that you'd like. And:

YOU CAN'T BE A WRITER IF YOU AREN'T A READER.

After all, you wouldn't join an orchestra if you'd never listened to any music in your life. You wouldn't decide to become a chef if you'd only ever eaten toast.

There's plenty of advice about particular types of writing throughout this chapter, but remember:

YOU'LL NEVER BE A WRITER IF YOU AREN'T A READER.

What you will be assessed on

In both of your pieces, the markers will be looking at two particular areas of your writing skill: your **content** and your **style**.

- Your piece should have the right **content**. This means that you will stick to your chosen **purpose** and write something that fits your chosen audience. You will be skilled at writing in your chosen genre.
- **Style** includes being able to use the features of your chosen genre skillfully. Your word choice and expression will be confident and varied. The structure of your piece will enhance its **purpose** and meaning.

To meet the requirements for a mark of 7 or more out of 15, you must also show consistent **technical accuracy**. This is a measure of how well you use the English language. Your paragraphs, sentences, spelling and punctuation will be mostly accurate, with very few errors, so that your writing is easily understood.

There are more particular assessment guidelines for each genre of writing. You will find these in the sections of this chapter that deal with those genres.

 Warning

The next few pages are going to contain lots of information about the course requirements for writing. Don't panic. You don't have to try to memorise all of this. As you read it over, just make sure you understand everything. You can check back to these pages at any time to make sure that you are following the rules and guidelines properly.

What you can write

Your portfolio should contain two pieces in two different genres. One piece should be what the SQA calls 'broadly creative', which means that you can produce any one of these types of writing to fulfil the requirements for this genre:

- a personal or reflective essay
- a piece of prose fiction
- a poem or a set of linked poems
- a dramatic script.

Later in this chapter you will learn more about two of these styles: prose fiction and personal writing. There is a limit to what this book can cover, but do look at again at the list above and at the other types of writing mentioned. Pupils often write successful poetry, drama scripts and monologues, and your teacher may give you an opportunity to try these types of writing too, or instead.

The second portfolio piece should be what the SQA calls 'broadly discursive', which means that you can produce any one of these types of writing to fulfil the requirements for this genre:

- an argumentative essay
- a persuasive essay
- a report
- a piece of transactional or informative writing.

Later in this chapter you will learn about the first two of these styles: argumentative and persuasive.

Length

Your portfolio pieces should each be no more than 1300 words long. This does not mean you have to write 1299 words to please the marker. A shorter piece can earn a high mark if it is well written and meets the criteria. However, if your piece is a lot shorter, it may not be the sort of developed work that Higher markers want to see. If your piece is too long, you may be rambling, and if you go over by more than 10% (in other words, if you write more than 1430 words), marks will be taken off.

Your title, any footnotes and any bibliography or list of sources are not counted. If your piece contains quotations, these are regarded as part of the word count.

Authenticity

Because your portfolio is worth 30% of your marks, quite a sizeable chunk of the entire Higher course, it is vital that the SQA can be sure that every pupil is working in the same way and under the same conditions, so that marking can be fair. Your portfolio has to be your own work, and at Higher level you are not allowed to have too much support or detailed input from your teacher.

You will work on your portfolio under what the SQA calls 'some supervision and control'. This is a way of saying that your teacher should always know that the work is entirely your own. There are various ways your teacher can be sure of this: you might be asked to keep a checklist of your work, and will certainly be asked for a list of sources you consult. Many schools get pupils to write first drafts in class, which is a good way for your teacher to be sure the work is yours.

What you can do	What you can't do
Benefit from teaching that extends your knowledge, understanding and appreciation of a range of genres	Rely heavily on ideas or wording that you found in a printed or electronic source
Use printed or electronic sources to find background information or ideas	**What your teacher can't do**
Use a dictionary, spell-checker or thesaurus	Give you detailed notes, or a specific plan, or a model so detailed that you wouldn't be coming up with your own structure
Discuss your topic and/or ideas with your teacher as part of your planning	Pick out and correct mistakes in your expression or your technical accuracy
Be given written comments on your first draft and discuss that draft with your teacher	Give you detailed advice about how to re-structure or re-word your first draft
Be given broad suggestions for how to improve your first draft	Read, mark or give feedback on **more than one draft** of the same piece

This might all sound very detailed and strict. You can check back at these regulations at any point in your work. Remember that their overall purpose is to get you to do what you should want to do anyway — to use your own ideas to write your own piece that shows your own interests and abilities.

Sources

You'll probably need to refer to outside sources as your write your discursive piece. These must be acknowledged.

- If you have used a newspaper or magazine article, give the title of the piece and the publication, name the writer and give the publication date.
- If you use information from the internet, give the name of the site and the specific page address.

- If you quote from a book, give the page number, title, author, publisher and publication date.
- Any quotations should be inside quotation marks.
- You **absolutely cannot, ever** copy and paste, or retype, exact wording from a website or from anywhere else and pass it off as your own work.

Drafting and redrafting

All real writing is drafted and redrafted. However, because your Higher portfolio is a test of how well you can write, and to make sure that everyone is being tested fairly, you are only allowed to produce one first draft and one final redraft of each piece you submit. You will find more advice about drafts and redrafts at the end of this chapter.

Well done! You've made it through the pages of rules and guidelines. Did you understand it all as you read it? Remember that you can refer back to these pages at any time. In fact you should keep coming back to these pages and double checking that you are following the rules.

Technical accuracy

You have already read that your portfolio work must show consistent technical accuracy. Your paragraphs, sentences, spelling and punctuation should be mostly accurate, with very few errors.

This book cannot teach you technical accuracy. There just isn't space. If you have difficulties with using language in this way, your teacher will certainly notice this and can recommend other books or exercises you can use.

What we can do here is prove to ourselves that technical accuracy matters. It changes meaning. Look at this sentence:

He baked an extra, large cake.

It tells us that a male person, who had been baking cake, made one more cake and that this additional cake was large.

However, if you change the punctuation, you get this:

He baked an extra-large cake.

Which suggests what you see in the picture.

The writer of this book once received some publicity from a company in which she had invested a lot of money. At the top of the page it said:

Were here to help you!

Can you explain why the writer didn't feel reassured? What went wrong with the company's use of punctuation?

Active learning

Work your way through the following tasks. Each one demonstrates how important technical accuracy is in affecting meaning.

1 Look at the following sentences. Draw a cartoon to illustrate each one, so that you show the difference in meaning.

> Careful! Children crossing
>
> Careful children crossing

2 At the start of Shakespeare's *Macbeth*, a wounded soldier tells King Duncan about a battle. These are the words the king says about this soldier after he has listened to the report:

> Go, get him surgeons.

What does the king want his staff to do?

Now, imagine the sentence had been punctuated like this:

> Go get him, surgeons!

What does it mean now?

Read the two different versions out aloud so that your tone and pace show the different meanings.

3 Look at the following sentences. Draw a cartoon to illustrate each one, so that you show the difference in meaning.

> This is Andrew. Who could be more attractive?
>
> This is Andrew, who could be more attractive.

4 You go to stay in a small hotel. Which is the right version of the sign on one of the doors?

> RESIDENTS LOUNGE

OR

> RESIDENTS' LOUNGE

What does the wrong version mean?

5 Look at the following sentences. Explain what each means.

> The factory made boys' and girls' toys.
>
> The factory made boys, and girls' toys.

6 Read these two sentences. Both use all the same letters and words in the same order; it is just the punctuation that has changed. Can you explain the two very different meanings?

> Let's eat, Grandma.
>
> Let's eat Grandma!

You might be thinking that some of those examples were pretty silly, and they were, but that's the point. Technical errors can weaken otherwise stylish and skillful writing, so you have to learn not to make them.

Ideally, you will be a skilled enough user of language that you don't make a lot of mistakes as you write. You should also be able to check over your own writing before you hand it in to your teacher, and to notice and correct any errors. If your teacher still finds mistakes when he or she marks your work, you should be able to correct these.

Many schools use a correction code. Teachers put these marks in the margin, to show that there is a mistake on that line of work. Here's one example of a correction code.

sp	spelling	^	something missing
caps	mistake in use of capitals	**rep**	repetition
S	sentence error	✓	something good
NP	new paragraph	**exp**	not clearly expressed
p	punctuation mistake	**?**	what does this say?

Active learning

You are going to see an example of work which a teacher has marked using the correction code.

1 Identify each specific mistake the pupil has made.

2 Correct the mistakes.

caps	Safely tucked Up In Bed
sp	I vividly recall that day I babysat for my cosins. The older one,
	Katie, was at Brownies, leaving me and five-year-old Connor to play
	games until she returned.
S	When I arrived I was greeted by a shy little Peter Pan Connor
	was, as usual, wearing one of the many fantastic costumes he owns.
exp	He keeps them in a wooden toy box that sits against the wall his dad
p	painted for him four years ago. Connor loves that box. Its one of
✓	the few things he has to remind him of his dad.
	As I smiled warmly at him, he declared, 'You have been taken
NP	prisoner!' 'This'll be interesting,' I thought. Little did I realise I'd
	be spending the next half hour tied up with Katie's skipping
	rope as her little brother hurled plastic tat at me.

By the way, if any of your writing contained as many mistakes as that extract, you would certainly not meet the standard for technical accuracy in your portfolio pieces.

Active learning

Read the next part of the piece. Decide where the teacher would mark errors. What would the teacher write in the margin each time?

'Stop chucking toys' I yelled, as a Barbie narrowly missed poking my eye out. Connor stopped lobbing and insisted quietly, 'They are cannonballs!' Nevertheless I managed to untie myself and get him to help me tidy up. I wrestled him into a firemans lift and he squeeled and wriggled as I carried him up the stairs, threatening to tickle him if he didn't get straight into his pyjamas.

This was actually a fairly easy task as over the month or too since I had started babysitting the children had learned to get changed when I told them to. In fact they are always very well behaved when i look after them. They are always good when I'm in charge.

Occasionally Connor and Katie will mention their dad in passing conversations, such as, 'I have sums to do tonight.' PAUSE 'Daddy was good at sums.' This never fails to make my throat tighten. I still get angry that two young, innocent children could lose their dad so suddenly.

They were both still under five years old when my uncle had a major heart attack and didn't recover, my auntie was in her late thirties and my uncle David was only thirty-seven. He was perfectly fit and healthy, led an active life, and loved his family more than anyone else I know. I think that's why, when we got the phone call, I couldn't believe the bad news. It still seems so unfair. Remembering times I spent with him makes me think about how I saw him — a tall, strong, clever man who never failed to make people laugh I always looked up to him.

As the kids grow up they remind me more and more of dad. Connor looks like him in every way and Katie has his bright eyes and sharp mind.

Now that we've worked through all this, let's move on to the fun part, the writing itself.

At the start of the chapter we saw that the SQA wants you to write in two different broad genres, **creative** and **discursive**, and that these break down into various types. There isn't space in this book to deal with every possible genre of writing, but we will look at the four that most pupils are most likely to want to write: **prose fiction** and personal writing from the creative genre; and **argumentative** and **persuasive writing** from the discursive genre.

Prose fiction

You already know that the marker will be looking at the **content** of your writing. When you write prose fiction, your writing should show strong creative qualities and a skilful command of the genre. The marker will also be assessing your **style**. This means you should use features of your chosen genre to create impact on the reader. Your expression will be confident and varied. Keep this in mind as you work through this part of the chapter.

There are many different forms of imaginative writing, including poetry, description and all sorts of script for stage and screen. However most Higher pupils who tackle imaginative writing do this by creating a piece of prose fiction.

The wide genre of prose fiction includes all short stories and all novels. However we can often tell that the fiction we are reading belongs to a more particular genre. For example, George R.R. Martin and J.R.R. Tolkien's books belong in the fantasy genre; Hilary Mantel and Philippa Gregory both write historical novels. Each genre has its own rules and conventions (the way things usually happen) and these can be very helpful for writers.

Active learning

Work with a partner or small group. Make a list of all the fiction genres you can think of. Next, share your answers with the whole class and build up a bigger list.

In this chapter, we are going to find out about one particular genre: **crime fiction**. You may have heard of Ian Rankin, Anne Cleeves, Val McDermid, Jo Nesbo and Peter May, who write in this genre. The makers of television programmes love this genre too.

Going deeper

The rest of this part of the chapter is going to be about writing crime fiction. It will prepare you to write the first chapter of a crime novel as a possible portfolio piece.

If you choose to do this, the chapter will give you examples, advice and support. But you can, of course choose to do something different:

- You might research the conventions of a different fiction genre and write an opening chapter in that genre instead.
- You might write a short story that fits a particular, different, genre rather than writing an opening chapter.

- You might write a story very much focused on a character dealing with an issue or problem in their life: feedback from Higher examiners tells us that pupils often write well about young people dealing with the challenges of life.
- You might use the classic structure of a short story, building up action from an initiating incident towards a climax and final resolution. (If your school has the book *National 4 & 5 English* by Jane Cooper, you can read much more about this in the chapter on the National 5 writing portfolio. All the advice is there, although as a Higher pupil you would need to write a more sophisticated story.)

Active learning

Work with a partner or small group.

- Make a list of all the crime writers you can think of.
- Now list all the television programmes you can think of that are about crime or detection.

Next, share your answers with the whole class and build up a bigger list.

Don't panic. You're not going to be asked to write a whole novel. You're just going to write the first chapter.

Active learning

Work with a partner or small group. Make a list of answers to this question:

What do you think a writer needs to do in the first chapter of a novel? (Don't think specifically about crime novels for the moment, just list what you think every novelist should do at the start of their book.)

Next, share your answers with the whole class and build up a bigger list.

Active learning

Work again with your partner or small group. Make a list of answers to this question:

What particular things do you think a writer needs to do in the first chapter of a crime novel?

Next, share your answers with the whole class and build up a bigger list.

Read the following text. It's just the first two pages of a book, not the whole chapter.

Beware of the Dogwalkers

'We should just round up all the dogwalkers.'

'Ma'am?'

'The dogwalkers. Haven't you noticed it's always them who finds one of these? Very suspicious if you ask me.'

'Quite, ma'am. Anyway, what would you like me to do?' Perhaps this was just the DCI's little joke. It was P.C. Harry Stevens' first murder, but he'd heard that officers who saw this kind of thing all the time developed a sort of black humour, a coping mechanism.

'Bring me the dogwalker,' said DCI Heather Barnes wearily. 'Just the one dogwalker. The one who found her.'

'Certainly, ma'am.' Stevens began scrambling up the slope away from the burn and towards the footpath at the top where a shaky-looking middle-aged woman was sitting on a fallen log. She was clutching her spaniel as if it might bring her some comfort — unlikely, as the dog was too busy yapping at the growing crowd. How could a crowd form in a place like this? Stevens liked cities, bars, and shops. To him this pathway at the edge of a village might as well have been the Gobi desert, but a crowd was forming nonetheless. Already he could see three other uniforms, two bio-suited members of the MO's team and a local television news crew. News crews were bad news.

Heather Barnes knew this too. 'And get rid of that camera crew!' Stevens heard her yell as he approached the dog lady.

The body was lying, as in Heather's memory they always seemed to, half buried. The dog had scurried through the leaves in its excitement and she couldn't be sure how much it might have disturbed the scene. The MO's men should be able to tell her. 'I'm sorry,' she said to the dead girl. 'I will find out who did this.' It was what she always said to the dead.

At the top of the slope, Harry Stevens was wishing he felt more authoritative. 'I must ask you to step back and cease filming. You'll have an opportunity to ask the DCI any questions you like at a proper briefing later.' The few minutes he'd spent with the dead girl seemed to have made him smaller and quieter and the news crew weren't really paying him much attention.

'Just a couple minutes. Yeah? Local colour? Early reactions?' The reporter was wearing a slightly too shiny suit under his slightly too red anorak. His wellingtons worried Stevens most of all. The man was keen. Any minute now he might head off down the slope towards the boss.

Impatient at last with waiting for the walker to be brought to her, Heather Barnes was on her way back up the slope, having left the body with the team in the white suits. She made straight for the reporter. 'Mr Morton. You have an amazing instinct for these sorry scenes.'

'Just doing my job, Heather. People have a right to know when there's a maniac on the loose.'

'MISTER Morton,' she said firmly. 'We are at the very early stages of what will be a complex investigation …'

'So you're saying you won't be able to find this guy quickly?'

'I'm saying,' she said through gritted teeth, 'that it is far too early for you to be using words like loose and maniac, or even assuming that we are looking for a guy.'

'So you have no leads whatsoever? Viewers will find that very disturbing.'

'A discovery has been made Mr Morton. At this stage I am unprepared to say more.'

'But it's a girl isn't it?' persisted the reporter. 'And she's been murdered.'

Heather had had enough. 'Mr Morton you are not helping. In fact you are actually stopping me at this moment from doing my job at all. I need to interview the woman who found the body.'

'So you're at least prepared to confirm that the girl's dead then? Not just sleeping?'

'Enough, Morton.'

As she walked off, the reporter turned to his cameraman. 'Anything we can use?'

'Not much. But I did get a little sound clip earlier on when I was setting up the levels. Something odd that DCI said to her PC. You should take a listen.'

Active learning

Do you want to add anything to your list of what you think a crime writer needs to do in his or her first chapter?

Now read the rest of Chapter 1 of *Beware of the Dogwalkers*.

Heather was in the incident room when she saw that night's news. It started well. The staged press conference was clear and brisk. She could see herself putting across the facts: a dead body, that of a woman probably in her late teens, had been found by a local person. Early indications were that the victim had been lying there for less than twelve hours. Residents were asked to report anything that might be significant to the investigation. Police were especially hoping to hear from anyone who was worried about a missing friend or relative as this might help to identify the deceased.

All of that was fine. The next item was more of a problem. A number of animal welfare groups, the Kennel Club and the local chapter of the Association of Professional Dogwalkers and Petsitters had all joined together to issue a strongly-worded statement. They utterly condemned the suggestion that the killer might have been a dogwalker.

This called for an exceptionally strong coffee. The pot that held the proper stuff was empty, as usual. Nowhere in the serious crime manual did it say who was in charge of the coffee pot, so it was always empty. Heather reached into her desk drawer and found a jar with about half an inch of granules solidified at the bottom. Poking them with a fork — there was no sign of a spoon either — did no good. Sighing, Heather tipped boiling water straight from the kettle into the jar, screwed the lid on, and was shaking it vigorously when the Super strode in.

'Now Heather!'

'Sir?'

'The wife's furious. I've just had her on the phone. She can't believe what you said about dogwalkers. You know how fond she is of wee Angus and Rosie.'

'With respect, sir …'

'DCI Barnes, people only say that when they're about to say something very disrespectful, and you know that I hold my dear wife in the highest regard.'

'Yes, sir, and I'm sure you're very fond of her dogs too, but wouldn't it be more appropriate for your wife to be furious about the fact that someone has been killed?'

'Just so, Heather. Anything in that jar for me?' The Super, having delivered his message and done his domestic duty, was now back to his usual avuncular self.

'Not really, sir, not unless you like tar with your shortbread.'

'Better come to my office then. I've got a pot of Colombian on the go.'

Superintendent Bruce Henderson's office was legendary. His dog-loving wife, Olive, was famed for keeping him far under her thumb, but she was a lovely homebaker. Bruce's office was both a haven from her iron rule, and a source of delicious aromas that sometimes reached as far as the holding cells. Heather accepted a mug of Colombian, a brownie, and a small cheese scone. Apparently Olive was practising for a bake off.

'So what do we have, Heather?'

'Pretty much what you heard me say at the news conference, sir. There's a dead girl but we don't know who she is. No ID, no match to any current missing person's report. MO's team think she was killed somewhere else and dumped there shortly after she died. We didn't tell them that.'

'Anything else you didn't tell them? Do you know how she died?'

'Blunt force trauma to the head. Hit two or three times but the first blow was probably enough to kill her.'

Henderson took a deep bite from his brownie. A walnut piece dropped onto his napkin. 'So what can we do about the dog thing?'

Heather sighed. 'I didn't know they were listening, sir. I was down the bottom of the slope with Harry Stevens. He was looking a bit green. His first body you see. I thought a wee joke might help. Bloody directional microphones.'

'Absolutely. But we'll have to do something, just to calm them down and get the attention back on the real story. We've no clues and we need the public to help, not to be told by that idiot Morton that we're about to round up all the pet owners.'

'I suppose I could make a statement. Say how much we appreciate the fact that the dog-walking community have always helped us with our enquiries.'

Henderson sucked in his teeth, his current mouthful of coffee, and a number of deliciously chocolaty crumbs. 'I don't think that's quite the way to put it. Isn't helping us with our enquiries what people do when we arrest them — because we've got a strong suspicion that they actually might have killed someone and dumped the body?'

'Yes, sir.'

'Yes, Heather. I think some kind of gesture might be called for.'

★ ★ ★ ★ ★

She felt stupid. The force's media team had suggested she'd 'play more sympathetically with the public' if she wasn't alone when filmed. 'I won't be alone,' she'd insisted. 'I'll have two west highland terriers, that idiot Peter Morton and his fat cameraman. Plus I've just been told to expect some guy who used to present Countryfile and a team from the dog channel!'

But they'd made her take Harry Stevens too. He'd been sent home to put on something that wasn't uniform, but it was obvious to everyone that the whole thing was staged. Heather's office suit looked wrong on the footpath and wrong beside Harry's designer jeans. Angus and Rosie clearly had no respect for her authority and were winding themselves around her ankles. Olive Henderson had handed them over with a long list of instructions and a stern look and was now hovering just out of shot.

They'd chosen a neutral location of course, a country park. All the footpaths radiated from what had once been a Victorian mine owner's country lodge and was now a nature interpretation centre and ranger station.

They'd been walking for about ten minutes when the path they were on turned towards a burn and the ground grew wet and slimy. Morton and his cameraman, slithering along behind them, were not happy. 'Slow down, can't you? I'm sure we've got enough footage now.'

'But Peter,' she grinned, 'I think we're far enough from the road to let these wee rascals off their leads.' Bending down she unhooked the two little white dogs, who darted off immediately in quite opposite directions.

Within moments she'd lost sight of Angus in the undergrowth by the water. She gave Stevens a look.

'Yes, ma'am.'

He was back horribly soon. 'Ma'am, I think you'd better come and take a look.'

The film crew caught up with them just as Heather was reaching for her mobile.

Active learning

Discuss the answers to these questions:

- What has the writer done in this first chapter to make you want to read on into Chapter 2?
- What do you think the police have found at the end of this chapter?
- What do you think is going to happen in Chapter 2?
- What do you think is going to happen in the rest of the novel?

You should have noticed that the writer is doing more than just setting the plot — the crime story — in motion. She's also establishing characters and letting us see the relationships between them. Because the story mostly sticks to Heather's point of view, we can tell that she is the main character, and is someone we are supposed to like and sympathise with. We see that she has a difficult relationship with the reporter, but a mostly good one with her own boss, Superintendent Henderson, and that she and the uniformed PC, Stevens, aren't quite used to working together yet.

Active learning

Something to think about

Although the genre is usually referred to as 'crime fiction', almost all crime novels, and most crime dramas on TV and film, are about the same crime: murder.

● Why do you think this is? Discuss this with a partner, and then share your answers with your class.

As this book was being written, there was lot of discussion about whether *Beware of the Dogwalkers* was a suitable chapter to use as an example. It features a murder, and the victim is a young woman.

Some people might say that to write about murder at all is a cliché. It's overdone. Some people might say that having a young woman as a victim of this violent act is a more disturbing cliché.

Before you begin to think about your own plans and ideas, take some time to consider this.

Teacher's task

To prepare your pupils for this task, photocopy the following pages, preferably onto thin card, and cut up the copied sheets into individual small cards. You need at least as many cards as there are pupils in your class, so you may need to copy each page more than once.

Give out the cards, one per pupil, face down so that they can't see what they are getting.

Victims of violence might actually find it helpful to see characters in crime fiction survive these situations and see criminals being brought to justice and punished.	Speaking out against writing that features violence against women is one way of speaking out against actual violence against women.
Victims of violence might have traumatic memories triggered by reading about violence or seeing it in TV programmes and films.	We should be able to write about all of life's important experiences. This includes writing about violence in general, and against women.

Writing about violence is not the same thing as actually being violent.	Most fictional victims of violent crime are women, often young, pretty ones. It's not representative of real life, where most victims of violent crime are actually men.
Are there any crimes that should never be written about? Why? Perhaps there are some crimes that are just so terrible, they should always be 'no-go' areas for writers.	It's possible to write about violence in a way that is thoughtful and thought-provoking. Good writers will think carefully about how they tackle difficult subjects and take care not to glorify violence.
There's no such thing as a bad subject to write about: there's only good writing or bad writing.	A lot of writing about violence — or about its aftermath — is just nasty and titillating, with the only intention being to provide a cheap thrill for the reader and sell lots of books.
Crime fiction is often too formulaic and gives the impression that the 'bad guy' is always caught and punished. In real life, this isn't the case. It gives a false sense of security and is misleading.	Just as *To Kill a Mockingbird* challenges racism by writing about racism, so the best way to challenge violence is to write about violence, not to ignore it.
Writing about violence, or reading crime fiction, allows us to consider why people do these terrible things.	Writing crime fiction about violence is an overused cliché — there are so many other crimes to write about that would also let us consider and explore human nature.

There's enough horrible violence in the world; why would anyone want to read about this for fun? It's just distasteful.	Since most victims of sexual violence are women, it would be an overly optimistic view of the world if crime fiction didn't reflect that.
In fiction where victims are female, detectives and other agents of justice can be written as female too, so that women aren't only shown as vulnerable but also empowered.	Reading about or watching violence can desensitise audiences, so that we stop being shocked and horrified by these terrible acts.
Reading about or watching violence can be a bad example, and might actually provoke violence in weaker and more susceptible readers or viewers.	Good crime fiction, in print and on film, allows readers and viewers to reflect on the impact and consequences of crime.

Active learning

First, your teacher will give you a card with an opinion or question on it. Some of the cards advocate writing about violence in crime fiction, while others are against this kind of writing.

- Have a look at your card. Does it make a point in favour of this kind of writing, or against it?
- Do you understand the point your card is making? Ask your teacher if you need help.
- Try to rewrite that point or idea in your own words. It might help if you can use examples from crime fiction you have read, or have seen on TV or in film, to help you illustrate the idea.

Next, find someone in your class whose point sits on the opposite side of the argument about violence in fiction. Discuss the ideas on your cards with each other.

- Can you see each other's point?
- Which idea do you find more convincing?

Finally, get back together as a whole class.

- Does your class think that crime fiction should deal with violence? Take a vote.

What have you learned from this exercise that will help you all to plan and write better crime fiction? Agree as a class on **three key pieces** of advice you would like to give yourselves.

People often ask writers where they get their ideas from. The writer of *Beware of the Dogwalkers* got the idea from a country walk, when she realised that she was in the kind of place where dogwalkers always seemed to find bodies.

You might be worried that you'll have trouble coming up with an idea of your own, especially when so many other people have written detective novels before you. To prove that ideas can come from anywhere, it's time to play a game.

Active learning

Close your book. This game will only work if you don't know what comes next. As long as your teacher has a copy of the book and can tell everyone in the class what to do, it'll work out fine. Go on, close your book.

The only person reading this now should be the teacher. This exercise uses randomly chosen words to set up the plot of a story in which there is a suspicious death. The use of random words in this task is actually very structured, so it's important that you take your pupils through this task in order, and that they follow the instructions carefully.

First, put your pupils into pairs and get them to choose two random nouns. It works best if the words they choose are common nouns, names of things. Make sure every pair has time to choose their two nouns before you explain the next step.

Then explain the following: the two words they have chosen are to be used to create the scene or setting of a crime story. (For example, if they chose the words *cage* and *stain*, the set-up could be that a man was found dead just outside the tiger cage in a zoo with a strange green stain on his shirt.)

Give them a few minutes to work their scenario out. At this stage they do not have to decide exactly how the victim died; they are just creating a situation.

Next, get your pairs of pupils to choose a further three random nouns. Give them plenty of time to do this before you go on to the final step.

Now tell them that these words are the clues. They must now use these words to construct a reasonable hypothesis, using these clues to explain how the suspicious death took place and who might have done it. (For example, if the second set of words went *rhino, pen, bucket*, the explanation could be that the man, a zookeeper, was on his way to take a bucket of corn to the chickens when he was charged by an escaped rhino. The green stain came from a pen in his pocket that burst when he was crushed by the charging beast.)

Last, get your pupils to share their answers with the class, first of all saying what their words were, then explaining what scenarios or solutions they came up with. Finally, tell them they can open their books again!

I hope you can see that ideas can come from anywhere and that the oddest things can sometimes get you going on a story. Let's look a little more specifically now at one particular element of your chapter — the crime scene.

You'll find one of these in the first few pages of nearly every crime novel, or before the first advert break in any television crime drama. Certain elements — what we might call genre markers — come up again and again:

- The senior detective arrives to find other police force staff already at work.
- The senior detective usually has a more junior colleague.
- The place setting is described to create atmosphere.
- There is a detailed description of the victim.
- A police doctor or pathologist is at work.
- The detective starts noticing clues, asking questions and drawing conclusions.

As you read the following two crime scenes, look for the above elements.

The first crime scene comes from one of Ian Rankin's Edinburgh-set novels about Inspector John Rebus. During the Edinburgh Festival, something nasty has been found under the Royal Mile.

'You know where we are?' the constable asked.

'Mary King's Close,' said Rebus. Not that he'd ever been down here, not exactly. But he'd been in similar old buried streets beneath the High Street. He knew of Mary King's Close.

There were ducts and pipes, runs of electric cable. Signs of renovation were all around. Rebus pointed to an arc lamp. 'Can we plug that in?'

The constable thought they could. Rebus looked round. At the end of the hallway he could see a wooden toilet, its seat raised. The next door along led to a long vaulted room, the walls whitewashed, the floor earthen.

'That's the wine shop,' the constable said. 'The butcher's is next door.'

So it was. In its ceiling were a great many iron hooks, short and blackened but obviously used at one time for hanging up meat.

Meat still hung from one of them.

It was the lifeless body of a young man. His hair was dark and slick, stuck to his forehead and neck. His hands had been tied and the rope slipped over a hook, so that he hung stretched with his knuckles near the ceiling and his toes barely touching the ground. His ankles had been tied together too. There was blood everywhere, a fact made all too plain as the arc lamp suddenly came on, sweeping light and shadows across the walls and roof. There was the faint smell of decay, but no flies, thank God. Dr Galloway swallowed hard. Rebus tried to steady his own heart.

Though it was against regulations he leaned forward and touched the young man's hair. It was still slightly damp. He'd probably died on Friday night and was meant to hang here over the weekend, time enough for any trail, any clues, to grow as cold as his bones.

'What do you reckon, sir?'

'Gunshots.' Rebus looked to where the blood had sprayed the wall. 'Something high velocity. Head, elbows, knees and ankles. He's been six-packed.'

From *Mortal Causes* by Ian Rankin

This second crime scene is deliberately bizarre. In this novel, nursery rhyme characters are real people, mostly living quiet lives in the suburbs. Should any 'nurseries' become involved in crime, either as victims or suspects, Detective Inspector Jack Spratt and his Nursery Crime Division investigate them. In the following extract, Humpty Dumpty has suffered a fatal fall.

The yard was shaped as an oblong, fifteen feet wide and about thirty feet long, surrounded by a high brick wall with crumbling mortar. Most of the yard was filled with junk — broken bicycles, old furniture, a mattress or two. But at one end, where the dustbins were spilling their rubbish on the ground, large pieces of eggshell told of a recent and violent death. Jack knew who the victim was immediately, and had suspected that something like this might happen for a number of years. Humpty Dumpty. The fall guy. If this wasn't under the jurisdiction of the Nursery Crime Division, Jack didn't know what was. Mrs Singh, the pathologist, was kneeling next to the shattered remains dictating notes into a tape recorder. She waved a greeting to him as he walked over but did not stop what she was doing. She indicated to a photographer areas of particular interest to her, the flash going off occasionally and looking inordinately bright in the dull closeness of the yard.

Humpty's ovoid body had fragmented almost completely and was scattered among the dustbins and rubbish at the far end of the yard.

The previous night's heavy rain had washed away his liquid centre, but even so there was still enough to give off an unmistakable eggy smell. Jack noted a thin and hairless leg — still with a shoe and sock — attached to a small area of eggshell draped with tattered sheets of translucent membrane. The biggest piece of shell contained Humpty's large features and was jammed between two dustbins. His face was a pale white except for the nose, which was covered in unsightly red gin blossoms. One of the eyes was open, revealing a milky-white unseeing eye, and a crack ran across his face. He had been wearing a tuxedo with a cravat or a cummerbund — it was impossible to say which. The trauma was quite severe and to an untrained eye his body might have been dismissed as a heap of broken eggshell and a bundle of damp clothing.

Jack kneeled down to get a closer look. 'Do we know why he's all dressed up?'

Mary consulted her notebook.

From *The Big Over Easy* by Jasper Fforde

Active learning

Discuss the following questions with a partner, a group or the class:

- Did the writers use all the genre markers you expected?
- Did the writers use any ideas or techniques that surprised you?
- Which did you prefer, and why?

Active learning

At this stage, it's a good idea to also watch at least the opening 20 minutes or so of a television crime drama. There's almost certainly something suitable on television this week, or your teacher might show something to your whole class. You should watch until you get as far as a 'scene of the crime' moment like those above.

We're going to leave crime fiction on one side for a little while and look at some more general writing skills that will help to bring your chapter to life.

First, we're going to look at a skill that's often summed up in the words: **show, don't tell**. To make that clear, have a look at the following sentences.

> I came into the room. I saw Alan. I greeted him and sat down in a chair.

Now look at these sentences.

> **I stormed into the room. I glared at Alan. I grunted at him and flung myself into a chair.**

How does the speaker feel about Alan? Angry of course. But notice, he never **tells** us, 'I felt angry with Alan.' Instead, by changing the simple verbs like *came*, *saw*, *greeted* and *sat* into more expressive ones like *stormed*, *glared*, *grunted* and *flung*, the narrator **shows** us the emotion.

Active learning

Go back to the first basic set of three sentences beginning, 'I came into the room …' Rewrite them to show the following emotions:

- The narrator is afraid of Alan.
- The narrator finds Alan very attractive.
- The narrator is surprised to find Alan there.

As you can see, the difference between showing and telling often comes from choosing interesting vocabulary. By using the right words to put across how characters move, act, appear or speak, we can show what they are like, or how they are feeling.

Active learning

Copy and complete the following table. It'll help you create a bank of words and phrases.

	How might the character speak?	What might their face look like?	How might the character move?
angry			stamping slamming storming grabbing
sad	stuttering sighing moaning		
happy			
scared		white faced eyes wide mouth tight	

One more task on showing, not telling. This one will take us back towards the crime novel.

Write a paragraph to describe, in as much detail as possible, a desk in a police station. The way you describe the desk, the things you put on it and how everything has been set out, should start to show the life and character of the detective who works at that desk. For example, if there are photographs of children on the desk, we can guess that the detective is probably a parent. Lots of dirty coffee cups and an empty painkiller box suggest one kind of person, a nearly-empty desk with a ticked 'to do' list on it suggests quite another.

Don't use any characters, action or speech in your writing, just description. When you've written your piece, swap with a partner and see what you can work out about each other's characters.

Looking at a real example

You are going to see a piece of detective fiction produced by a real pupil. First of all just read through the piece of writing. You may wish to do this aloud around the class, or you might want to read it on your own.

Chapter 1 – Rock-A-Bye-Baby

When the phone rings before dawn, it rarely brings good news. When that phone belongs to a Detective Inspector, it never brings good news.

Leah Stark grunted a greeting. Less than five minutes later she had pulled herself out of bed, dressed and was rushing out the door, leaving her husband sleepy and confused.

It was a bitterly cold morning. Leah stepped out of the car and hurried over to her colleague. He was behind the local supermarket, where the dumpsters sat and deliveries were dropped off.

'Morning Leah,' smiled Detective Sergeant Toby Smith. They had worked together on many cases.

'Hey Toby. What's going on?' Leah asked as he led her over to the dumpsters. All she had been told over the phone was that 'a death' had been reported.

Toby stopped between two dumpsters and pointed. 'That's what's going on.'

Leah sucked in a breath as she crouched down. A woman, probably in her mid twenties, was huddled on the ground, her arms clutching a blanket. Her head was bent, and her chin sagged onto her chest, leaving her dark hair falling over her face. Frost had formed on top of her head and shoulders. Inside the blanket, a hand enclosed in a tiny mitten could just be seen. Leah had to fight against her maternal instinct as she looked at the little hand. She stood up, fists clenched at her sides, struggling to keep her face from betraying her emotions as she asked 'Any idea what happened?'

Toby shook his head, 'We're not sure yet. Pathologist's on his way, but nobody's touched the bodies or even had a good look at the mother's face. The most obvious explanation would be that they froze overnight. Temperatures were below zero.'

Leah bit her lip, thinking of her own little girl, still safely tucked in her bed. She was about to comment on how horrible the situation felt, knowing Toby would understand, when they were joined by the pathologist. Jim Roberts was well into his fifties and had been in his profession nearly thirty years, much longer than either of them. His silver hair looked like the frost on the ground.

'Somebody want to fill me in?' Jim asked, looking at them through his half-moon glasses.

'Unidentified female, still holding her baby. Looks like they froze, but nobody's had a good look at either of them. Store worker found them this morning when he was preparing for the shop to open. He's inside at the moment, very shaken. Absolutely crapped himself when he came across them. He's only seventeen. Leah and me will go talk to him while you do your thing out here.'

Toby tugged on Leah's arm and half-dragged her into the supermarket through the back door. 'Sorry, but I couldn't feel my toes anymore. Been here longer than you have. Still, the manager's letting us use his office. I bet it's really warm in there.'

Leah rolled her eyes and opened the door to the office. It was extremely tidy, not a sheet of paper out of place. The bin didn't even have anything in it. A boy sat on a plastic chair, looking very out of place. In contrast to the scarily tidy surroundings, he had very scruffy hair, rather dirty hands and a shirt that was only half tucked in.

'I didn't do it, I swear!' the boy cried, almost as soon as Toby and Leah walked through the door. His eyes darted around their faces, looking for any sign that they were there to arrest him.

'Relax, would you? Nobody's blaming you for anything. We just want to take a statement. Tell us what happened this morning.' Leah tried to smile encouragingly at him.

The boy swallowed and looked at her, his pale blue eyes still searching her face. His braces glinted as he answered her, talking very quickly. 'I came in this morning, stocked some of the shelves, went to chuck out the packaging and then I saw her. Them. They were just curled up there, not moving or anything. I totally freaked out and called you lot. Didn't realise I'd end up getting involved, but I didn't touch her, or the body, or move the buckets or anything. My name's Andy, by the way. Andy Nichols.'

Leah smiled at him again as Toby said 'Thanks, Andy. It'll just be a couple more questions, then you can go home. We checked with your boss, he's OK if you want to leave early.'

Andy swallowed again, his Adam's apple bobbing visibly in his skinny neck. 'Boy,' he said, looking a little shocked, 'I always wanted a half day. Didn't know I had to find a dead person before it would happen.'

* * * * *

Jim Roberts knelt down and touched the woman's hand. It refused to move, clutching the baby tightly even in death. Rigor had almost completely set in but, given the extreme temperature, that put her death at around five hours ago, in the small hours of the morning. That fitted in with Toby's theory that they had frozen.

Jim pushed the woman's hair aside. There, on her neck, was an angry looking purple line, clearly from some kind of ligature. He sighed. The investigation had just changed from a tragically wasteful death into a murder case. He gently prised her eyelids apart, and had his ideas confirmed. In the whites of her eyes, there were little pinpricks of blood. Petechial haemorrhaging, consistent with asphyxiation. The poor girl. He couldn't think of any reason anybody would do this to her. And to leave her here so her baby froze too …

Jim worked her elbow just enough until the rigor broke with a pop. He did the same to the other arm and lifted the baby, still wrapped in its many blankets. He peered inside the bundle, hoping against hope that the infant would not show the same signs of violence as the poor mother.

He pushed the blanket away from the baby's face.

'Mary, mother of God,' he murmured. He pulled his phone from his pocket.

* * * * *

Leah and Toby were still gently questioning Andy, but it was hopeless. The boy had no idea what had happened. He was shocked and upset and clearly just wanted to go home. Leah heard the sirens first. She looked out the window and watched with some confusion as an ambulance pulled into the yard. Surely it was a bit too late for all that?

Her silent question was answered as Jim Roberts burst through the door to the office.

'What the …,' Toby started.

Jim cut him off. 'Did anybody think to check for a pulse?'

'No … we just assumed … it was so cold last night …' Leah stammered, hope beginning to rise in her.

'Idiots!' Jim shrieked, 'You completely useless turds! You had no other way to be sure!'

Andy stared at the older man, his mouth open.

Jim closed his eyes and pinched the bridge of his nose, trying desperately to regain some composure. He looked at Andy, Toby and finally settled his eyes on Leah. Quietly he said, 'The mother was murdered. She was strangled. But the baby … the baby, somehow, is alive.'

Now that you have read the story once, you are going to analyse it in more detail. Consider these questions.

1 Does the writer use the genre markers you expected?

2 Does the writer do anything that surprises you?

3 Write a couple of sentences to show what makes it a **good** piece of writing.

4 Suggest two things the writer could have done that would make the story work **even better**.

Planning your own first chapter

You need to plan, in quite a lot of detail, two main aspects of your story. If you've planned stories in the past, what you probably did was plan the **plot** of your story, the events that would happen in it. We'll get round to that later. First you need to plan, and get to know, your main **character**. It's time to create your detective.

Using the following questions and prompts, make a list of details that show that you know, and have carefully thought about, your main detective character.

- Male or female?
- Age?
- Appearance?
- Home/family situation?
- Main personality traits?
- Any unusual quirks, habits, hobbies?
- What is this person's background?
- What motivates them to do the job?
- Does this person always stick to the rules?
- Does your character work well with others, or prefer to go it alone?
- How does this person cope with the stresses of the job?

Once you have answered all these questions, you should know your character well, and if you know them well, you can write well about them. **Be careful!** That doesn't mean that you will actually use all these details in your writing. After all, you're only writing the first chapter of a novel. You should never end up writing something like:

> 'Heather could never forget her first case. She hadn't been able to catch the killer and she'd never forgiven herself. Now she felt she owed it even more to every victim to find the killer.'

Writing that would be a horrible example of telling when you should be showing. Instead, knowing that a failed case is what motivates Heather, the author of *Beware of the Dogwalkers* writes:

> 'I'm sorry,' she said to the dead girl. 'I will find out who did this.'
> It was what she always said to the dead.

Once you know your **character**, it's time to start thinking about your **plot**.

Active learning

First of all, choose one of the following rough shapes for your chapter. Each has three steps and each includes a crime scene.

Possible structure 1:

- Your detective arrives at the crime scene.
- The crime scene is examined and the detective gets information about the case from other characters.
- The story cuts to the detective following up some sort of lead.

Possible structure 2:

- Your detective arrives at the crime scene.
- The crime scene is examined and the detective gets information about the case from other characters.
- The detective leaves the scene with no real leads and facing a very baffling case. At the very end of the chapter, a clue or lead does come up.

Possible structure 3:

- The novel starts with somebody being attacked and killed. We may know who the victim is, but the identity of the attacker is not revealed.
- Your detective arrives at the crime scene.
- The crime scene is examined.

Possible structure 4:

- The novel starts with someone (perhaps a member of the public) finding a body.
- The novel cuts to your detective arriving at the crime scene.
- The crime scene is examined.

Possible structure 5:

- The novel starts with a description of a member of the public doing something quite normal.
- The novel cuts to your detective arriving at the crime scene.
- The crime scene is examined, and the reader now realises that the body being examined is that of the ordinary person they saw at the start of the chapter.

You should now have the very rough outline of the three main stages in your opening chapter and you should know your main detective character really well.

Spend about half an hour planning your first chapter carefully, bearing in mind everything you've worked out so far. Your plan might use headings, might be a bullet-pointed list or might be a spider diagram.

As you plan your chapter, remember the issues you reflected on earlier about violence, especially against women, in crime fiction. You should be trying to:

- avoid clichés
- stay away from gratuitous violence
- watch out for accidental sexism.

Make sure your chapter is going to end in a way that makes the reader wish there was going to be a Chapter 2. You might use a full-scale cliffhanger, where you shock your reader into turning the page because a character is facing a terrible threat or danger, or you might use a gentler hook like having your detective heading off somewhere so that we feel we want to go along too.

When your plan is finished, pair up with another pupil and explain your plans to each other. Don't be afraid to ask each other questions or to help your partner fix things that don't quite work yet.

Just before you write your story, here's some final advice:

1   Make sure you use dialogue in your chapter. If your characters don't speak to each other, they will never seem as if they are alive, and your story will feel completely flat and dull. Not only does speech give your story life, but the way characters speak and the words they use reveal lots about them.

2   British police detectives are known by their titles (Detective Constable, Detective Sergeant, Detective Inspector and Detective Chief Inspector, often abbreviated to DC, DS, DI and DCI) and are never just called 'Detective' as American characters would be. So, when you first introduce a character you would call them *PC Harry Stevens* or *DCI Heather Barnes*. After that you might call that person *Heather* if you want readers to sympathise with her or *Barnes* if you want her to feel like a more distant character.

3   British police tend to work in teams with a clear leader and a fairly strong sense of rank. The head of a murder investigation would be at least a DI, or even a DCI. Unlike the detectives you may have seen in American films or dramas, British police don't really have partners.

4   Detectives are in a police division called CID. They wear smart, plain clothes. Uniformed police have different titles. It's likely that your crime scene would have a number of uniformed PCs at it, taking statements and securing the site.

It's now time to follow your plan and write your piece.

When you've written it, read your work over before you hand it in to your teacher. Think about the three areas the markers are looking at, content, style and technical accuracy, and ask yourself the following questions:

Content:

- Have I stuck to my purpose and written for my audience?
- Have I used the conventions of my chosen genre?
- Does my writing show my creativity?
- Have I developed my ideas in some depth?

Style:

- Is my expression confident and varied?
- Does my style fit my chosen genre?
- Have I used structural devices like hooks, cliffhangers, flashbacks and cuts to give my work impact?
- Have I made the reader believe, and wish, that there could be a second chapter?

Technical accuracy:

- Are my spelling, grammar and punctuation all accurate?
- Is my work properly paragraphed?
- Can my work be clearly understood?

Once you have checked over your work, hand it in to your teacher. He or she will mark it and give you feedback and suggestions for ways to improve it for your portfolio.

Personal writing

In a piece of personal writing you will focus on a specific event or situation, and on your reaction to this. This is a genre of writing that many pupils do very well in. It is also one that you have probably worked on earlier in your school career.

You already know that the marker will be looking at the **content** of your writing. When you write a personal piece, your writing should show a skilful command of this genre. You will explore your ideas, feelings and experiences with mature reflection, self-awareness and insight. Your writing will give a strong sense of your personality and individuality. Your themes will be skilfully introduced and developed. The marker will also be assessing your **style**. This means you should use features of your chosen genre to create impact on the reader. Your expression will be confident and varied. Keep this in mind as you work through this part of the chapter.

Active learning

Your teacher needs to divide the class into two halves. Once you know which half you are in, your half needs to organise itself into small groups, with about three people in each group. Work in these groups for five minutes.

The groups in one half of the class should list all the reasons why they think people do well at personal writing. The groups in the other half of the class should list the particular features that we look for in a piece of personal writing.

Each group should share their answers with the rest of the class.

It is likely that your personal writing will focus on a specific experience or situation and, crucially, on your reactions to and reflections about this. It is that process of reflection and reaction that makes this a piece of personal writing. To give you an example to bear in mind as we work through the next few pages about skills for personal writing, read this piece by a Higher English pupil. It deals with fostering and adoption, which may be sensitive subjects for some readers. You may wish to read this at home rather than in class.

At first glance our family — mum, dad, daughter and son — appears as normal as any other but it is, in fact, quite different. My brother is adopted. It took a number of attempts before we were able to finalise this arrangement. Before my brother, Euan, there were two other foster brothers, Richard and Ian, who were unable to remain a part of our family life.

Richard came to us when he was six years old. Sadly, like many adoption cases, Richard had been mistreated. My first impression was of a distant child. Although he wasn't really part of our family, he wasn't not a part of it. He seemed more like the family pet than a brother but I accepted it all the same.

He adjusted surprisingly well considering: perhaps this was a result of his young age. Although Richard remained with us for four years I don't remember much about our relationship, but he was particularly close to my father who had always wanted a son. I can recall the silence in our house when his mother took him back, a silence broken by my father saying he'd always be welcome in our home.

Richard had, for some strange reason, believed it was his fault his mother had left him and so jumped at the chance to return to her. Six months later he was again rejected, thrown out of the house, his belongings sold and his bank account emptied — his mother kept all the proceeds. The offer of help that my father had given Richard could not be taken up — we had another 'brother' by then and Richard soon became little more than a memory.

As I look back on these events, I realise the influence and the pain that his mother had inflicted upon him. Because of these, Richard could never have allowed himself to become part of our family.

The other 'brother' was a boy called Ian who was nine when he came to us. Ian made the biggest impression on me in the three years he lived with us — I was older then and was able to remember more. Like Richard, Ian had been in care. Unlike Richard, this had been since he was two. It took some time to realise the full extent to which this 'care' had affected his life.

Suddenly I had the protection of an older brother. Wherever he went I followed, with the intensity of a besotted fan. For me, Ian was more than just a foster brother. We grew close as we shared our childhood and it was this that hurt so much when Ian left.

My mother said she could no longer cope with him because he was 'just an empty shell,' and showed no emotion. According to her, Ian hid a cold-hearted nature behind a mask of childhood innocence. I don't remember seeing this side of him at all. I look back on the day that he was taken away and I recall the tears that he cried. I think perhaps that Ian never truly realised how much he had until he was taken away. I imagine the pain my mother must have felt as she watched him go and realised that it was her who had decided his fate. If I sound bitter I don't mean to because I'm not, but I just think it was wrong to have given up so easily: perhaps it is because of this that there are so many foster children still in care while childless couples pursue some idea of a 'perfect' family.

When Ian left, our family drew into itself for a time, but my father still had his dream of having a boy and so, once again, we contacted the social services. This time we got a toddler, eighteen months old, called Euan. His young age was perhaps a blessing as it enabled him to adjust well. He doesn't remember anything now about his previous life, and so he isn't curious about his real parents, or about the reasons for his separation from them.

At first, because of the large age gap between us, it seemed like Euan was more my own child than a brother and I took an active part in teaching him to read and write and telling him what I knew about life. I remember certain events during his early childhood that a mother usually remembers, such as his first day at school and his first tooth falling out. I think that my position in the family as only child after Ian left gave me more responsibility, and it was this that contributed to the feeling of protectiveness when Euan came along.

I think that he has had a lot of pressure placed on him by my parents to be better than Ian and Richard and I believe that their expectations are too great for such a young child. The problems that Ian and Richard faced have nothing to do with Euan's life and it is in this sense that I believe the past should be forgotten and we should all look to the future.

As Euan has settled into the family, I have begun to think about the role of the social services and the awe-inspiring power that they hold. They literally decide on the fate of the child in care. The social services have the power to make or break a family according to their whims while the child plays piggy in the middle. This often ends with the foster family, hurt and having been rejected once too often, giving up hope and watching as the social worker drives off down the road with their dream in the back seat.

Rejecting Ian was a cruel thing to do, especially to a child who had been in care all his life, and after reflecting I believe that it would have been handled differently had my parents been his real parents. I think that parents who have difficulties with foster children tend to give up easier than they would if it had actually been their own child and it is because of this that there are so many children languishing in care today.

It seems, now, that our family has come to the end of its emotional drama and the search for a little boy is over. It is through this search that I have become strangely older and wiser and I am able to stand back from my life, and look at how it has affected me and my family. I wonder, if my parents had realised what they would have to go through to fulfil their dream, would they still have pursued it?

However through all of this one thing remains true — a family is not the people with whom you are born but the relationships you form with them and how you, yourself, make it work. At times I feel nostalgic and wonder what happened to my other 'brothers'. Maybe one day I'll know.

We'll return to that piece as we work through this chapter. For the moment, just keep in mind that this is the kind of thing you are aiming to do.

Choosing what to write about

It shouldn't be too hard for you to choose a topic. After all you know yourself better than anyone else does. You are unique, interesting and well worth writing about.

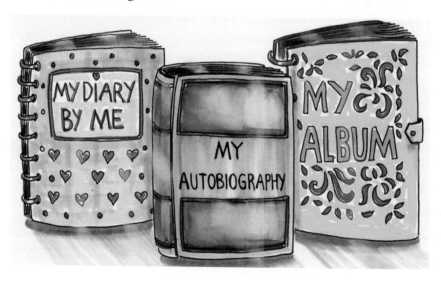

And you do have to choose your own topic. Not only is your teacher not allowed to give you an exact subject to write about, in this case your teacher just can't. Only you have lived your life and you are the only person in the world who has had your particular set of experiences. You are the only person in history who ever had the exact set of family and friends that you have. Your brain is the only one in the entire universe to hold your set of memories, thoughts and feelings.

Active learning

Stop and think. Is there an experience you have had which matters to you very much, one that you'd like to write about in your personal essay? If you can think of such an experience, make a note of it now. If not, read the next section and follow the prompts.

Narrowing down your ideas

If you don't already have a subject in mind, then it may help you to think very quickly about a lot of different experiences you may have had, and see if any of them are suitable for a longer piece.

Active learning

Take the question 'What is the … thing that has ever happened to you?' and insert each of the seven options below in turn. Whenever one of the options applies to your life, write a couple of sentences to answer the prompt.

1 worst

2 hardest

3 happiest

4 saddest

5 most frightening

6 strangest

7 most confusing

Active learning

For those options below that apply to your life, write a couple of sentences to answer the prompt.

Which event or situation in life …

1 has most shaped you?

2 made you grow up or mature?

3 most changed your family?

4   was the biggest challenge for you?

5   was when you experienced great loss?

6   was when you experienced great success?

7   was when you experienced failure?

8   was when you had to take responsibility?

9   made you feel most isolated?

10   made you feel different from those around you?

11   made you feel you were being stereotyped?

12   showed you the best of people/someone?

13   showed you the worst of people/someone?

Active learning

Now you are going to think about these nine ways a person could make an impact on your life. Again, for those options below that apply to your life, write a couple of sentences to answer the prompt.

Which person …

1 has most influenced you?

2 has most helped you?

3 has most hurt you?

4 has least understood you?

5 do you miss most?

6 have you been in most conflict with?

7 have you had the most complicated relationship with?

8 have you had a very changeable relationship with?

9 are you most glad to be rid of?

Active learning

Now you are going to think about some aspects of your identity — of the way you see yourself in the world. How much does each of these shape and influence you?

1 Your gender?

2 Your sexual orientation?

3 Your nationality or ethnic background?

4 Your religion?

5 Your social class?

6 Your position in the family?

7 Your experience of mental and emotional health?

8 What do you most like about yourself? What are your best qualities?

9 What do you find difficult about yourself? What are your worst faults?

Active learning

Lastly, think about these slightly surprising ideas:

1 What's the best mistake you ever made?

2 What has been your most disastrous success?

Did you notice that every one of those 40 prompts and questions used the word 'you' or 'your'? That's because this really is a **personal** writing task. Whatever you write, including pieces where the original impetus comes from thinking about another person, the piece is about you and you are writing to explore and reveal yourself, your thoughts and your personality.

You should now have many short paragraphs in front of you. Read them over. Is there one you could write about in depth in your personal essay? Remember you need not only to focus on an event or situation, but also to explore your reactions to and reflections on it.

Although you won't be writing your essay for a while, it's a good idea to choose your topic now, so that as you work through the rest of this chapter you are doing it with your subject in mind.

There are other ways you might come up with topics. You could look through some photographs to see if that sparks anything off. If you keep a diary or blog, have a look at that. If you have a Twitter account, look through past tweets. Check your Instagram or your Facebook timeline. Are there recurring themes, or ideas that you keep coming back to? A good piece of personal writing doesn't have to be based on something huge: if you flip forward to page 48 you'll find an essay called *Class Room* which arose from a number of small incidents that got the writer thinking.

Good writing techniques

Thoughts and feelings

Your personal writing will really come to life when you include your thoughts and feelings. No one else knows these. Only you can tell the reader about them.

To show you what I mean, let's look at an example from a book called *Touching the Void*. The writer, Joe Simpson, was climbing in Peru when he broke his leg. In this extract his climbing partner, Simon, is about to begin lowering the injured Joe down the mountain on a rope.

I lay on my chest immediately beneath Simon, and edged down until all my weight was on the rope. Initially I couldn't commit myself to letting my feet hang free of the snow. If it crumbled we would be falling instantaneously. Simon nodded at me and grinned. Encouraged by his confidence I lifted my feet and began to slide down. It worked!

He let the rope out smoothly in a steady descent. I lay against the snow holding an axe in each hand ready to dig them in the moment I felt a fall begin. Occasionally the crampons on my right boot snagged in the snow and jarred my leg. I tried not to cry out but failed. I didn't want Simon to stop.

In a surprisingly short time he did stop. I looked up and saw that he had receded far from me, and I could make out only his head and shoulders. He shouted something but I couldn't make it out until three sharp tugs explained it. I was astounded at the speed at which I had descended 150 feet. Astounded and pleased as punch. I wanted to giggle. In a short time my mood had swung from despair to wild optimism, and death rushed back to being a vague possibility rather than the inevitable fact. The rope went slack as I hopped onto my good leg. I was acutely aware that while Simon was changing the knot over we were at our most vulnerable. If I fell, I would drop a whole rope's length before it came tight onto him, and he would be whipped off the mountain by the impact. I dug my axes in and stayed motionless.

Active learning

Simpson is obviously feeling a mixture of emotions, some positive, some negative. Copy and complete the following table to help you explore the emotions in the extract. You should be able to find a wide range of emotions.

Emotion	Evidence	Positive or negative
Hesitation	'Initially I couldn't commit myself to letting my feet hang free of the snow.'	Negative

Interestingly, people often write extremely well about hard experiences. If we go through sad, difficult or tragic events, we are strongly aware of how we feel at the time. Sad situations affect and shape us. We have to keep working with and processing the memories, thoughts and feelings that go with these events. We are acutely aware of our reactions.

Active learning

Go back to the piece of personal writing about adoption that was printed on page 32. Pick out that writer's thoughts and feelings.

Details and description

Because your memories are important to you, when you bring them to mind they will be full of tiny details; things you noticed at the time. Many of these details might not be very important in themselves, but they are important in your writing because they bring that memory to life.

To let you see what I mean, here's a piece from the start of *Touching the Void*, before Joe Simpson breaks his leg.

> I was lying in my sleeping bag, staring at the light filtering through the red and green fabric of the dome tent. Simon was snoring loudly, occasionally twitching in his dream world. We could have been anywhere. There is a peculiar anonymity about being in tents. Once the zip is closed and the outside world barred from sight, all sense of location disappears. The sounds of rustling, of fabric flapping in the wind, or of rainfall, the feel of hard lumps under the groundsheet, the smell of rancid socks and sweat — these are universals, as comforting as the warmth of a down sleeping bag.
>
> I felt a homely affection for the warm security of the tent and reluctantly wormed out of my bag to face the prospect of lighting the stove. It had snowed a little during the night, and the grass crunched frostily under my feet as I padded over to the cooking rock. There was no sign of Richard stirring as I passed his tiny one-man tent, half collapsed and whitened with hoar-frost.

This short passage is stuffed with tiny details. Simpson manages to use nearly all of his senses to bring the description to life.

Active learning

First **list** your five senses. Then **re-read** the Joe Simpson passage above. Next, **note down** the details that fit each sense. Which sense has the writer not used in this extract?

It's easy to use your sense of sight as you describe what you remember in detail, but Simpson's example is a good reminder to bring in as many of our other senses as is appropriate.

Active learning

Now read this third extract from *Touching the Void*. Although Joe's accident hasn't happened yet, he and Simon have already had a difficult time, being caught in a storm just after reaching the summit of the mountain. They've spent the night in a cave they dug in the snow. As you read, make a list of the small details that make it seem vivid and convincing. Again, look for the writer's use of different senses.

I had the stove burning away cheerfully by my side, and could look beyond it through a hole in the snow cave. The early morning sun etched the ridge lines with shadows and danced blue shadings down the edges of the mountain face. For the first time in the last four days the tense concentration in my body relaxed. The anxious struggles of the previous night had been forgotten.

It was cramped in the snow hole. Simon was still asleep, lying on his side close by me, facing away. His hips and shoulders pressed up against my side, and I could feel his body warmth seeping through my sleeping bag. I moved carefully to avoid waking him and felt myself smiling. I knew it would be a good day.

I dressed and geared up first, before climbing out of the cave. Simon was slow getting ready, and it wasn't until he joined me outside that I remembered his frostbite. My good humour vanished to be replaced by worry when he showed his fingers to me. One fingertip was blackened and three other fingers were white and wooden in appearance.

Did you notice that, as well as the descriptive detail you were looking for, Simpson again uses a mixture of positive and negative emotions in his writing?

Active learning

Go back to the piece about adoption on page 32. What are the details that bring it to life?

Using dialogue
Something else you can do with this genre of writing to bring it to life is to put speech into it. Just as dialogue makes stories vivid, it does the same for personal writing. Don't worry if you can't remember the exact words you and other people said; you can make up something which seems close enough.

In this extract from her book *The Reading Promise*, American writer Alice Ozma remembers how her father, a school librarian and single parent, tried to understand the subtleties of dressing for a high school prom.

'Does it have to be a "gown"? Can't you just wear something you already own?'

'There's a dress code. Plus, I'll feel really weird if I'm underdressed. I'll stick out in a bad way.'

'What about a nice skirt, and a button-up shirt? Would that fall under the dress code maybe?'

Single fathers of girls have a lot of tricky issues to face. They deal with puberty, boys, and dating as best they can. I give them, and especially my father, enormous credit for this. My grandmother passed away when I was thirteen. My sister moved out when I was in middle school. My father was too proud to ask his sister for advice. So with relatively little female input, he found his way through the maze of teenage girlhood right beside me, learning to trust me and, eventually, the boys I chose to date. I am proud to say that most of the time, he fully understood what he was doing and made reasonable, logical decisions. I chalk some of this up to all the books we read about young girls. They were almost entirely fiction, but they were usually quite realistic and gave us both great insight into what 'normal' girls and 'normal' families did. Even with all of our reading though, some things still absolutely baffled my father. As my senior year of high school came to a close, I realised that prom was one of those things.

My father just didn't understand the hype.

'It's one night!' he kept repeating whenever he saw the list of things I needed to buy and do.

My list was actually quite modest, compared to most girls I knew: I wanted my hair done, only because I didn't know how to do it myself. I wanted a dress. So far, that was it. I didn't feel the need to bother with shopping for a purse, or jewellery, or even shoes. I was fine with hunting around my closet for something that would come close enough. But things kept popping up.

'Stephanie says I should get my nails done,' I mentioned over breakfast one morning shortly before the big night, 'but it seems like a waste of money. What do you think?'

'"Done"? What do you mean by "done"? Painted?'

'Well that's one option.'

'They're too stubbly. You chew on them like you've got the secret to eternal youth in your — what's the white part called? The tip?'

'I could get fake nails I guess.'

'Oh my goodness no. They look like cat claws, and when the teachers at school get them they make this awful clicking sound whenever they type. It's enough to drive a person batty.'

'I wasn't planning on typing very much at prom.'

He let air out of the corners of his mouth dramatically.

'Still,' he said. 'Who would even notice if you had them? In your prom photos, is anyone really going to look at your fingernails?'

Notice that the dialogue here does more than just bring the writing to life. It also shows us what the two characters, father and daughter, are like, and lets us see something of the relationship between them.

Active learning

First, just to show why it is better to use dialogue, try to rewrite the above piece so that we get all the same information, but without either of the characters speaking.

Now think about the piece that you are planning to write. Where could you use speech to bring it to life?

Using storytelling techniques
Earlier in this chapter, when you were preparing to write your piece of prose fiction, we looked at the technique of showing, not telling. This is just one of many storytelling techniques (and the dialogue that you just worked on above is another) that will help make your personal writing better.

Active learning

First, go round the class and give everybody a letter, A or B. All the letter A pupils should re-read the piece of writing about adoption which was printed on page 32. All the letter B pupils should re-read the three extracts by Joe Simpson and the one by Alice Ozma (pages 38–42).

As you re-read your piece(s), look for and note down evidence of the writer using any of these techniques:

- dialogue
- showing, not telling
- imagery
- starting at a moment of action
- flashback
- short sentence or paragraph for impact
- minor sentence
- jump/cut to a different scene or action
- repetition
- use of incident or anecdote.

Also, think of one technique you think your writer could have used but did not. When could he or she have used that technique? How would this have improved the piece of writing?

Now find someone with the other letter, who has read the other piece(s) — not someone who sits near you in class. Share what you found with each other.

Reflection

When you have worked on personal writing before, you probably concentrated most on bringing the experience to life. Now that you're working at Higher level, your reactions and responses should go further. It might help if you think of the piece of writing like this:

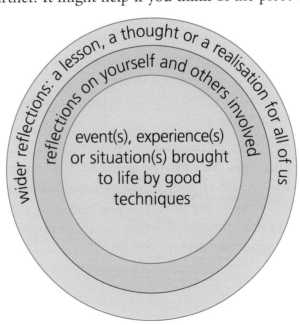

wider reflections: a lesson, a thought or a realisation for all of us

reflections on yourself and others involved

event(s), experience(s) or situation(s) brought to life by good techniques

Reflections on yourself and others

To do well in this task, you need to do something only mature and insightful writers are able to do: **examine yourself**. If you stand in front of a mirror, you can examine yourself pretty thoroughly by looking at your reflection. Every spot and blemish will be visible, but you'll also be able to see all your good features and everything that you like about yourself; that you have poise and posture, that you have an intelligent face.

If you apply this idea to your writing, it means that you might question and criticise yourself. On the other hand, you might realise that you handled a situation well. You may realise that certain experiences have shaped you and made you into the person you are, just as growing up changes the way your face looks in the mirror.

Often events in our lives make much more sense once they are over and we are older and wiser. Perhaps when something happened to you it was a really terrible experience, but now you realise that you benefited from it in some way. Events may be confusing when they happen, but when you look back on them they may make more sense.

As well as examining and reflecting on yourself, you can reflect on others. You may be aware of how events and experiences have affected other people as well as you. It may be that you disagreed with someone at the time, but you now realise they did the right thing. On the other hand, when we are young we sometimes accept the things adults do without question, but as we grow up we are not so sure about their motives.

Below is a list of phrases that can be used in reflection:

- Looking back …
- On reflection …
- With hindsight …
- In retrospect …
- Nowadays I feel/think/ believe …
- If I could do this again …
- If this happened now …
- I learned …
- I realise …
- I understand …
- I should have …
- I could have …
- I wish I had …
- Because of this I am …

- Since this happened, I …
- When I think back on this …
- Thinking about it now, I feel …
- At the time I … but now I …
- If I could change things …
- It was a … thing to do because …
- I wish this had never happened because …
- Now that I've been through this …
- I grew through this experience because …
- This made me think about …
- This experience shaped me by …
- I'm glad this happened because …
- That's when I realised …

Although these phrases can be used to start sentences and paragraphs, your writing will actually be more subtle, and therefore better, if you don't use them quite so blatantly.

> **Despite the loss of her friendship, I grew through this experience because …**

is better than

> **I grew through this experience because, although I lost a friend I …**

and

> **I was unable to admit to anyone that I was in the wrong, but on reflection …**

is better than

> **On reflection, I realise I was in the wrong …**

Active learning

Go back to the subject that you thought of earlier, the topic you have chosen to write about. Spend some time making reflective notes. What lessons have your experiences taught you about yourself and those around you? How have these experiences shaped and changed you?

Reflecting more widely

When tackling this kind of task at Higher level, you should take your reflections wider still. You need to show that your experiences have taught you something about life, about society, or about people in general; that you now have a lesson, a thought or a realisation for all of us.

Look at this extract from the piece you saw earlier. The writer, having described the effects these events had on her own family, begins considering the wider 'system':

As Euan has settled into the family, I have begun to think about the role of the social services and the awe-inspiring power that they hold. They literally *decide* on the fate of the child in care. The social services have the power to make or break a family according to their whims while the child plays piggy in the middle. This often ends with the foster family, hurt and having been rejected once too often, giving up hope and watching as the social worker drives off down the road with their dream in the back seat.

Most of the writer's wider reaction and response comes near the end of the piece:

I think that parents who have difficulties with foster children tend to give up easier than they would if it had actually been their own child and it is because of this that there are so many children languishing in care today …

However through all of this one thing remains true — a family is not the people with whom you are born but the relationships you form with them and how you, yourself, make it work.

The writer considers how foster or adoptive families react to difficult children, and ends the piece by challenging us to rethink our definition of what a family might be.

Active learning

In your own words, sum up this writer's wider reflections. What did the writer learn?

Here's another extract from Joe Simpson's *Touching The Void*. Again this comes from the early part of the book. Joe and his climbing partner, Simon, have just reached the summit of a mountain in the Peruvian Andes called Siula Grande.

Active learning

As you read, look for and note down:

- any times when Simpson is examining himself
- any times when Simpson reacts or responds in a way that lets him take a wider look at human nature.

We took the customary summit photos and ate some chocolate. I felt the usual anticlimax. What now? It was a vicious cycle. If you succeed with one dream, you come back to square one and it's not long before you're conjuring up another, slightly harder, a bit more ambitious. I didn't like the thought of where it might be leading me. As if, in some strange way, the very nature of the game was controlling me, taking me towards a logical but frightening conclusion. It always unsettled me, this moment of reaching the summit, this sudden stillness and quiet, which gave me time to wonder at what I was doing and sense a niggling doubt that perhaps I was inexorably losing control — was I here purely for pleasure or was it egotism? Did I really want to come back for more? But these moments were also good times, and I knew that the feelings would pass. Then I could excuse them as morbid pessimistic fears that had no sound basis.

Active learning

Go back to the subject that you thought of earlier, the topic you have chosen to write about. Spend some time making notes on how you could use this experience for wider reflection. What lessons have your experiences taught you about life, about society, or about people in general?

Looking at a real example

You are going to see another piece of personal writing by a pupil. Ideally you should have a photocopy of this piece, as that will help you with the later stage of this task.

This piece, *Class Room*, is an example of a piece focusing on the writer's reaction to a number of apparently small but thought-provoking events, rather than to one big event or experience.

First of all, just read through the piece.

Class Room

'You're so lucky Paula*, you can just get your dad to pay for it.'

Aged eight, I watched my parents' marriage fall apart due to the stress caused by work and financial crises. Money was evil. However, I also watched them build their careers back up and turn into happier people. Money was the catalyst for this.

So, I have always been aware of money, but this comment by a classmate was the first time someone had directly flagged up the issue of my class. I couldn't help thinking that it was inappropriate. I don't think he meant to leave me feeling exasperated and irritated, but he did. It was his declaration of my supposed status. He was referring to my dad's financial situation, not mine. His preconception was an unjust remark; he had no idea about my father's job.

I had been categorised.

I began to wonder if I had always been aware of the divide between rich and poor — the divide between those who are financially comfortable and those who struggle. Have I been living in a bubble all my life? Perhaps I have, always aware but choosing to ignore it, ignoring the less fortunate.

When I think back to that boy's comment, I am reminded of a classroom – a microcosm of society in which people from different walks of life must interact with each other.

His assumption got me thinking: what is my own preconception of class? At this age, my exposure to society and the various types of people in it boils down to my experiences in school, in music groups and in swimming clubs.

For example, when I would meet up with other members of these clubs, in particular after the summer holidays, I would share the experiences I had on my holidays. I would tell my friends and teammates the adventures I had been on.

But in recent years I have restricted myself and held back on the stories I tell. I have become more aware of the many people who do not get the opportunity to do such things, go such places, and who are not as lucky as I am. This makes me wonder: did I ever think of the people who didn't go on holiday when I recalled my adventures each August when we were all back at school? Did I see them sitting quietly as they compared their lives to mine? Did I take into account that I was bragging — did I even realise I was bragging? Maybe they thought if they shared the stories of their summers they would be judged and frowned upon. Was I sensitive to their feelings? These moments now fill me with embarrassment, making me feel uneasy about my younger self and the ignorance I was lucky to enjoy.

Memories often resurface of people less fortunate than me, and I wonder how some of the less privileged people I have encountered in life are doing today. I remember one such scenario vividly. We were playing the 'stand up' game in school and my teacher called out various items — we had to stand up if we owned them. One day she used houses for the game: detached, semi-detached, terraced, bungalow and flat.

Now a flat of course is a perfectly common residence. However, in the context of that particular school, surrounded by wealth and luxury, a flat was not considered to be the norm. When 'flat' was called out, one boy stood up and the class started to giggle. He must have felt isolated, exposed and embarrassed.

Why did the teacher think this game was a good idea? Was she living in a naïve bubble? Why didn't she think ahead to the possible outcomes of this scenario? She encouraged a separation between the wealthy children and the boy. Just as I felt prejudged by the boy in my class who had categorised me into a comfortable class bracket, so too must have the boy who lived in a flat.

I live in Edinburgh — one of the UK's wealthiest cities. Everywhere I go I am reminded of my own social status and that of others. To reach the city centre from my house I travel through extremes. It baffles me that, just minutes down the road from an area of severe deprivation, I pass houses worth over a million pounds in one of the most desired postcodes in the nation. It makes me wonder how rich and poor live alongside each other and what one must think of the other. There is no happy medium — no group of 'less wealthy' but 'not so poor' houses to bridge the gap between the very rich and the poverty-stricken.

On a recent school trip I was forced to ask myself how much Edinburgh still lives in the past of its rich ancestors and poor forefathers. We were learning about the old buildings that make up our city. A trip to a house called Gladstone's Land on the Royal Mile allowed us to view these buildings firsthand, and my eyes were drawn to a bell. I asked the guide what it was and he explained that the wealthy residents of those houses would ring and their maids would have to emerge from the depths of the house and rush to tend their masters' needs.

It struck me that these bells still exist in modern society — not perhaps in the form in which they used to exist, but it is still a common occurrence to have maids and cleaners working in the homes of the wealthy. Even though we think we've come so far since the time of our ancestors, the social divide in the 21st century is still prominent. All we need to do is look around us; open our eyes on the bus; acknowledge the existence of the homeless on Princes Street or the range of backgrounds in our children's classrooms.

The divide between rich and poor is not only apparent — it is embedded within us. We are all programmed to decode our classmates or workmates and to subconsciously make snap assessments of their social standing and backgrounds.

I was irritated when this happened to me; I didn't like it. However, I too am a product of this socially aware society. I would like to say it is not a prerequisite that my friends come from a particular background; I would like to say my school helps to reinforce the value of diversity, yet I know we all still judge each other, and that we feel at our most comfortable surrounded by people who are actually quite a lot like us.

*Names have been changed to protect the writer's privacy.

Active learning

Now that you have read the piece of personal writing once, you are going to analyse it in more detail. The easiest way to do this is to have a photocopy of it in front of you. You'll also need pens and pencils. If you have a variety of colours, that's even better.

You'll need to use the following symbols:

1 Every time you find the writer sharing **thoughts**, draw a **think cloud** beside this in the margin.

2 Every time you find the writer sharing **feelings**, draw a **heart** beside this in the margin.

3 Every time you find the writer using **detail or description**, draw an **eye** beside this in the margin.

4 Every time you find the writer using **dialogue**, draw a **speech bubble** beside this in the margin.

5 Every time you find the writer using **a storytelling technique**, draw an **open book** beside this in the margin. Write the name of the technique on the pages of the book.

6 Every time you find the writer **discussing or sharing her reflections**, write a **bold capital letter R** in the margin. If you think the writer is **reacting more widely**, put a capital **W** before the **R**.

7 Write a couple of sentences to explain what made it a **good** piece of writing.

8 Suggest two things the writer could have done that would have made the work **even better**.

This is a useful example piece. It shows that you can build a thoughtful essay from a number of smaller moments — that you don't have to have something huge happen to you before you can write about it.

Going deeper

By the way, if you'd like to look at one more example of a personal essay before you plan and write your own, read *Shooting an Elephant* by George Orwell. (You'll find it easily on the internet, or your teacher may have a copy in school.) He uses all the skills of personal writing. He brings an incident to life in detail; tells us about his own reactions, thoughts and feelings at the time; reflects on his own behaviour and that of others around him and thinks more widely about the nature of empires. All of this makes his piece an excellent example of personal writing.

Planning your personal piece

You've had a chance now to look at two long pieces of personal writing produced by Higher pupils and at a number of shorter extracts from published books. Reading and examining all these pieces has shown you that you need to use all these genre features:

thoughts	feelings	detail and description
dialogue	storytelling techniques as appropriate	reflections on yourself and others
wider reflections		

It's time now for you to plan your piece. There are many ways you could do this. Some people make spider diagrams. Some people list their ideas. Some people write paragraph-by-paragraph plans. All of these ways are useful; you should do whatever is best for you and for the way your brain works. Here, however, is one possible plan you might want to use.

Active learning

You'll need a photocopy of the blank plan on the following page. You should have lots of ideas by now, so ask your teacher if you can have a copy in A3 size.

Use the prompts and shapes to help you plan your piece of personal writing. The shapes are those you used to annotate the piece entitled *Class Room*, but they are bigger this time so that you can write your ideas on them.

What event(s) or experience(s) are you going to write about?

Which storytelling techniques will you use, and at which points in your writing?

Reflections on yourself and others

Wider reflection

Active learning

If you feel comfortable about doing so, and using your plan to help you, explain your ideas to another pupil whom you trust.

Your teacher may also want to see and discuss your plan. Remember that he or she should keep a copy of that plan as evidence that your portfolio is your own work.

Active learning

It's time now to follow your plan and write your piece.

When you've written it, read your work over before you hand it in to your teacher. Think about the three areas the markers are looking at — content, style and technical accuracy — and ask yourself the following questions:

Content:

- Have I stuck to my purpose and written for my audience?
- Have I used the genre conventions for personal writing?
- Have I reflected on myself, on other people, and more widely?
- Are my ideas, feelings and experiences expressed and explored maturely, with insight?
- Does my writing show my personality and individuality?

Style:

- Is my expression varied and confident?
- Does my style fit my chosen genre?
- Have I chosen a structure that helps me fulfil my purpose and put across my meaning?

Technical accuracy:

- Are my spelling, grammar and punctuation all accurate?
- Is my work properly paragraphed?
- Can my work be clearly understood?

Once you have checked over your work, hand it in to your teacher. He or she will mark it and give you feedback and suggestions for ways to improve it for your portfolio.

What we've done so far

So far in this chapter we have found out about the rules and guidelines for Higher writing. We found out about the genre that the SQA calls **broadly creative** writing. This covers four sorts of piece:

- a personal or reflective essay
- a piece of prose fiction
- a poem or a set of linked poems
- a dramatic script

and we learned in detail about the personal essay, and about one particular prose fiction genre.

Now it's time to go on to the other major genre, which the SQA calls **broadly discursive** writing. Remember that, in your portfolio, you need one piece from the creative genre and one from the discursive.

Discursive writing

The second portfolio piece should be what the SQA calls **discursive**, and you can produce any one of these types of writing to fulfil the requirements for this genre:

- an argumentative essay
- a persuasive essay
- a report
- a piece of transactional or informative writing.

We're going to work on the first two of these in detail.

In **argumentative** writing you explore an issue or topic. You will explore two (or more) points of view about this subject, and you will usually come to a conclusion at the end, while still allowing the reader to decide for themselves.

In **persuasive** writing you start with a clear belief or strongly held point of view. In this kind of piece, you will try to use evidence and language to make the reader agree with you.

You can't really decide whether your piece will be argumentative or persuasive until you've chosen a subject, so let's deal with that issue first.

Choosing a topic

Whether your writing ends up being argumentative or persuasive, you need to pick a topic about which people have strong opinions. It should also be a topic in which you have a genuine interest: your finished piece of writing should show real engagement with the ideas or issues you are writing about, and should also show that you understand these well. Feedback from SQA markers shows that pupils often write very well about topics which are current, or which deal with local issues. You need to sustain and develop your ideas for up to 1300 words. You'll only manage all of this if you pick a topic you care about.

So how do you choose a subject?

- You could ask yourself which subjects you are interested in or care about: these will often be tied in to the things you choose to spend your time on.

- You could visit your school library: some publishers produce special series of books where each book contains articles on one controversial subject. Without even reading the books themselves at this stage, just finding out which subjects they deal with might help you think of a topic.
- You could watch television news programmes, read newspapers and use news websites.
- You could ask your teacher about topics that pupils have written successfully on in the past.

Active learning

You shouldn't go any further, or spend any time on research, until you know that your teacher thinks your subject is a good one. Once you have chosen a topic, write it down and give a note of it to your teacher.

If you know already which approach you want to take — two-sided argumentative or one-sided persuasive — write this down along with your subject. If you're not sure which approach to take yet, don't worry. It will become much clearer after you've done your detailed research.

Researching

Whether your piece of writing is one-sided or two-sided, and no matter how much you think you already know about the subject, you need to do some research. Everything you eventually write will be based on this and it is time well spent.

Your first port of call will probably be the internet. You could visit the websites of charities and pressure groups who have an interest in your topic. If, for example, you are writing about development issues, you could visit the sites of organisations like Oxfam or Christian Aid.

Many newspapers have excellent websites. These can be very useful if your topic has been in the headlines recently, and often give real-life examples you can use. One very good site is www.theguardian.com/uk. It is free to use and easy to search.

You need to take far greater care with the online reference source Wikipedia, because it is written by the people who use it. This means that, though the contributors are genuinely interested in their subjects, some of it can be quite biased. You shouldn't use Wikipedia as your only source, and you should check anything you find there against other sources to make sure it is accurate.

If you don't know which sites you want to use, you'll need to begin by using a search engine such as Google™. Try to use only one or two keywords for your search. The computer doesn't know what you are thinking, or why you are looking these words up, so be as precise as you can about what you want.

If you're using a phrase, put double quotation marks round it. Let's suppose you are writing a persuasive essay in which you contend that Formula 1 motor racing should not be regarded as a sport. Looking for "Formula One" will find web pages using that complete phrase. This might be just what you want to know:

> **One factor which surely suggests that Formula One is not a sport is that contestants take part sitting down.**

If you type the same two words without quotation marks you will get all the pages that have the word *formula* and the word *one* anywhere on the same page. This isn't so helpful:

> **One chemical formula used a particularly vile combination of noxious liquids.**

This is good time to go back to your school or local library and ask the staff for advice about the most suitable sources of information on your topic. One thing you will find there is an encyclopedia. These can be very good on established factual information but, as huge books like this take many years to write and put together, they are not great sources for material on current controversial topics. For that, you may be better going back to the internet.

Depending on your topic, you might also speak to people about their own experiences. If you are writing about the rights and wrongs of organic food and you know a farmer, speak to him or her. If you are arguing that young people nowadays are put under far too much pressure to achieve at school, ask a teacher, youth worker or counsellor what they think.

By the way, and just in case you think you don't have to, or in case you think your topic doesn't call for it, everyone needs to do research. Even the most personal persuasive essay will only persuade, will only convince the reader, if what you write is supported by facts, statistics, experiences and anecdotes.

Using your own words

There was one very important note of advice in the guidelines at the start of the chapter: you **absolutely cannot, ever** copy and paste from a website or from anywhere else.

You are allowed to get ideas and information from sources, but you can't use someone else's words and pass them off as your own. This is called **plagiarism** and if the examiners think that you have cheated in this way, the consequences can be very serious.

To help you avoid accidentally falling into plagiarism, here's a useful piece of advice to follow during the research stage:

> ### Warning
>
> It's OK to read, underline or highlight someone else's words, but **WHENEVER YOU MAKE A NOTE, DO THAT IN YOUR OWN WORDS**. It doesn't matter if you type the words or handwrite them, **WHENEVER YOU PUT WORDS ON A PAGE, THEY SHOULD BE YOUR OWN**.

I hope all those bold and shouty capitals got the point across. The advice is only useful, of course, if you know how to put something into your own words. This skill is called **paraphrasing**. It's worth practising because it won't just be useful to you in your discursive writing. You also need to be able to do this to demonstrate your understanding in the Reading for Understanding, Analysis and Evaluation exam, where lifting words straight from the text will mean you get no marks, even if you have found the right information.

There's a third reason for making sure that you can paraphrase all the ideas and information you find. You're not just avoiding plagiarism, and you're not just practising a skill you'll use elsewhere, you're also making sure you understand what you have read. The best way to prove that you really grasp something is to be able to explain it yourself in a different way.

Look at this sentence found by a pupil who decided to research global climate change:

> **The overwhelming consensus among climate change scientists is that human activities are responsible for much of the climate change we're seeing.**

The pupil needed to put this in his own words, which he did like this:

> **Those who research this subject believe our own actions are the main cause of the climate change we are experiencing. They are in almost complete agreement about this.**

This pupil used a lot of different tactics as he paraphrased.

First, he changed some important words or expressions.

You will see a list of expressions from the original sentence. How did the pupil change each one?

- overwhelming consensus
- climate change scientists
- human activities
- responsible for
- much of the
- we're seeing

Second, he changed the number of sentences from one to two. Third, he put the two ideas in the original sentence the other way round. All of this shows that he has understood and can process the information.

What he didn't change was the phrase *climate change* itself. Because that is his subject, and that is what his whole essay is about, he can keep using those words.

Active learning

Here are five more extracts pupils found while researching different topics. Remembering the techniques above, paraphrase each extract. The subject of each extract is given for you at the start.

1 [The death penalty] Those who believe that deterrence justifies the execution of certain offenders bear the burden of proving that the death penalty is in fact a deterrent.

2 [Raising the legal age for buying alcohol] In the US, the age to drink legally is 21. However, it is naive to assume that there is no drinking problem. University students attend house parties where binge drinking is the norm. They lack the protection that would come from being in a bar or nightclub. In addition, attending such parties usually requires transport, which is a key reason why so many American students drink and drive.

3 [Having a curfew for teenagers] It is impossible to solve antisocial behaviour by using repression. If the British government enforces this law, rebellious teenagers will merely become convinced that society is actually against them.

4 [The pros and cons of same-sex schooling] Thirty years ago, the popular belief about same-sex education was that it upheld outdated stereotypes about gender, such as women should study nursing and men should study engineering. Experts at that time believed that coeducation dispelled those gender myths.

5 [Whether footballers are overpaid] Football has become an industry, and its employees — the players — have taken their places alongside the world's elite of movie and rock stars. Across the planet, football has slowly grown to become the world's biggest and most widely followed sport. It is only natural, therefore, that some of the huge profit that the football league makes each year finds its way into the hands of its key assets: the players.

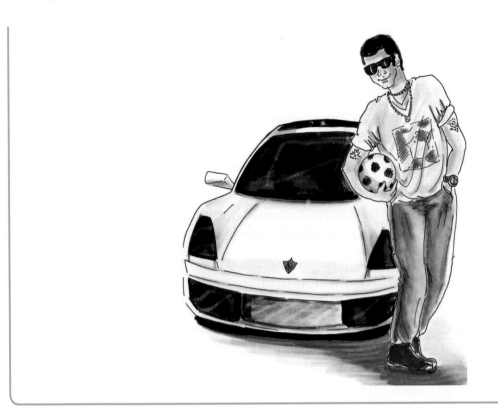

Citing your sources

Another of the authenticity guidelines we saw at the start of the chapter was about being able to show where your information came from. As you research, take a note of all these things. You will need to list them in a **bibliography** at the end of your essay.

- If you have used a newspaper or magazine article, give the title of the piece and the publication, name the writer and give the publication date.
- If you use information from the internet, give the name of the site and the specific page address.
- If you quote from a book, give the page number, title, author, publisher and publication date.

Active learning

If you haven't already discussed with your teacher whether your essay will be two-sided argumentative or one-sided persuasive, now is the time to do so. Read over your notes and consider what approach you are going to take. These prompts should help you decide:

- If you find your topic interesting, but you're genuinely not sure what your stance on it is, or if you think it's a highly complex issue without a straightforward answer, you should go for the argumentative approach.
- If you've developed a genuine opinion on the subject, and if you think you can put it across in a way that makes you sound engaged and committed, go for the persuasive approach.

Using your research to support opinions

Once you have collected your information, you should try to find a way to make each fact or idea you have found support an opinion. Facts can be proved. They are true and nobody can argue against them.

Pizza is made by baking cheese, tomato sauce and perhaps other toppings on a bread base.

Opinions are more personal. They are what people think, and different people can have different opinions about the same thing.

Never mind the calendar, central heating and public sanitation, the best thing Italy ever gave the world was pizza.

In **persuasive** writing, organise the facts to support what you believe. In **argumentative** writing, organise them to support the two different sides of the argument.

Here's an example from a pupil who is writing persuasively about his belief that footballers are overpaid.

FACT/EXAMPLE FROM RESEARCH

The typical Premiership footballer earns £60,000 a week. The salary for a newly qualified police constable is less than £24,000 a year.

HOW THIS SUPPORTS MY OPINION

The fact that some footballers can earn over 150 times as much as police officers, who do a valuable and dangerous job, shows they are overpaid.

Active learning

Look through the notes you gathered during your research. Remember, these should be in your own words by now. Organise your material as shown above, picking out the useful facts and working out how each one could be used to support an opinion.

A good writer will be able to 'spin' facts to support their opinion. Two newspapers could have two very different opening sentences at the start of their front-page stories.

A tram scheme that will turn the city centre into a building site and cause years of traffic chaos was revealed today.

A tram scheme that will provide rapid, low–carbon public transport and cut journey times across the city was revealed today.

They're both reporting the same fact, that the city has announced plans for a tram scheme, but they have spun this to suit their own opinions.

Being able to bend facts towards the direction you want to go is especially useful in persuasive writing, when you are trying to make your readers agree with you.

Planning two-sided, argumentative pieces

In these essays you should show that you understand the arguments on both sides. At the end you can give your opinion and your readers can decide on theirs.

We'll look at two ways you could structure these essays. We'll look first at the **simple structure**. It would be more impressive though if you used the complex structure, and we'll go into that in more detail later. The simple structure works like this:

Step 1 A one-paragraph introduction to the topic:

> **Although Britain abolished the death penalty in the 1960s, there are frequent pleas for its reintroduction, usually after the details of some grisly multiple murder are splashed across the tabloids.**

Step 2 Write a link sentence, explaining which side of the argument you will begin with.

> **Those who advocate the return of capital punishment have many firmly held beliefs.**

Step 3 Now take all of the points on one side of the argument. Each point should be in a separate paragraph, and these points should be backed up with facts, observations or personal experiences. Use **topic sentences** and the **PEE structure**. (You will find out more about these soon.) Start with the strongest, most convincing arguments and work your way down to the weaker ones. You should aim to have at least three or four paragraphs on the first side of the argument.

Step 4 Write a link sentence showing that you are about to switch to the other side of the argument.

> **Those on the other side of the argument are just as passionate in their belief that there would be no benefit in executing even our most notorious criminals.**

Step 5 Now do the same on this side of the argument as you did at Step 3 above, working again from the stronger points down to weaker ones.

Step 6 Finally, in your conclusion, briefly sum up what you have written. Now say which side you agree with and why. Show which arguments convinced you, or refer to an experience in your life or the life of someone you know that has convinced you that a particular side is right. You may wish to leave the reader with something to think about.

> It is clear that both sides have strong arguments. Having examined them, I feel that on the whole we will not create a better Britain by executing our criminals. Any system that says it is wrong to kill people, but then tries to prove that by killing, is misguided and wrong.

The **more complex structure** for two-sided pieces makes you look more skilled at handling your material. It works like this:

The introduction and conclusion are the same as they are in a simply-structured essay. However, in the main body of the essay, you begin with the strongest argument from one side of the argument. Then, in the next paragraph, you work through a point on the opposite side that contradicts what you have just written about. You can organise these paragraphs with **topic sentences** and the **PEE structure**, which will be explained later in this chapter.

To illustrate this, let's imagine an essay on the issue of assisted dying. Here's a point in favour of this practice:

> Perhaps the strongest argument for allowing terminally ill patients to choose how and when to die is that this may prevent great suffering. Not only can people in the final stages of a long illness experience terrible pain, they may also suffer the indignity of being unable to take care of their own most basic needs. The right to die could spare them all of this.

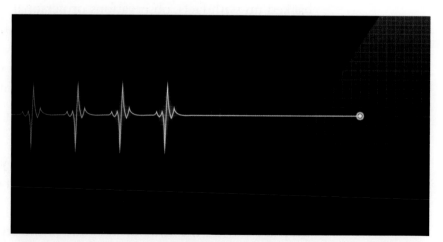

Now here's the answering point from the opposite side of the argument:

> However, this assumes that dying patients are somehow not being properly cared for. This is not true. Modern advances in pain control mean that even the last days of life can be made comfortable,

allowing patients to spend longer with their loved ones. Many say that we should demand not the right to choose when we die, but the right to die with dignity.

Then take the second strongest point from the first side of the argument. Explain it, and then challenge it by making another point from the opposite side to contradict it. Keep going, following this pattern.

You may find that some of your points cannot be paired up in this way. You can deal with them just before you start your conclusion. All the remaining points can be rolled into two short paragraphs, one for the ideas that support one side of the argument, for example:

There are other valid reasons why many people think that we should allow the terminally ill to choose when to end their lives …

and the other for the evidence that concludes the other side of the argument, for example:

Those who are against this also have further important points to make …

Active learning

If you know that you are going to write an argumentative essay, decide now which of the two structures, simpler or more complex, would be best for you to use.

Structuring persuasive writing

Organising this kind of piece is very similar, but simpler. In persuasive writing you don't have to switch from one part of the argument to the other, because you are always trying to defend your own point of view.

Step 1 A one-paragraph introduction to the topic. Make clear straight away what you believe about the subject. Use your wit and passion to grab the reader's attention from the start.

Our supermarkets, corner shops, even our petrol stations are filling with brightly coloured celebrity magazines. We seem to have become so used to them that we never question their place in our lives. However, I firmly believe Britain would be a better place if we gathered up every copy of *Heat*, *Hello*, *OK*, *Grazia* and all their shiny little clones and dumped them in a recycling facility. Somewhere offshore. The mid-Atlantic should do it.

Step 2 Using the points you've planned, set out your argument. Each point should be in a separate paragraph, and these points should be backed up with facts, observations or personal experiences. Use **topic sentences** and the **PEE structure** whenever you can. (You will find out more about these soon.) Start with the strongest, most convincing arguments and work your way down to the weaker ones. Plan to write three or four paragraphs of this type, for example:

> **What's most striking about these magazines is their overwhelming similarity. The same faces crop up week after week, and a trawl of any given week's offerings will throw up (and that vomit reference is deliberate) perhaps five or six versions of the same story about the same botoxed fembot having boozy second thoughts during her tacky, Sahara-themed hen night. With so few characters to go round, and so little of interest to say about them, do we really need more than a dozen weekly magazines all trying and failing to say it?**

Step 3 Although you are always defending your own position in this kind of writing, your argument will be stronger if you can show that you understood the other side's position and can disprove it. Plan to write one or two paragraphs where you start by acknowledging what those who disagree with you would think, and then go on to dismantle their points. For example:

> **Some readers will defend these tatty comics, and the creatures they tirelessly report on, by saying that they bring celebrities down to Earth. What *Heat*, *Grazia*, *More*, *OK* and the others claim to do for us is show that celebrities are nothing different. They are just like little old us. But they aren't. In real life divorce is a heartbreak not easily cured by taking a dozen friends on a get-over-him holiday in the Maldives. When real people lose or gain half a stone in weight they buy a new pair of jeans. They do not get papped in their bikini and splashed across the front page. Real women do not marry three times before their thirtieth birthday and get a different paper to pay for every tastelessly themed celebration.**

You may find that some of your points are not strong enough to be dealt with in their own separate paragraphs. If you still feel they are valuable and want to use them, then you can deal with them just before you start your conclusion. All the remaining points can be rolled into one short paragraph:

> **As if all of this is not enough, we also have to remember …**

Step 4 Finally, in your conclusion, briefly sum up what you have written. End with a strong, clear statement that shows again why you believe you are right. You may also want to challenge the reader to think or respond.

> **Sweeping the celebrity magazines from the shelves would make the world a better place. We'd fill our minds with higher thoughts, we'd have a much clearer view of what normal adult behaviour looks like, and we might even read more books. Do you really need to know how much a television presenter weighs?**

Structuring your paragraphs

As well as structuring and ordering your whole essay, you need to have a clear structure in each paragraph. One good way to do this is to use **topic sentences** and the **PEE pattern**. You can also use these when writing critical essays about the literature you've read, but they apply just as much here.

Topic sentences

A topic sentence is called this for two reasons:

1 It refers to the topic of the essay.
2 It introduces the topic of its paragraph.

The topic sentence is usually the first in the paragraph. Look at the following paragraph from our writer on the death penalty. The topic sentence has been underlined. The words that tie that sentence into the topic of the whole essay are in bold.

> <u>Some wish to see the **death penalty reintroduced** as a punishment for murder because they see it as a way of making the punishment fit the crime.</u> **If someone is guilty of taking a life, they argue, that person should then forfeit his own life. Any other punishment is too merciful, too lenient in the harsh light of what the criminal has done. This argument is strongly advocated by some Christian commentators as they believe it fits the Biblical principle of 'an eye for an eye'.**

Using PEE

As you write your discursive essay, within each paragraph of it (apart from the introduction and conclusion) you could use the **PEE structure**, which goes like this:

- **P** – Make a **POINT** that is relevant to the topic of your essay. This point is the topic sentence at the start of the paragraph.
  One reason why celebrity magazines should be terminated is because this would actually make the lives of celebrities better and happier.

- **E** – Give **EVIDENCE** to back up the point you are making. This should be either a fact you found out during your research, something you have noticed, or something you have experienced yourself.
  A flick through just three of these, all published in the last week, revealed a total of 32 photographs which had obviously been taken by paparazzi photographers without the subject's permission, and at times clearly without even their knowledge.

- **E – EXPLAIN** this. If you are writing to persuade, show how it adds to your argument. If you are doing a piece of argumentative writing, show how the point and evidence contribute to this side of the topic.

  It can do no good for anyone's mental health to know that they are being constantly stalked, and that even to put the bin out or nip to the shops for a pint of milk is regarded as an invitation to invade their privacy.

Direction markers

Certain words and phrases signal the direction of the argument in a piece of discursive writing, or emphasise the writer's point of view in persuasive writing. Most of these words and phrases appear at the start of a paragraph or sentence.

Active learning

You may wish to work with a partner or small group. Look at these four headings:

- These expressions move the argument forwards.
- These expressions let the argument change direction.
- These expressions allow the writer to sum up.
- These expressions show the writer is sure he is right.

Now look at the expressions below. Each one fits best under one of those headings. Get a piece of A4 paper and divide it into four large boxes. Put each heading at the top of a different box. Underneath the heading, list the expressions that fit there. Check any new words with a dictionary as you go.

nonetheless	rather	in contrast	instead
without a doubt	undeniably	surely	definitely
thus	otherwise	moreover	yet
nevertheless	finally	on the contrary	obviously
likewise	conversely	on the other hand	whereas
unquestionably	therefore	however	next
despite	similarly	in spite of	absolutely
at the same time	without question	and	alternatively
in retrospect	without doubt	significantly	but
in conclusion	first(ly)	accordingly	although
also	in brief	second(ly)	indubitably

in addition	furthermore	as a result	equally
consequently	third(ly)	because	
on the whole	to sum up	to balance this	
what is more	in other words	certainly	

Finally, still working with your partner or in your group, see how many words or phrases you can think of to add to each list.

Some other useful words

If you want to refer to another argument so you can knock it down, one useful word is *claim*. Using this word hints that you do not believe something the other side says. Read the following paragraphs:

> The footballer **claims** to be a dedicated family man and a devoted father to his two young sons.

> She reached her current position after unusually fast promotion through the company, a firm in which she has a very close relationship with the chairman, Sir Antony Blackadder. She **claims** that Blackadder merely recognised her potential and mentored her to help her fulfil it.

What is the writer suggesting about the footballer and the businesswoman mentioned above?

Some words are useful if you can't prove something for sure. These words are also useful for suggestions and rumours. These words include *reported, rumoured, alleged, believed, could, likely, would, reported* and *may point to*. For example, here's a piece of gossip that may have very few provable facts behind it:

> It is **believed** that troubled television presenter Sonia Summers **could** again be struggling with the addiction problems originally **reported** earlier this year. It is **rumoured** that her use of alcohol and painkillers **could have** risen once again to the worrying heights that **allegedly** led her to seek treatment in January. It is **likely** that television bosses, who pay her £1 million a year to present 'A Healthy Mind In A Healthy Body' **would be** very unhappy if she were facing such issues. The television star's close friends are **reported** to be very concerned. Summers's unexplained non-appearance on last week's episode of 'Lightly Come Prancing' **may point to** continuing problems with substance misuse.

Some particular techniques for persuasive writing

Persuasive writing tends to use certain techniques. Some of the most common are:

- **repetition** of words or phrases
- dramatic-sounding **short sentences**
- including the reader by using **'we' and related words**
- asking **rhetorical questions** — which do not need an answer but make the reader think
- using what's called **'the rule of three'** — doing something three times over; this might be three examples, three rhetorical questions, three uses of the same word or phrase and so on
- use of an **anecdote** or **personal experience** to justify why the writer holds a certain opinion
- an appeal to the reader's **emotions**, or **emotive language** which stirs up the reader's feelings
- offering the reader a **vision** of success or achievement.

Active learning

Read the following text. It is by the food writer and television presenter Hugh Fearnley-Whittingstall. From the starting point of a conversation with his young son, he takes the perhaps unexpected stance of persuading people that it's better for animals if we are NOT vegetarian. As you read the piece, look for examples of each technique being used.

Vegetarians With Teeth

'How do you know stegosaurus is a vegetarian?' asked Oscar.

'You can tell from his teeth,' I said, feigning confidence in my hazy paleontological recollection. 'Dinosaur experts think they weren't the right teeth for eating meat.'

'But Ned's got the right teeth for eating meat, and he's a vegetarian too,' said Oscar.

Good point, I thought.

'Well, Ned has a choice, because he's a human being. Animals either are vegetarians, or they're not.'

'I'm a shoe-man bean. Does that mean I can choice?'

'Yes,' I said.

'Well, I'm going to choice to eat meat then.'

'Why's that?' I asked.

'Because I like it.'

'Me too,' I said.

What I didn't say to Oscar is that I have been thinking a fair bit recently about the whole vegetarian/carnivore thing. Why exactly do I eat meat? I don't think it's particularly good for me (partial as I am to the fattier cuts). I abhor the way most of it is produced. And, much as I enjoy eating it, I don't imagine life without it would be completely unbearable. So you see, I am not an untroubled carnivore. So why haven't I become a vegetarian?

Well, I guess there's my image to think of. Connoisseur of obscure body parts. Enthusiastic muncher of small furry animals. But honestly, I'd give it all up — even the bacon — if I was properly convinced it was the right thing to do. Recently, I've been considering the matter in some depth for a book I'm working on. Soon I hope to have resolved the matter to the satisfaction of my own conscience — one way or another.

But in the meantime, there's one thing I'd like a bit of help with. And perhaps there's a vegetarian out there who can oblige. (Or more likely, a vegan, because what vegans understand, to their credit, is that the dairy industry is the meat industry — or at least the beef industry.)

My questions are these: what would the vegetarian Utopia look like? And would anyone seriously want to live there? How would vegetarians set about dismantling the mixed farming system? What would happen to all the farm animals?

One possible response is that because killing animals is simply wrong, a moral absolute, questions like mine are irrelevant (as well as irritating). But that really isn't good enough. Because if enough of us were genuinely persuaded of the wrongness of killing animals for food (which is presumably what vegetarians would like to happen) we could then choose democratically to live in a meat-free society and these questions would become very real.

Would vegetarians be in favour of the mass slaughter of farm animals, to accelerate the arable revolution? And if so, would the carnivorous minority be allowed a last supper of the slaughtered corpses? Presumably the answer is 'no' on both counts.

More likely, the WPTVB (Working Party for the Transition to a Vegetarian Britain) will favour a gradual scaling down of stocking, to a point where small populations of a wide range of breeds are managed, by man, in 'Tame Life Parks'. Here they are well looked after and preserved for their educational and historic interest. Meanwhile the countryside is turned over to the cultivation of fruit and vegetables — grown, of course, without the aid of animal manures, and therefore with the input of huge quantities of chemical fertilisers.

But the matter cannot quite rest there. What happens when the sheep and cows get a bit long in the tooth? Or short in the tooth, as is the problem with ageing livestock. They can't feed properly, and quickly lose condition. In the absence of predators to finish them off, they will die a lingering and stressful death. Will the vegetarians allow human, and humane, intervention? Can we 'put them out of their misery'? And, incidentally, do we incinerate their carcasses? Feed them to our pets? To the worms? Or, as a sop, to those appalling carnivores, for an occasional 'treat'?

I guess what it boils down to is this. All animals must live some kind of life, and die some kind of death. And having died, they will be eaten, whether it's by a maggot, a crow, or a person.

The carnivore's position, and mine until you persuade me otherwise, is that the best, most morally acceptable way to co-exist with our dependent, domesticated livestock is to take care of them when they are alive, ensure that they have a quick and, in relative terms at least, stress-free death. And then eat them.

I accept entirely that, through industrial farming practice, we are guilty of a gross abuse of our responsibility of care, and a treatment of farm animals that is often morally without defence. But surely reform, and not abstinence, is the answer?

If you're a sheep, the question of who ends up eating you when you're dead is the very least of your worries. And, in the long run, you'd probably rather be a sheep than a stegosaurus.

Active learning

Now try this: First, share your answers with the rest of the class. Next, give examples of any other techniques you found Fearnley-Whittingstall using to make his argument effective.

Active learning

It's time to plan your piece. (You may already have done quite a lot of planning after the research phase if you organised your material into what the facts were, and how each fact could be used to support an argument.) Look back at all the material you gathered from your research. Double check that you did put everything you found into **your own words**.

Following all the advice this chapter has given you, prepare a paragraph plan for your piece. Think about these things:

- What will you do to grab your readers' attention in the introduction?
- For each body paragraph, make sure you know:
  - what your topic sentence will be
  - what evidence you are going to use
  - how your evidence backs up the idea in your topic sentence.
- How will you give impact to your conclusion?

Remember, you have a choice of simpler or more complex structures if you are writing a two-sided, argumentative essay.

It's now time to write your piece. Don't forget the bibliography of your sources at the end.

When you've written it, read over your work before you hand it in to your teacher. Think about the three areas the markers are looking at — content, style and technical accuracy — and ask yourself the following questions:

Content:

- Have I stuck to my purpose and written for my audience?
- Is there evidence that I have researched the subject and selected relevant ideas?
- Do I clearly understand my topic and have I shown that I am engaged with it?
- Does my writing have a clear line of thought?

Style:

- Is my expression confident and varied?
- Does my structure enhance the purpose and meaning of my essay?
- Have I used features of the discursive genre to inform, argue, discuss and/or persuade, as appropriate?
- Does my writing show depth and complexity of thought?
- Am I objective, or persuasive, at the right times?

Technical accuracy:

- Are my spelling, grammar and punctuation all accurate?
- Is my work properly paragraphed?
- Can my work be clearly understood?

Once you have checked over your work, hand it in to your teacher. He or she will mark it and give you feedback and suggestions for ways to improve it for your portfolio.

Your final portfolio

It may take most of your Higher English year to prepare and complete your portfolio, which will be sent away for marking in March, a couple of months before your exam. You may write a number of first draft pieces before deciding, in consultation with your teacher, which two to redraft and send.

The two pieces you finally submit should be clearly distinct from each other. So, though your discursive piece might use anecdotal evidence, or a personal essay might touch on an issue that has affected and shaped you and your experience, there shouldn't be any feeling of overlap or common ground between the two pieces. The Higher markers want to see the breadth and depth of your writing skill, and therefore there must be a clear difference between your creative and discursive writing.

Throughout this process, your teacher should keep a note of your titles and ideas, and should also keep your plans, and the marked first drafts, for the two pieces you eventually redraft. Doing so is part of the 'supervision and control' mentioned earlier.

Your teacher is allowed to write comments and suggestions on your first draft, and can discuss these with you, but cannot mark mistakes in detail. It's up to you to be able to correct these. It is also very clear in the SQA documentation for this course that your teacher is allowed to mark only one draft of any piece, and that you are allowed to produce only one redraft. This makes the process fair for every pupil in every school.

You will need to sign a declaration to say that your portfolio is your own work. The two pieces that you send away should be produced under conditions that help to ensure that the work is your own. In practice, the easiest way to do this is to write your first draft of each piece in class. Your teacher can then compare that draft to any later versions to make sure that the work, as it improves and develops, is without a doubt still your own.

Presentation

Your portfolio has to be submitted to the SQA according to a very exact format, pasted into a special template sheet. You can find this on the Higher English page of the SQA website (at www.sqa.org.uk, under the heading 'Coursework'); your English teacher may also be able to give you a link to the file or a downloaded copy of it. The file gives you a virtual 'page' that you can type straight into, or you can copy and paste the work from elsewhere.

Your portfolio pieces should be typed and printed in black. Use a clear standard font in 12 point. You should use one-and-a-half line spacing, with a double return for new paragraphs. Make sure your writing stays inside the margin of the format page. Put the word count for each piece at the end of the piece. Your second piece should start on a new page, but still in the same document. Your Scottish Candidate Number and a page number go in boxes at the bottom of each page.

CHAPTER 2 The Spoken Language Performance

The **spoken language performance** tests your skills in talking and listening. As you discovered in the Introduction to the book, this is the only part of the Higher English course that is assessed internally, in your school or college. It is also ungraded; you won't get a mark or score for this task, you only have to achieve the standard, which you must do to get an award at Higher.

What you will be assessed on

You must do at least **one spoken language activity**. This can either be:

- a group discussion
- an individual presentation to an audience.

You will be assessed on **four** aspects of your spoken language and you have to achieve them all.

1 **Content:** your ideas and information should be detailed and complex, and put across using a structure that suits your purpose and audience.
2 **Style:** you should communicate effectively by selecting and using detailed and complex language.
3 **Non-verbal:** you must use aspects of non-verbal communication.
4 **Listening:** you will demonstrate your listening skills by responding to the spoken language of others.

Although there is no rule about how long your presentation should be, or how long a group discussion should take, you need to speak for long enough to let your teacher see you demonstrate all the above skills.

You do not have to do this all on one single occasion; you don't need to worry that your assessment rests on just one group discussion, or on just one presentation to the class. Although this book will deal with these as two separate, individual tasks, as that's the easiest way to explain them, your teacher can make a much more holistic judgement based on your spoken language on a number of different occasions.

Your teacher may use a number of different methods of assessing your work and of recording these judgements. He or she could:

- assess your work against a detailed checklist
- make video recordings.

Spoken activities

Notice that the SQA says you will be taking part in a spoken language **activity**.

Even if you are mainly standing up at the front of the room giving an individual presentation, you should be *interacting with* the audience, not *talking at* them. You need to engage and involve the audience, and show that you are involved with them. Remember also that you are being assessed on **both** talking **and** listening. In a group discussion, you should actively listen and respond, as well as talk; in an individual presentation, you should take questions from your audience.

Some people do feel very nervous about talking, especially about individual presentations to an audience. That's completely understandable. For every raging, egomaniac extrovert in your class who just loves being listened to, there's going to be someone who wishes the carpet would open up and swallow them.

But the reason talking is assessed in the Higher English course is because it is a valuable life skill, one you will use in your further study, at work, and in your daily relationships.

Individual presentations

You might deliver your individual presentation to your whole class. However, it is also possible to talk to a smaller audience, perhaps by speaking to a group while the rest of your class is working on something else. If you are particularly anxious about individual presentation, discuss with your teacher whether you can be assessed in this way.

But, the best way to overcome nerves is by being ready. So, in this part of the chapter we will focus on the three Ps of **preparing**, **practising** and **presenting** your talk.

First though, an inspirational example:

Malala Yousafzai speaking to the United Nations in 2013

Malala Yousafzai was a schoolgirl in Pakistan when she became known for campaigning for the right of girls to have an education. She wrote a blog for the BBC, was filmed by a US documentary crew, gave media interviews, and was nominated for the International Children's Peace Prize.

One morning, Taliban gunmen boarded Malala's school bus. They asked for her by name, and shot her in the head. Critically ill, she was brought to Britain for surgery and intensive medical support.

Far from giving up her campaign, she became the focus for a worldwide movement to give all children everywhere, and especially girls, an education. In October 2014, Malala became the youngest person ever to win the Nobel Peace Prize and has been named as one of the 100 most influential people in the world. She met the Queen, and former US President Barack Obama, and marked her sixteenth birthday by making a speech to the United Nations.

So, if Malala Yousafzai can speak to hundreds of people at the UN, on her birthday, under the gaze of the world's media, just seven months after a brain injury, and can do so in English — which isn't even her first language — what's stopping you from talking to your classmates?

We're going to use that event as an example. First, your teacher needs to do a little preparation.

Teacher's task

- Search online for 'Malala UN speech' to find the film of this event.
- Your pupils will also need a written version of the speech, which you can find by searching for 'Malala UN speech transcript'.
- Each pupil in your class also needs a copy of the next page of this book to write on.

Active learning

Start by working on your own. The whole broadcast speech is quite long. Get your teacher to play it up to the 6 minute, 50 second point, just before Malala talks about her feelings for the Talib who shot her.

As you watch, make notes on your sheet to record your observations. The wording on the page comes from the assessment standards for talking at Higher, which means your teacher might also eventually use something like this page to take notes while assessing you.

For example, under the heading for language choice, you might notice Malala's repeated use of the 'Honourable … Respected …' form of address. Under the heading for ideas and content, you might notice her gratitude to those who have helped and supported her.

Now join up with someone else and compare your notes. What did your partner spot that you did not?

Next, still working with your partner, read the transcript of the speech. This will really let you focus on two features: the speaker's ideas and content; and her language choice. Add to your notes on the sheet.

Speaker: Topic:

Detailed and complex ideas and content, using a structure suitable for purpose and audience:

Selecting and using detailed and complex language

Non-verbal communication

Going deeper

You can do this task again in class or on your own by watching or reading other inspiring examples of talks, speeches and presentations.

John F. Kennedy speaking at his presidential inauguration

- If you'd like to read the text of a historical talk, look for the Gettysburg Address, delivered by Abraham Lincoln in 1863 during the American Civil War. This famous oration is just ten sentences long.
- For another US presidential source, search out John F. Kennedy's inauguration speech from almost a century later in 1961. Listen out for what he says about '*your country*'.
- To read the words of a man unafraid to lay down his life, find Nelson Mandela's statement from the dock at his trial in 1964. This is a very long speech, but the last few paragraphs have become especially famous. Or, look for the shorter speech he gave when inaugurated as South Africa's president in 1994.
- For a speech by a younger, female speaker, look for actress Ellen Page addressing the Time To THRIVE conference or Emma Watson talking about the HeForShe initiative.

Ellen Page

- To watch a speaker engaging with a young, inner-city audience, look at rapper LL Cool J addressing the I Have A Dream Foundation.

Now that you are thoroughly inspired, it's time to work on the first of the three P stages mentioned earlier.

Preparation

The best way to use this section on individual presentations is to prepare one as you work through the next few pages. Before you start to do this, it's helpful to know two things:

1 **Who** will your audience be? Your whole class? A small group? Some other audience altogether?
2 **What** will your talk be about?

Your teacher can help you clarify the *who*. Let's take some time to think about the *what*.

You know that you have to use detailed and complex language. Also, your audience will most likely consist of Higher English pupils, who should be listening to detailed and complex language. One way to make sure you use this sort of language is by picking a subject that is, in itself, detailed and complex.

Your teacher may give you a topic, or at least an area to think about. Here are some other suggestions. For some of them, you'll see how they might be an evolution of, or a move on from, topics you might have covered in National 5.

At National 5 you might have spoken about a favourite film, speaking about what happens, who is in it, and why you like it. You could still focus on just one film, but deal with it far more deeply, with thorough analysis and by making use of appropriate film studies terminology.

You might choose a film director and present an introduction to his or her work. This would include looking at aspects of this director's style, recurring themes and ideas in the work, and so on.

Or, at National 5 you might have spoken about a book. Again, you could still deal with just one book at Higher, but taking a far deeper and more critical approach.

You could choose to discuss the work of a particular writer. This would include looking at aspects of this author's style, recurring themes and ideas in their work, and so on.

You might talk about a writer you are studying for your Critical Reading exam. For instance, once you have become familiar with some of this author's work, you could investigate a new area: a new poem or short story, a later extract from a novel or play. In your talk you would share your discoveries with the class, thereby introducing them to that text or extract.

You could deliver a revision lecture to your class about a text they have studied for the exam.

Your talk might be based on the research you have done for the discursive essay that goes in your portfolio.

You might pick an issue that is currently in the news and present a deeper viewpoint: for example, if a conflict has broken out somewhere, you could research and explain the underlying historical causes; if the government has launched some new policy or programme, you could investigate the ideas behind this.

These are just some suggestions. Any topic that gets you to be thoughtful, critical or analytical is likely to be a rich source for your talk. Once you have an idea, discuss it with your teacher and make sure she or he thinks it will be suitable and will give you enough to say.

Here's an idea for you to think about:

> **The holy grail of public speaking is rehearsed spontaneity.**

Have a chat with your partner. What do you think this means? If you understand this, you will understand what the preparation and practice stages are for.

Active learning

The first step is to create a rough outline for your presentation. The easiest way to do this is to make a list of headings. For example, if you were talking about a writer, your headings might be:

- Introduction — who this is, why I chose him/her
- Brief overview
  - biographical detail
  - significant works
- Key themes and ideas — how these are handled
    1
    2
    3
- Key aspects of style
    1
    2
    3
- Critical responses/reception
- My own response to this author
- Conclusion

You can then write out what you want to say under each of these headings. Even at this stage, try to do this by writing notes rather than full sentences. Use short phrases, keywords and bullet points. This will lower the risk of you just getting up and reading your notes out to the audience. This isn't a reading aloud assessment, it's a talking one!

Now that you have your raw material, let's look at how to shape it into a successful presentation, one you know you have rehearsed, but that will come across as spontaneous.

Good openings

You want to engage your audience right away — to draw them in or intrigue them, to get them thinking or to startle them.

Look at the two openings that follow. Which one do you think belongs to the National 5 presentation, and which one begins a presentation by a Higher pupil?

'First, do no harm,' said Hippocrates, which is all very well for him sitting quietly in ancient Greece, but rather more daunting for a sixteen-year-old in an ill-fitting set of scrubs.

Doctors, nurses, patients… As you've probably guessed, I spent my work experience week in a hospital.

You should have spotted that the first one is the Higher one. While both speakers draw the audience in, the National 5 speaker starts by saying something rather predictable. The Higher speaker, though, shows off knowledge of the foundation of all medical ethics, then undercuts that seriousness with the self-deprecating image of herself in the borrowed hospital clothes.

There are many ways you can give your opening impact. Here's writer and broadcaster Sandi Toksvig:

> A man once offered two camels for my hand in marriage. I was making a documentary in the Nubian desert in Sudan when I caught an older gentleman's eye. He made the offer to my male producer, who very kindly suggested he would split the proceeds with me if I agreed. Never one to rush a decision, I went off to look at the proffered creatures. I'm no camel expert, but they seemed rather dapper for fellows with many miles left in them. In the end, however, I graciously declined and we all had mint tea instead.

Toksvig starts with a very striking opening sentence, a statement the audience can't ignore. She goes on to tell a story, as an introduction to her text.

So, by looking at the opening from the pupil who did her work experience in a hospital, and from that by Sandi Toksvig, we already have five techniques you can use:

1 use a quotation
2 use humour
3 paint a picture with words
4 make a striking statement
5 tell a story.

You could also do one or more of these things:

6 ask a question, either a rhetorical one or one you want the audience to answer
7 share a thought or observation
8 jump right into the middle of the action.

Active learning

Look back at the notes you have made so far for the presentation you are preparing. Rewrite your opening to have more impact on the audience.

Language and vocabulary

One of the things the assessor will be looking at is the language and vocabulary you choose to use. These, remember, should be **detailed** and **complex**.

First of all, you should **vary your vocabulary**, choosing interesting, less common words rather than more ordinary and predictable ones. So Sandi Toksvig in her opening used words like 'proffered', 'dapper' and 'declined' rather than the more straightforward 'offered', 'smart' and 'refused'.

Active learning

This pupil is talking about his favourite film director. His language at the moment is a little unsophisticated. Can you re-write this section of his talk to make the language more detailed and complex? You should be helping him to do these three things:

1 use more interesting vocabulary
2 avoid repetition of the same words or phrases
3 use longer and more complex sentences.

Wes Anderson's next film was his most successful so far. This film was *The Grand Budapest Hotel*. In my opinion it is also his best. Every frame is full of detail that makes you wish you could rewind it and watch it again. Wes Anderson has used lots of bright, light colours such as pinks, creams and blues. These colours almost make the film feel like a bright and tasty box of chocolates for the viewer to pick from. This is very suitable as one character works in a bakery making incredible cakes and pastries. Part of the plot involves two characters using the bakery van to sneak their way into the hotel.

As well as working on varying your vocabulary, and using more complex structures, think about how you will use language to shape your presentation and give it direction. Words like *therefore*, *furthermore* and *however* can act as links and connections within your talk. (You already saw a lot more of these useful words and phrases on pages 66–67, in the section of this book that dealt with discursive writing.)

Look back at the notes you have so far for the presentation you are preparing. Check over your vocabulary. Are there places where you could vary words? Remember, variety can mean both avoiding boring repetition and also showing the breadth of your word choice. Are there places where you could use longer, more complex sentences?

As well as generally varying your vocabulary, there are other language techniques you can use to engage your audience and give impact to your talk.

Register

Register is the choice of language you make to suit your purpose, your audience, and the situation in which you are speaking. At its simplest level, register is often about choosing how formally to speak. As being assessed is one of the most formal parts of school life, and as your language at Higher should be detailed and complex, you should be choosing a fairly formal register for your individual presentations and for group discussion.

That doesn't mean informality is always wrong, just that your choice of register is a choice about technique. What you say has to work as an interesting speech, and you should always be trying to engage your audience while fulfilling your purpose. But it can be hard to handle detailed, complex ideas if you use overly simplistic and informal language.

This pupil is giving a revision lecture about the poetry of Norman MacCaig. Read the two possible versions of what he might say:

We have to concede MacCaig is a marvellous poet. He conveys his dislocation and unease while dazzling us with his mastery of technique. This writer's depiction of New York allows him to paint a portrait of the city as he experienced it, but it also offers him a way of addressing the darkness in human nature.

You have to say he's great. He makes you feel his emotions at the same time as basically just dazzling you with his technique. His take on New York is brutal. You can see how he's using the city to say important stuff about us humans.

Did you notice the second bubble uses *you*, a lot? Using *you* in speech, and in writing, can be a problem. It's rather vague, and too impersonal. The pupil is talking about a poet he has studied. Why is he using *you* as if only the audience knows about MacCaig? If you are talking about yourself, say *I*. If you are talking about people in general, say *we* or *us* to involve the listeners.

Register goes a little further than just choosing how formal to be. You should also be able to use a little bit of slang, or dialect, or informality, to gain certain effects and to make your speech vivid. Furthermore, your choice of register may also involve using specialist vocabulary: words, phrases and terminology that pertain to a certain subject matter or area. All of this would give evidence of your ability to choose the best words at the best time.

Active learning

Look at the groups of words and phrases. Which subject or area of interest does each belong to?

A mise en scène, representation, institutional factors

B jurisprudence, precedent, duty of care

C enjambment, assonance, rhyme scheme

D bond, hedge fund, annuity

E grind, carving, wipe out, 360

F fold, sauté, ballotine

For answers see page 205.

While it's important that you use a register that suits your subject matter and your purpose, remember that, for the sake of your audience, you might need to define or explain some of the terms you use. If you use specialist language that your audience can't understand, that's not communication, it's just showing off.

Humour and anecdote

One of the easiest ways to win over your audience is to give them something to laugh at — especially if that something is you. Being funny to order may sound like a hard thing to do, but we all make our friends laugh all the time in real life by using **anecdotes**. An anecdote is a brief story, often an amusing one.

Look back again at the introduction by Sandi Toksvig that appeared on page 82. She's telling a personal, gently humorous anecdote. But she goes on in the rest of her text to discuss the more serious subject of how marriage, and society's definition of marriage, has changed in recent years.

You don't have to personally star in each anecdote that you use. An anecdote can just as easily be something you observed, or an experience that you know happened to someone else. Nor do anecdotes all have to be funny. If you listen to correspondents on longer radio news programmes, like Radio 4's *Today* or *PM*, you will often hear them telling anecdotes about one person's experience as a way of illustrating a wider story. For instance, an anecdote about one lorry's journey to Britain from the port of Calais was used as part of an exploration of the ongoing problems caused by people traffickers.

Hyperbole

Hyperbole is the more formal and literary term for exaggeration, and it's another technique that can bring life to the language of your talk. Here's the next part of Sandi Toksvig's piece. Can you spot the hyperbole?

> **I wonder what the world would have made of me if I had suddenly become the wife of a Nubian nomad about whom I knew nothing? He was a man, I was a woman. Did that make it a pleasing union for all concerned? I suspect even the most rabid proponent of 'traditional' marriage might think not, but the offer was entirely in keeping with the origins of matrimony. Historically, marriage had nothing to do with love. It was a legal contract and was all about alliances, getting the right in-laws and adding to your property. Things have changed. Now marriage is about love, or at least it should be.**

Active learning

Go back to your notes again. Decide if there are places where you could use anecdote or hyperbole.

Rhetorical questions

We have already seen how you can use questions — **rhetorical** or otherwise — to engage your audience at the start of your talk. These can also be used throughout to challenge your listeners or to get them thinking. You can see one in the Sandi Toksvig extract above:

> **He was a man, I was a woman. Did that make it a pleasing union for all concerned?**

'Of course not,' think the audience members, knowing marriage is about much more than binary biology.

Emotive language

One technique that can be particularly helpful in serious or persuasive talks, or in ones dealing with controversial subjects, is to use **emotive language**.

Emotive words are strong ones, ones that rouse the listeners' emotions. If you read tabloid newspapers, listen to politicians, or read the advertising sent out by charities, you will often find a lot of emotive language in use.

Active learning

Some emotive language aims to cause negative emotions such as anger or disgust. Look at the words in the box on the left. How many similar ones could you add to the box on the right?

disturbing
terrifying
horrendous
scandalous
contemptible
alarming

Some emotive language aims to cause more positive emotions. Look at the words in the box on the left. How many similar ones could you add to the box on the right?

excellent
superb
remarkable
astounding
magnificent
extraordinary

Active learning

Go back to your notes. Try to find a couple of places in your presentation where you could change statements into rhetorical questions, or where you could use emotive language.

Good endings

Endings matter too. When you did National 5, you probably concentrated on making sure that you wrapped up clearly so that the audience knew that you had finished. You will have made sure that you summed up your presentation, and perhaps thanked the audience or invited questions.

You can take this further at Higher. Think of it as **finishing with a flourish**.

Do you remember the techniques we said you could use for your opening? Many of them will also work equally well for endings, particularly:

- quotation
- making a striking statement
- asking a question
- sharing a thought or observation.

There are other ways you can make your ending effective too. You could refer back to something you mentioned earlier in your presentation. You could bring the whole thing back round by returning to a detail from your opening.

Here's the ending of Sandi Toksvig's piece. Having discussed how marriage, and society's view of it, has changed, she looks ahead to her own upcoming celebration:

> **Marrying is one of the greatest things that has ever happened in my life. I know it's traditional to have doubts on the big day, but I confess to just one tiny niggle. I am worried that I am never going to get that camel.**

You could also refer to a person, story, or example that cleverly embodies or epitomises an idea that was in your talk.

Active learning

Look back at the notes you have so far for the presentation you are preparing. Rework your ending so that you can finish with a flourish.

Using notes

There's nothing wrong with using notes. However, you do have to use non-verbal communication, such as gesture and body language, and the way you handle your notes can affect these.

Your notes are there to support you if you need them. You should never just read your presentation out — this is not what you are being marked on. The best way to avoid this is to keep your notes as short as possible, so that you **can't** just read them.

On page 81 you saw the outline for a talk about a writer. Let's focus on the section giving a brief overview of the writer's life and work. The outline for that point looks like this:

- Brief overview
  - biographical detail
  - significant works.

Imagine you were going to talk about George Orwell. You want the audience to hear something like this:

Orwell was born Eric Arthur Blair in Bengal, then part of British India but now the independent nation of Bangladesh, in 1903. He later described his background as 'lower-upper-middle-class'.

The family returned to England when Orwell was three. He was sent to boarding school aged eight on a scholarship, and later went to Eton, also on a scholarship: facts which demonstrate both how clever he was, and how little money his family had. One might assume that attending Eton – an exclusive and prestigious private school which has produced 19 British prime ministers – would have turned Orwell into an establishment figure. On the contrary, he always felt like an outsider, unworthy and very aware of how little money his family had.

After school, rather than going to university, he joined the Indian Imperial Police and served in Burma from 1922 to 1927. He spent much of his time there feeling disillusioned and frustrated, and returned to Britain 'conscious of an immense weight of guilt that I had got to expiate'.

After leaving Burma, he lived for a while among poor and marginalised people in Britain and France, taking low-paid and dirty jobs. He wrote about this later in a book called *Down And Out In Paris And London*. He spent most of the rest of his life writing, not only essays but also journalism, longer non-fiction books and novels. Two of his most famous books are *Animal Farm* and *1984*, and in the latter he created two ideas that have become part of our culture: the notion that Big Brother is watching us, and the idea of a Room 101 where the things that upset each of us most can be found.

If you get up to deliver your presentation with all these words written out, you may just read them. The next step is to reduce the notes to keywords, first by underlining or highlighting the most important words and phrases.

Orwell was born <u>Eric Arthur Blair</u> in <u>Bengal</u>, then part of British India but now the independent nation of Bangladesh, in <u>1903</u>. He later described his background as '<u>lower-upper-middle-class</u>'.

The family returned to England when Orwell was three. He was sent to boarding school aged eight on a <u>scholarship</u>, and later went to <u>Eton</u>, also on a scholarship: facts which demonstrate both how clever he was, and how little money his family had. One might assume that attending Eton – an exclusive and prestigious private school which has produced <u>19 British prime ministers</u> – would have turned Orwell into an establishment figure. On the contrary, he always felt like an <u>outsider</u>, unworthy and very aware of how little money his family had.

After school, rather than going to university, he joined the Indian Imperial Police and served in <u>Burma</u> from <u>1922 to 1927</u>. He spent much of his time there feeling disillusioned and frustrated, and returned to Britain '<u>conscious of an immense weight of guilt that I had got to expiate</u>'.

After leaving Burma, he lived for a while among poor and marginalised people in Britain and France, taking low-paid and dirty jobs. He wrote about this later in a book called <u>*Down And Out In Paris And London*</u>. He spent most of the rest of his life writing, not only essays but also journalism, longer non-fiction books and novels. Two of his most famous books are <u>*Animal Farm*</u> and <u>*1984*</u>, and in the latter he created two ideas that have become part of our culture: the notion that Big Brother is watching us, and the idea of a Room 101 where the things that upset each of us most can be found.

However if you speak from notes like these, you may still have to do a fair bit of scanning to find your keywords. The next step is to write them out on small cards or slips of paper. Using strong colours and large print, write out your keywords. You can also use layout to show the connections between ideas.

Your last card might now look like this:

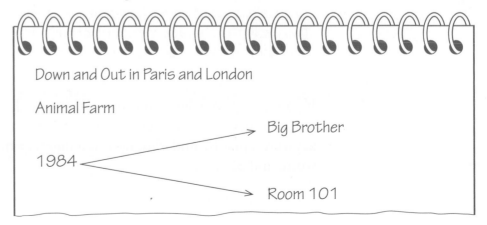

Active learning

Create cue cards for the rest of the material about George Orwell.

Hint: think carefully about what to do with the two exact quotations you plan to use.

By the time you get to this stage, you'll know your material so well that a quick glance down at the few words in your notes will bring up all you want to say.

Active learning

Go back to your notes. You should be able to set your whole presentation out on cards, using colour, keywords and simple symbols to bring everything quickly to mind.

Using props

As we saw earlier, you should be interacting with your audience, not just talking *at* them. The more ways you can find to interest them and to engage with them, the more interactive you are being.

It can be a very good idea to use props in your presentation. For instance, if you are talking about an author, you could bring copies of books by that person. If you are exploring the background of a current news story, you could bring papers whose headlines show them covering that issue.

Holding a prop gives you something to do with your hands, which may help you control signs of nerves. Passing a prop around is interesting for the audience and connects you more strongly to them. If your presentation is well prepared, then using props may even remind you of everything you want to say and help you to speak without notes.

Active learning

Go back to your planned presentation. Is there a prop you could use in your delivery?

Using PowerPoint and other technology

If you are speaking to your whole class, or some other roomful of people, rather than a small group, you may decide to use a PowerPoint to accompany your presentation. This can be a fantastic way of bringing more interest and interactivity to your talk.

A word of warning here. Many PowerPoint users make a classic mistake: instead of talking to the audience, they just read out what can be seen on the screen.

Orwell's key works include *Down and Out in Paris and London, Animal Farm* and *1984*

This is just repetition, and it will bore your audience. Instead, use PowerPoint to support your words and don't feel the need to have a slide for every single thing you're going to say. The pupil talking about Orwell could put up a picture of the writer, or a map showing the locations of Bengal and Burma.

The same goes for DVD clips, YouTube videos and any other visual material. They should be doing something you cannot do in words, not repeating something you have already verbalised.

You shouldn't use PowerPoint, or any other technological prop, unless you are absolutely sure how it works and how it operates in your school or college. Even if you know how it would run on your computer at home, even if you know how to bring up a clip on your own device, make sure you get a chance to set up and practise on the equipment you'll be using at school.

Now that you have your notes set out on cue cards, have chosen any props and have made your PowerPoint or other visual aids, your talk is prepared. It's time to think about the next two stages.

Practising and presentation

We're going to look at these two steps together, because any practice of your talk is, in itself, a little presentation.

Eye contact

Eye contact is one of the key aspects of non-verbal communication.

If you've produced good notes as discussed already, then you are on your way to good eye contact, because you should not **need** to keep looking down. If you feel that you might **want** to keep looking down, there's a section coming up on dealing with nerves that you'll find helpful. If you want to look up, but you're not sure how to, keep reading.

If you are talking to your whole class, your teacher will be part of the audience. If you're speaking to a group, your teacher will be sitting among you, or nearby. As you talk, the teacher will assess you: maybe by making notes or following a checklist, or by filming your talk.

Lots of pupils make the mistake of staring at the teacher, or at the camera. Some others look at a friend, because they know that person will support them. Others just look straight ahead.

Try this instead. Imagine you are a lighthouse. Although you are standing still, your eyes — the lamp of the lighthouse — can move, sweeping across the class like the light sweeps across the sea. Whenever you are able to look up for a few seconds, sweep your eyes across the class, taking in most of the room. You might notice that this is what your teachers do when they talk to their classes. The reason this works so well is that it makes everyone in the audience feel they should pay attention to you all the time, because they know you could look at them at any second.

Active learning

This game will give everyone in the class a very quick chance to practise eye contact. Everybody needs a small slip of card or paper. Get each person to write down a nice, simple, straightforward, common noun and then fold their paper in half. Get someone to collect the cards in a bag.

One by one, each person should take a card and talk for 30 seconds about the word on it. (You may need to give people a minute or two to think about what they are going to say.)

When each person comes up to speak, they should try to keep their eyes on the audience at all times, moving their eye contact around the room like a lighthouse as they do so.

Body language

This is another aspect of non-verbal communication, one that is rather more significant if you will be standing up talking to your whole class than if you will be sitting presenting to a smaller group.

Think of a television presenter who is good at their job. (It should be someone who stands up to speak, and doesn't just read from a prepared script, so not a newsreader.) Now try watching them with the television sound muted so you can focus only on what they do and not what they say. Carefully notice the gestures they use. Can you work out, from their gestures alone, what they are talking about, or how they feel about that subject? Can you tell how they feel about any other people in the studio or in the shot with them?

You should find that the television presenter's body language helps him or her to put across the message. Unfortunately, bad body language can adversely affect your talk, and there are a few things to avoid.

Some people fidget terribly. All sorts of 'head' fidgets, like earring twisting, ear rubbing, nose scratching and hair twiddling are really your subconscious mind trying to send your hands to cover your mouth and stop you talking. These fidgets muffle what you say, and they display your nerves to the whole audience.

Some people, both girls and boys, hide behind their hair. If yours is long, tie it back. If your fringe tickles your eyes, just for as long as you are up there talking, don't keep flicking your head to get it out of the way — you'll look like a pony being annoyed by a fly!

Some people stand awkwardly, twisting their arms behind their backs or crossing their legs while standing up to talk. Try to plant your feet firmly, about shoulder-width apart. Otherwise the audience won't be able to concentrate on your presentation, they will just be waiting to see you tip over sideways.

If you have to hold onto your notes, keep them in one hand and use the other for gestures. If your classroom has a lectern or book stand, try putting your notes on that. You could even borrow a music stand and use it. This way you can lightly place your hands on the stand and move them when you want to make a gesture.

Gestures

These are any movements that you make that support the meaning of your presentation. It can be a little bit hard to plan these – if they work, it is usually because they have come naturally. Let me give you some examples:

- A pupil talking about film director Alfred Hitchcock slapped his own (much slimmer) stomach while talking about Hitchcock's famously recognisable fat silhouette, which Hitchcock used almost as a logo.
- A pupil discussing the history of politics in sport gave the Black Power salute given by two American athletes at the 1968 Olympics.

Any uses of good eye contact, suitable body language or appropriate gesture will make your presentation more interactive. They connect you to the audience and make the listeners feel more interested.

Voice

We've thought a lot about visual elements of your presentation: props, PowerPoints, eye contact and body language. But your voice is a key tool. It needs to be varied and interesting. There are several ways you can do this:

- vary the speed of what you say, speaking more slowly to create moments of emphasis and tension, or to highlight what is most important, speaking a little more quickly to indicate excitement
- increase the volume of your voice at moments of excitement
- speak a little more softly to draw your audience in
- use intonation for emphasis, leaning more heavily on the most important words: this is the spoken equivalent of using bold in your writing
- use a rising tone to suggest questions.

If your audience sat there with their eyes shut, they should still find you fascinating.

Active learning

Find a partner. Ask this person to sit with their back to you. Practise your talk, or a section of it, so that your partner can hear you but cannot see you. Ask for feedback on your use of voice. Then swap roles and do this again.

Other ways of interacting with your audience

Remember the best way to engage your audience is by giving an interesting presentation that they feel they want to listen to. The advice so far about visual aids, body language, eye contact and voice will all help you with that. However, here are a few other hints and tips to help you get the audience on your side:

- As mentioned above, one way to do this is by showing them something. This can be something electronic that you show on screen, or a real prop you pass round.
- Try asking them questions, not only rhetorical ones but perhaps also ones where you clearly expect one or two of them to answer.
- Use a quiz, perhaps at the start of your presentation, to find out how much they know about your subject, or at the end to see what they have picked up and learned from you.
- Get them to raise their hands to vote on something you've said, or to show that they have had a similar experience to the one you are describing, for example, 'How many of you have ever read a novel with a historical setting?'
- Get them to laugh, and show them you appreciate that laughter by not talking over it.
- Use language that includes them, for example, 'I'm sure **we** have all at some point in **our** studies this year found **ourselves** puzzled by **our** first encounter with a new text.'

Taking questions

Remember, this is something you must do at some stage in your presentation as it's how you demonstrate your listening skills. The way you respond to these questions will show that you have listened to what audience members have asked.

The most obvious point at which to do this is at the end of your talk. The room is still yours and you are still in charge. It is up to you who you take questions from and whether you allow them to ask follow-up questions once they've heard your initial answer. Make sure your answers still use that detailed and complex language we expect to find at Higher.

Dealing with nerves

Although we've left this to last, it's actually the first thing that comes to mind when many people find out they have to do a presentation. If you've followed all the advice in this chapter so far and prepared well, that should help you to feel less nervous and more skilled. Remember also that you do not necessarily have to talk to a whole room full of people, and that if this is a worry

for you, you should discuss it with your teacher. Another way to defuse nerves is to practise on other people.

Active learning

Pair up with someone else from your class and practise your presentations on each other. Be sure to include times when each listener asks the speaker some questions. Get your partner to time what you say. Then ask them to tell you two things that were good about the talk, and one thing you could improve. Also, ask for one suggestion of a way you could add length and detail to your presentation.

Now join up with another pair to make a group and all take turns to practise again. This will help you to get to know your material even better, as well as giving you a chance to practise lighthouse eye contact. After each person has spoken, give the same kind of feedback mentioned above.

When you get up to give your actual presentation, remember this: **The audience wants you to succeed**. They know you, and they want you to do well. They also want to be a good, receptive audience for you, because they'll have their own talks to do too, and they'll want you to be part of a friendly and receptive audience for them when their turn comes.

Think of your talk as being shaped like a little hill:

SPEAK

SMILE   SMILE

STAND   STAND

STAND there, nice and still

SMILE at your audience

SPEAK to them, giving the presentation you've prepared and practised

SMILE again at the end

STAND and wait for the applause

You're ready to do your presentation now. Good luck!

Group discussion

If you've worked through the section on individual presentation, then you already know about the skills you will use in group discussion too.

However, the group situation does introduce a few differences:

- You may have less choice in what you talk about. Your teacher might provide you with a discussion topic or set of questions.
- Remember, your teacher can assess your spoken language on a number of occasions throughout your Higher course. So he or she might be making notes and observations while you are

discussing something as part of your wider learning, rather than setting up a specific 'test' of your discussion skills.

- You will probably have less time to prepare for group discussion than for an individual presentation. You may be given some advance notice, and if so you should use that time to gather together ideas and points, but you won't be preparing language in the way you might do for the sort of solo talk opportunity we have just learned about.
- You may or may not get to choose the other people who are in the group with you.
- You may be given a particular role to play in the group during the discussion.
- You need to show that you know how to behave in a group situation, respecting and interacting with the others in your group. This is how you will show the listening skills that you must demonstrate to pass your spoken language assessment.
- You must make sure you contribute enough to the discussion that your teacher can find evidence to assess you on. At the same time though, you must not take over the group. That's a tricky balancing act.

We'll deal with particular group roles later. First, let's look at how both your body language and your spoken language can be used to show that you are listening to others in your group.

Active learning

Imagine you had these two people in your group. Which person's body language shows that they are taking an active part in the group? Which one seems to have opted out?

So we can easily see how your body language shows that you are actively listening. However, you need to go beyond that.

During the discussion you should be doing more listening than talking. This doesn't mean staying quiet for as little time as possible until you can wedge in something that you have already decided to say. What you say when you do speak might support, develop, or challenge what you hear when you are listening. If you disagree with what you have heard, there are ways to express this without giving offence or seeming arrogant, and it's perfectly all right to disagree, even quite firmly, so long as you can do so respectfully too.

Active learning

The comments in the speech bubbles fit into two groups.

1 Some phrases show that you support the previous speaker and agree with what he or she has said.

2 Some of them will let you express disagreement, so that you can challenge the previous speaker.

First, work out which comments belong in which group.

I agree with you because …

On the other hand …

I don't agree because …

I think you're wrong because …

But in my opinion …

You're right to say that …

Next, see how many more ways you can think of to begin:

1 comments or sentences that show support for a previous speaker

2 comments or sentences that allow you to appropriately challenge another speaker.

As well as being able to support and challenge what you have heard from other group members, you should also be displaying these skills in your responses to others:

- developing
- summarising
- refuting
- justifying.

Active learning

Copy and complete the following table to show your understanding of these concepts.

Concept	What this concept means	What Pupil A might say	How Pupil B could respond
developing			*That's not the only reason why the government should address this. It also matters because …*
summarising			*You seem to be saying …*
refuting	Using evidence to prove that someone else is wrong.		
justifying	Using evidence to prove that you are right.	*I'm afraid I don't agree. I think X's films are overrated because …*	

Any comments or points you make during group discussion should be developed in some detail and should be backed up and supported.

Roles and contributions

In some group discussions you may be asked to take on a certain role. If so, make sure you understand what is expected of you. Here are some of the more common roles:

- **The chair** should lead the discussion and keep it moving along. The chair should also solve any conflicts or arguments and should try to encourage any shy group members, while trying to stop confident speakers from dominating. By the way, if your teacher expects your group to have a chair, he or she will be watching to see that other group members are listening to and acknowledging that chairperson.
- **The leader** has a similar role to the chair, but may also be responsible for reaching a decision or conclusion or having the casting vote if the group cannot reach a consensus.
- **The reader** may be asked to read out instructions, information or questions to the group.
- **The recorder** takes notes of what is said. Near the end of the discussion, it is a good idea for the recorder to read their notes back to the group so that people can agree that the record is fair.
- **The reporter** may be asked to give a verbal report back to the whole class on what the group talked about.

- **The timekeeper** may be responsible for keeping the discussion moving, or for ensuring that a conclusion or solution is reached within a given time.

Your own teacher may use different titles for some of the roles, but these are the main responsibilities that people are generally asked to carry out in groups. Just make sure you know what is involved in any role you are given, and you'll be fine.

You may also notice that someone in your group is not contributing much, or is having trouble getting a word in. Since your teacher will want to see all group members taking part, you need to find a way to draw out that quiet person (or perhaps to encourage other group members to become a little quieter!). Try using some of these phrases to help you:

I'm interested in hearing X's opinion about …

What would you like to say?

What's your opinion?

Is there anything you'd like to add?

What do you think?

It would be good to hear some other opinions about …

That's the end of this chapter. We have looked at individual presentations and group discussions, as these are the two ways that pupils' spoken language skills are most commonly assessed. Your teacher may give you all sorts of other talk opportunities, like debating or hot-seating a character from a text you're studying. In the end, as long as you eventually demonstrate all the skills, you will achieve this part of the Higher course.

CHAPTER 3 Reading for Understanding, Analysis and Evaluation

Reading for Understanding, Analysis and Evaluation is the formal name for the skill your teacher might also call 'close reading'.

You will be tested on this by sitting an exam in early May. Although this exam comes at the end of your Higher course, you will probably want to work on these skills throughout the year.

You already have a firm grounding in these skills from your previous work at National 5.

Active learning

Work with a partner.

Your school probably keeps past papers from recent exams. For this task, your teacher will need to give each pair of pupils two Reading for Understanding, Analysis and Evaluation past papers: one at National 5, one at Higher.

First check, or add up, how many lines of text you have to read in each paper.

- What do you notice about the difference between National 5 and Higher?

Next, read both passages. As you read them, note down any vocabulary that is new or unfamiliar.

- What do you notice about the difference in vocabulary between National 5 and Higher?

Then read the questions.

- What do you notice about the difference between how the questions are laid out and organised at National 5 and Higher?
- What do you notice about the difference between how questions are worded at National 5 and Higher?

Warning

There is one very significant difference between National 5 and Higher that you cannot see by looking at the question papers.

At National 5, every time you chose a suitable, appropriate quotation, you earned a mark. So, a lot of the 30 marks you were trying to earn in this task at National 5 could come just by quoting well.

At Higher, you earn **no marks for quoting** in your reading answers. Despite this, you do still have to quote. An answer without a quotation is like a building with no foundations: your explanation and analysis have no basis if you don't quote the ideas you are explaining or the language you are analysing. However, you won't get marks for what you quote. Remember:

All your marks at Higher come from explanation and analysis.

What you will be assessed on

In the exam you will be given **two** non-fiction passages, perhaps pieces of journalism or extracts from books. They will be written in the detailed and complex language you have come to expect at Higher and will be about the same topic or very closely linked topics.

You will have **one hour and thirty minutes** to read the passages and answer **30 marks'** worth of questions. These will be divided up as follows:

- **Passage 1** will be longer — usually 800–900 words. It will be followed by a series of short questions. Each question will probably be worth 2, 3 or 4 marks. The total number of marks available for Passage 1 will add up to 25 marks.
- **Passage 2** will be shorter — usually around 600–700 words and will be about some aspect of the same topic as Passage 1. Passage 2 will be followed by just one question, which will ask about both passages. This question will be worth 5 marks and will get you to show your understanding of where the two writers agree or disagree on their shared topic.

The exam tests your ability to **understand** the writers' ideas, and to **analyse** and **evaluate** the language they use to put those ideas across. You will also be expected to summarise the writers' ideas. You have, of course, already done all of these things at National 5 level; the difference is that you will be working at a more challenging level, and with more complex language.

This chapter will introduce you to the skills you need to pass this exam and to some of the types of questions you may be asked. You will see explanations and worked examples and then have a chance to try questions for yourself.

This chapter will teach you suggested approaches to questions. Although you will learn how to tackle various sorts of question, you cannot assume that all these question types will come up in the exam you sit. The examiners base their questions each year on what suits their chosen passage, not on a list of question types. Also, many of the questions you will meet don't easily fit into any particular type, and so there can't be a straightforward formula for answering them. The most important advice for the exam is always going to be:

ANSWER WHAT THE QUESTION ASKS!

Using your own words

If you can put something in your own words, you have understood it; if you don't understand something, you won't be able to express it in your own words.

This will be emphasised in some of the questions, where you may see **in your own words** or **use your own words** written in bold. Questions that ask you to *identify* or *explain* also expect you to use your own words.

This skill is so important that, even when the question does not say that you must use your own words, it is still best to do so as far as possible. A good general approach is to quote from the passage only when you know that you are going to go on and analyse the language of that quotation. We'll look at these more analytical questions later in the chapter.

Read the following article about homesickness:

Skype gives an illusion of closeness — homesickness, however, is as real as ever

1   Nostalgia used to be considered an illness. A word with a refreshingly certain etymology, it was coined by a Swiss medical student, Johannes Hofer, who in 1688 joined together two Greek words, *nostos* for homecoming and *algos* for pain or ache. The Swiss also knew it as *mal du Suisse* or *Schweizerheimweh*, later translated into English as the nationally unspecific '*homesickness*', a mental and physical malady that was found particularly among Swiss soldiers in foreign armies. It was to these mercenaries, fighting on the lowlands of France and Italy and missing the peaks and valleys of their homeland, that Hofer applied his impressive new word. Stomach pain, fever, anxiety, headache? Rather than blaming bad water, unfamiliar food or the sound of muskets, military doctors now diagnosed nostalgia: a yearning for the past, and not in a general, sentimental way (as it now tends to mean), but for a specific time and place: in this case, one where the sufferer might once have woken to the tinkle of cowbells.

2   The top deck of a number 19 London bus is a good place to listen to nostalgia, though of course you cannot be sure. The

phone conversation that lasts the half-hour from Tottenham Court Road to Finsbury Park might be about grandma's delicious Christmas recipe for roast carp, or how auntie prepared couscous in the High Atlas, but then again it might just be about *The X Factor* or nuclear physics. Somali, Bengali, Russian, Bulgarian, Moldovan, Latvian: the averagely insular native English speaker on the number 19 can easily hear all of them (and more) without understanding a word.

3   **Whatever the people on the bus are talking about, they are talking about it with someone who shares their language and — probably — their customs and traditions and country.** An interesting question then arises: has technology — mobile phones, Facebook, Skype — lessened nostalgia or increased it? Does technology give the illusion of closeness, or does it sadden the caller by reminding them sharply of what they have left behind (which is why parents were discouraged from phoning their children too often at English boarding schools)?

4   More thought than you might imagine has gone into this question and others like it, universities being what they are. Researchers at the University of Southampton, for instance, have developed the Southampton Nostalgia Scale, a universally accepted measurement produced from a standard list of questions such as 'Specifically, how often do you bring to mind nostalgic experiences?' The answers available to be ticked range from 'at least once a day' to 'once or twice a year'; as the university defines nostalgia as 'typically a fond, personally meaningful memory', it seems inconceivable to me that such recollections could be rationed in any human being to once a week, never mind once a year. And yet, as a US history professor, Susan J. Matt, recently pointed out in the *New York Times*, certain kinds of modern personality find it better to suppress or eliminate the backward glance. Explicit discussions of homesickness are now rare, Matt writes, because the emotion was typically seen 'as an embarrassing impediment to individual progress and prosperity. This silence makes mobility appear deceptively easy.'

5   **In the 19th century, by contrast, immigration made America the most openly homesick society in the world.** 'Victim of Nostalgia: A Priest Dies Craving for a Sight of his Motherland', ran a headline over a story about the death in 1887 of an Irishman in Brooklyn, demonstrating that neurology had hardly moved on since 17th-century

Switzerland. But who could deny that mobility carried high emotional costs? By 1900, American commentators wanted to believe, in the words of one of them, that homesickness had grown less common 'in these days of quick communication, of rapid transmission of news and of a widespread knowledge of geography'. Facts denied such a hopeful view — according to Matt, at least 50% of migrants from Greece and southern Italy went home (not necessarily, of course, from nostalgia) — and she is sceptical that new technology has made much difference: **like the phone call from the fretful parent to the boy or girl boarder, frequent contact may actually heighten feelings of displacement**.

6   Matt feels that the persistence of homesickness shows the limitations of the cosmopolitan philosophy that 'celebrates the solitary, mobile individual and envisions men and women as easily separated from family, home and the past'. It may do, but that looks to be a poor brake on the migratory urge. A recent Gallup World Poll suggested that 630 million adults or 14% of the world's adult population would move abroad permanently if they had the chance, while another 1.1 billion would move temporarily for better-paid work.

7   **The multilingualism of the London bus remains the most obvious manifestation of this great multicultural city.** Twenty years ago, the measure of difference was how people looked. With the mobile and cheap call rates, it has become how people sound.

8   For those of us who were here before, another kind of nostalgia presents itself. **We remember the years when the top deck was filled with cigarette smoke**

and passengers who, if they spoke at all, confined themselves to small remarks about the football or the weather.

9   This kind of nostalgia — the way we were — can be the seedbed of the narrowest nationalism, and therefore we must watch our step. To anyone who has sat for half an hour behind a shouter in Russian, however, the memory of men in hats coughing quietly over their Capstans can seem as seductive and beyond reach as a tinkling cowbell did to a Swiss trooper struggling across a mosquito-infested plain.

Adapted from an article in the *Guardian* by Ian Jack,
20 December 2013

By the way, you may think this is a very London-centric passage to use in a textbook for Scottish schools. Although he does not mention it in this passage, Ian Jack's regular readers would know that he himself is Scottish, and moved to London some years ago. So he too is someone who left 'home' to move to that faraway city.

This sentence from paragraph 7 of the article:

The multilingualism of the London bus remains the most obvious manifestation of this great multicultural city.

could also be expressed as:

The fact that people on the bus speak so many different languages is the clearest example of what a mixture of cultures London is.

Active learning

Several other sentences or parts of sentences in the article have also been printed in bold. Rewrite each one in your own words. You don't have to change every single word, and you may find that some long sentences can be reworded better as two or even three shorter ones.

Showing your understanding

You won't meet a question in the Higher exam that just asks you to put part of the passage in your own words. The reason you need to use your own words, as we've seen before, is to prove your understanding. The exam questions will usually want you to demonstrate your grasp of the writer's ideas and of what the passage is saying.

Active learning

Answer the following questions, using your own words as far as possible, to show your understanding. The number of marks available for each question will suggest how many details or ideas you need in each answer.

1 Read paragraph 1. According to the writer, what is the difference between the original meaning of *nostalgia* and what we now understand this word to mean?   2

2 Read paragraph 3. Explain the two different ways in which the use of modern technology may have affected our feelings of nostalgia.   2

3 Read paragraph 6. How does the remainder of the paragraph develop the idea that there is '*a poor brake on the migratory urge*'?   2

For answers see pages 205–6.

Questions about technique

Over the next few pages, you will have the opportunity to tackle questions about some of the key techniques that come up in the exam. There is quite a lot of variety in the way these questions are worded. Sometimes a technique or techniques will be named, for example:

> **Analyse how the writer uses both sentence structure and imagery to …**

or

> **By referring to both word choice and sentence structure, analyse …**

If you get a question like this, you must stick to the techniques named, and will only get marks when you analyse examples of the writer using those specific techniques. If two techniques are named, you must examine them both or you can't get full marks for your answer.

At other times, you will see a more general instruction, such as:

> **Analyse how the writer uses language to …**

or

> **Analyse how the writer's use of language …**

or

> **By referring to at least two examples, analyse how the writer's use of language …**

With these questions, it is up to you to identify which techniques and language features are worth commenting on in your answer. As you answer, you should make clear which techniques you have chosen to write about. You can do this through the way you word your response, for example:

The writer uses imagery in line 35 when she calls politicians the 'puppets' of big business ...

or you could do it by using a heading:

Imagery
The writer calls the politicians 'puppets' of big business. Just as puppets ...

As you work through the next few pages on key techniques, do remember that in the exam you are unlikely to get a question that names just one technique, and that some questions will not name specific techniques at all. We will learn about techniques one at a time, but you will usually have to answer about them in combination, and it may well be up to you to discern which techniques are most relevant.

Developed and undeveloped answers

Here's another idea you need to keep in your head as you answer Higher reading questions. You already know that all your marks will come from your explanation and analysis; you get nothing for quoting. That's a major difference between Higher and National 5.

Another major difference, another way that the Higher exam takes you further and makes you work harder, is the new idea that markers will be looking at how **deeply** you answer. The mark scheme — the set of instructions that the markers follow as they assess your work — says:

> **2 marks may be awarded for detailed/insightful comment.**
>
> **1 mark for more basic comment.**
>
> **(Marks may be awarded 1+1 or 2.)**

Each year, after all the results come out, the SQA prepares a report on how that year's exam went. This is full of advice for teachers to pass on to pupils to help them do well in future exams. This advice often highlights the fact that exam candidates do well at giving basic comments, but find it harder to make more insightful comments in their answers.

What can you learn from this? Two things:

1   Try to expand your answers so that you are responding in depth and getting 2 marks together.

but remember:

2   It is also perfectly fine to try to earn your marks one at a time. If a question is worth 4 marks, you can have four little sections in your answer, earning all the available marks 1+1+1+1. You'll see an example of this in the questions you are about to tackle on word choice.

Word choice questions

Of course all words that a writer uses are chosen in some way, but when we talk about **word choice** as a technique we mean that certain words are very carefully and deliberately chosen to obtain particular effects, or to suggest particular meanings.

Most words have two levels of meaning, a **denotation** and a more complex **connotation**. The denotation is the basic, simple, straightforward meaning. The connotations of a word are the ideas that the word suggests to us; some people think of this as the emotional meaning of the word.

For example, *wrote, scribbled* and *inscribed* all have the same denotation. They all tell us that someone used a hand-held implement to mark words upon a surface.

However, they all have different connotations. *Wrote* is merely factual; *scribbled* suggests speed or carelessness; *inscribed* implies that the words were put there with great care, and were perhaps engraved into the surface. The context in which words are used will help you to know more about which exact connotation to go for.

Active learning

You will see pairs or trios of words. In each group, the words have the same basic denotation, but different connotations. For each group, work out the denotation they share and the different connotations of the individual words.

doggie	hound	canine
pupil	scholar	student
book	tome	volume
procure	get	obtain
meticulous	controlling	
enthusiast	fanatic	
conservative	fundamentalist	
teased	taunted	
castle	fortress	

Now pick one of the pairs or trios of words that you examined. Draw two or three cartoons to illustrate the different connotations, just as the ones on the previous page illustrate *wrote*, *scribbled* and *inscribed*.

When you answer word choice questions, you will usually need to identify and quote the carefully chosen words the writer uses, then examine and explain their connotations.

Read the following news article about how the internet gets our attention:

The compelling web

1   The dirty secret of the internet is that distraction and interruption is immensely profitable. Web companies like to boast about 'creating compelling content', or offering services that let you 'stay up to date with what your friends are doing', 'share the things you love with the world' and so on. But the real way to build a successful online business is to be better than your rivals at undermining people's control of their own attention. Partly, this is a result of how online advertising has traditionally worked: advertisers pay for clicks, and a click is a click, however it's obtained. A website such as Mail Online doesn't care, at least in the short term, if you're 'hate-reading' — clicking in order to share your friends' outrage. Facebook doesn't really mind if you click a link by mistake because it's tweaked the design of the site overnight

without telling you. Advertising aside, commandeering people's attention, so that they click compulsively, is just a surer way to survive in the hyper-competitive marketplace of the web than trying to convince them intellectually that they ought to click a link, or that they'll benefit in the longer term from doing so.

2   And let's be honest: this war for your attention isn't confined only to Facebook or Twitter or Pinterest, or to the purveyors of celebrity gossip or porn. Higher-minded publications feel the same pressures. 'We're living in a moment when even institutions that used to be in the business of promoting reflection and deep thinking are busy tearing up the foundations that made these things possible, in favour of getting more traffic,' says Stanford University technologist Alex Pang, whose book on 'contemplative computing', *The Distraction Addiction*, will be published in August. 'Even universities and churches end up doing this when they go online, never mind newspapers and magazines.' The compulsiveness is given extra force, in social media, by the fear of missing out.

3   To explain what makes the web so compelling — so 'addictive' in the colloquial sense, at least — the advocates of what has become known as 'conscious computing' usually end up returning to the psychologist B.F. Skinner, who conducted famous experiments on pigeons and rats at Harvard University in the 1930s. Trapped inside 'Skinner boxes', equipped with a lever and a tray, the animals soon learned that pushing or pecking at the lever caused a pellet of food to appear on the tray; after that, they'd start compulsively pecking or pushing for more. But Skinner discovered that the most powerful way to reinforce the push-or-peck habit was to use 'variable schedules of reward': to deliver a pellet not every time the lever was pushed, but only sometimes, and unpredictably.

4   There's a slightly depressing view of the web according to which we're essentially just Skinner pigeons, compulsively clicking in hopes of a squirt of dopamine, the so-called 'feel-good' hormone in the brain. Once you've learned about Skinner, it's impossible not to see variable schedules of reward

everywhere you look online. When you click *refresh* on your email, or when you check your phone, you're not guaranteed a new message; when you visit Facebook or open Twitter, you might or might not find an update of the sort you'd been hoping for. This might even help explain the appalling quality of so much online content. Nine times out of ten, when you click on a Huffington Post link — 'PICTURE: Kate and Wills as OAPs', 'Simon Cowell Just Got Weirder' — it's a tedious disappointment. But if it predictably lived up to expectations every time, you might actually feel less compelled to click.

5   By far the funniest, or maybe the most horrifying, illustration of this situation is Cow Clicker, a Facebook game created in 2011 by the game designer Ian Bogost as a satire of undemanding 'social games' such as FarmVille. In Cow Clicker, you clicked on your cow and it mooed, and that was it: you then had to wait another six hours to click again, unless you were willing to part with real money (or virtual money, accumulated through clicking) for the right to click again immediately. Bogost's joke became a surprise hit: at its height, Cow Clicker had more than 50,000 users, some paying $20 or more for pointless 'improvements' to their cow, such as making it face the opposite direction.

6   'After a while,' Bogost told a US radio interviewer, 'I realised they're doing exactly what concerned me about these games' — becoming 'compulsively attached'. 'I began to feel very disturbed about the product.' Eventually, a few months after the launch, Bogost eliminated all the cows in a Rapture-like event he called the Cowpocalypse. After it, users could keep playing only by clicking on a bare patch of grass — and some actually did. Responding to a player who complained that Cow Clicker was no longer 'a very fun game', Bogost replied, 'It wasn't very fun before.'

7   It's this vicious Skinnerian cycle that conscious computing seeks to break. That's why one of the simplest pieces of advice — to check your email at fixed points during the day — works so well: if you're checking only occasionally, you're virtually guaranteed the 'reward' of new messages, so the lure of the variable reward dies away, and with it the constant urge to check. Something similar is going on with services such as iDoneThis, which lets you track the work you've accomplished by responding to a daily email. When it launched, its founder Walter Chen had the capacity to process the emails only once a day, so to put a positive spin on things, and mainly as a joke, he added a note: 'iDoneThis is part of

> the slow web movement. After you email us, your calendar is not updated instantaneously. But rest up, and you'll find an updated calendar when you awake.' It's hard to imagine Mark Zuckerberg approving a feature that actively encouraged making fewer visits to Facebook. But maybe we'd all be a bit happier if he did.
>
> Adapted from an article in the *Guardian* by Oliver Burkeman, 10 May 2013

Now look at this worked example of a word choice question:

Q Analyse how the writer's word choice in the final sentence of paragraph 1 (*'Advertising aside … from doing so.'*) emphasises the power of the internet.

2

A The writer uses the word 'commandeering'. This suggests that the internet has taken over the users, and that it controls them rather than them being in control of it. The 'command' part of the word has almost military connotations, suggesting that internet users are dominated and governed as an invading army might take captives.

A few pages ago, we introduced the idea that markers can give you 1 mark for a more basic answer, but 2 marks for a developed or insightful one. Let's exemplify that by unpicking this answer. You'll see the marker's thought process in red:

The writer uses the word 'commandeering'. **(The candidate has quoted suitably, but this earns no marks at Higher: nothing so far.)** This suggests that the internet has taken over the users, **(1 mark here, as this is a legitimate connotation of the chosen word)** and that it controls them rather than them being in control of it. The 'command' part of the word has almost military connotations, suggesting that internet users are dominated and governed as an invading army might take captives. **(1 mark here for expanded analysis of what the chosen word connotes/implies.)**

We also discovered that it is perfectly all right to earn the marks for a question one at a time. Here's an example of how you could tackle this question piecemeal:

The writer uses the word 'commandeering'. **(The candidate has quoted suitably, but this earns no marks at Higher: nothing so far.)** This suggests that the internet has taken over the users. **(1 mark here, as this is a legitimate connotation of the chosen word.)** The writer also uses the word 'compulsively'. **(The candidate has quoted suitably, but this earns no marks at Higher: nothing so far.)**

This suggests that internet users feel they have to keep clicking and have no choice. **(1 mark here, as this is a legitimate connotation of the chosen word.)**

As you work through the rest of the language questions in this chapter, and in the past papers and exams that you go on and do, remember that there are these two options for earning the available marks: go deep to get 2 marks together or pick them off 1+1.

Active learning

Now answer the following word choice questions about this passage:

1 Read paragraph 1. By referring to at least two examples, explain how the writer's word choice conveys the strength of competition between web companies for users' attention. **4**

2 Read paragraph 2. By referring to at least two examples, explain how the writer's word choice in the rest of the paragraph supports his statement that *'this war for your attention isn't confined only to Facebook or Twitter or Pinterest, or to the purveyors of celebrity gossip or porn.'* **4**

3 Read the first sentence of paragraph 4 (*'There's a slightly depressing view … in the brain.'*) How does the writer's word choice suggest the disappointing nature of the rewards the web offers? **2**

4 Read paragraph 6. How does Bogost's word choice convey his concern about the game he created? **2**

For answers see pages 206–7.

Active learning

Earlier in this chapter you learned about how to answer questions that show your understanding of the ideas and information in the passage. Now answer these:

5 Read paragraphs 3 and 4. How do the examples given by the writer in paragraph 4 develop the idea of *'variable schedules of reward'* as introduced in paragraph 3? **2**

6 Read paragraph 5. How can the Cow Clicker game be understood to be both *'the funniest'* and *'the most horrifying'* example of the compulsion to click? **2**

For answers see pages 207–8.

You will have more opportunities to work on word choice later in this chapter. Now let's move on to a technique that, in reading, often rests upon your understanding of word choice.

Tone questions

It's easy to understand what we mean by **tone** if we think of a speaking voice. When you hear someone speaking, you can tell if they are angry, confused, excited or fearful. These tones in the speaking voice are created by factors like the volume and speed of the speech, which words the speaker puts emphasis on, and how fluently or hesitantly the words come out.

It's a little harder at first to see how we can identify tone in written English, when there are no sounds, only words. But skilled writers can create a tone by their word choice and also by their use of features such as sentence structure and punctuation. First, let's look at the idea of creating tone through word choice.

Teacher's task

Twelve tones are mentioned below. Prepare enough separate cards for each member of your class to get a card each: this will probably mean you need two or three cards for each tone. On each card, write a different tone. Hand these cards out around the class, making sure your pupils do not show or tell each other what it says on their cards.

Active learning

Four tones have already been mentioned above:

angry	confused	excited	fearful

Here are some more:

defeated	hopeless	scathing	sceptical
critical	matter-of-fact	humorous	emphatic/definite

Your teacher should give each person a card with a tone on it. Don't let anyone else know what is on your card!

You have five minutes to write a short paragraph in this tone. Then, to make sure that you have created that tone through word choice alone, swap your writing with someone else. Get them to read it and tell you what they think the tone is.

Active learning

So far we have looked at how writers create tone through their word choice. But, as we've already heard, they can also use features such as punctuation and sentence structure to create tone.

Discuss the following questions with a partner or small group. Then share your answers with the class and check that you are all in agreement. Some questions will have more than one possible answer.

1 Name any tones that might be shown to us through the writer's use of
   a question marks
   b exclamation marks
   c lots of commas in a list
   d ellipsis (…).

2 Name any tones that might be shown to us through the writer's use of
   a a short sentence
   b a single-sentence paragraph.

Writers can also establish tone through the imagery they use. You will soon learn about how to examine and analyse images. When you do so, depending on what the image is and what it suggests to the reader, you may be able to see that it contributes towards tone, and you can mention this in your answer if it's relevant. **Remember**, you will only get marks for answering in a way that fits the question!

As we saw earlier with questions on word choice, in the exam tone will not usually be mentioned specifically. You may get a question that begins:

> Analyse how the writer uses language to …

or

> Analyse how the writer's use of language …

We are going to take the chance here to focus on tone as a distinct technique, but do remember that in the exam it will often be up to you to decide which features of the writer's language merit your analysis and to notice instances where the writer's tone is significant. (You will get the chance to work on some exam-style questions later in this chapter, after we have looked at more of the individual skills.)

When you are answering questions on tone, you will probably have to do a mixture of these different things:

1 **identify** a tone
2 **quote** the aspects of the writer's language that create that tone
3 **explain and analyse** how the language you have quoted creates the tone.

Liz Lochhead

Read this piece by poet Liz Lochhead about poetry and ageing:

1   The subject of how to care for the elderly and those suffering dementia has been very much in the air lately. We're all aware that the UK has an ageing population, whose care will have to be funded from a dwindling tax base. Some 10 million people in the UK are over 65 years old. (Hell, I'm joining them on my next birthday, my 66th, later this month. Me, in my mock Converse trainers and leopard-skin Bob Dylan bunnet, trying to convince myself that I'm an artist and I don't look back. Omigod, I'm actually, technically, One of Them.)

2   In 20 years' time, it's estimated there will be 15.5 million of us in the UK who are over 65, the number increasing to 19 million by the middle of this century. Little wonder the subject of how to pay for care proves so daunting to politicians. We hear the elderly described in terms of being a 'burden' on the welfare state. But if caring for the old is a burden society has to bear, then it had better bear it gladly.

3   The issue of funding often aggravates the complicated feelings — resentment, among others, let's face it — that 'the elderly' trigger. The people you meet in care homes when some combination of duty, family ties, honouring old friendship takes you there, come, of course, from an incredibly diverse range of backgrounds. They are retired doctors and nurses and teachers who once taught you, and joiners and butchers and builders and former soldiers; folk that never got a start and were 'on benefits' all their lives; parents, neighbours, widowers and divorcees; folk that 'fought drink', or were made redundant at 50. They were fly-men, head-hunters, bank clerks and church-goers and socialists and atheists and pacifists and harmless biddies and bonny-fechters, folk who followed their team and total chancers and ballroom dancers … They were big readers or avid cinema-goers or opera enthusiasts or rock fans or jazzers or into am-dram. They were artists or writers or musicians themselves.

4   It's hard, but we need to look closer, see the old as individuals. Their experience should be, could be, an asset. To us. And to them. They have a right to continue to enjoy things they've taken part in throughout their lives. They may be having to move into residential care, but their lives are not over. Maybe they will even finally have the chance to deeply engage with something that hasn't meant much to them so far. Creative solutions should be called upon — and I have to believe that

poetry, language at its most naked and most playful, must be a useful tool.

5   The Scottish Poetry Library and the Scottish Storytelling Centre have been collaborating on the pilot scheme of what we all hope is to be an ongoing project called Living Voices. Into care homes and sheltered housing complexes in three regions, they have been taking poetry old and new — wonderful texts full of recall, reminiscence, rhythm, rhyme, pieces spilling over with immediate, now, living, sensuous detail and distinct voices.

6   I'm told that a raw wee elegy for my mother, *Sorting Through*, detailing the universal, painful, intimate experience of dealing with a loved-one's things in the immediate aftermath of loss — a poem that I might have flinched away from reading aloud in such a setting myself — has been immediately popular and stimulated a whole lot of talk and communication. So it's not a matter of 'don't mention the war'. It's proven to be quite the reverse. They want words that deal with reality.

7   Certainly, a session can legitimately be about nothing more than pure escapism and entertainment. Pleasure. People who can't remember what happened half-an-hour ago can just come out with whole screeds of what, long, long ago, they learned by heart. And then they remember the English teacher who taught them it, and his skelly eye, and his fancy for the music teacher that everybody knew all about, and they remember who they were sitting next to in the class and what she did to Archie Esslemont with the point of her protractor and what their granny came out with when they did the poem out loud for everybody at teatime …

8   The scheme has proved its effectiveness. Well, we've long known that music and memory go hand in glove — music is memory, according to neurologist Oliver Sacks in *The Man Who Mistook His Wife for A Hat* — and, lo, poetry seems to work in exactly the same way. There is loads of anecdotal evidence from staff in the homes about marked, even miraculous, shifts of mood and engagement in certain individuals. One man who had been very withdrawn (depressed?) now 'joins in everything and has a lot to say to the others. Really connects'.

9   Of course, I'm not old. My survival strategy? Denial. Denial and a pair of rockabilly shoes in viper-green, tartan or leopard-skin. My hair might be white but, hey, I can think

platinum blonde if I like. I'll be playing with words, reading, drawing, 'keeping creative' if I can. Just as long as those proteins and neurons Alois Alzheimer discovered aren't already busily clotting and fusing and forming themselves into those terrible, twisted, tangled trees in my brain.

Adapted from a piece by Liz Lochhead in the *Sunday Herald*, 1 December 2013

Here are two possible tone questions on the start of this passage, along with suitable answers. Notice that in one of the questions you have to identify the tone, while in the other you only have to show how it is created:

Q1 How does the writer establish an authoritative tone in the first paragraph? **2**

A1 She uses formal vocabulary such as *'dwindling tax base'* and statistics, for example, saying how many UK residents are over 65 years old. The seriousness of this word choice, and the apparent reliability of the figures quoted, combine to make her sound authoritative.

Q2 What is the tone of the bracketed section in this paragraph, and how is this created? **2**

A2 The tone is a self-mocking one. This is created by her use of the phrase *'trying to convince myself'*, as if she knows she cannot keep pretending she is not growing older.

Active learning

Now try these tone questions. Remember, you can earn 2 marks together with a deep and insightful comment, or you can pick off the marks by earning them 1+1.

1 How does the writer establish a surprised tone in paragraph 1?   2

2 How does the writer establish a persuasive tone in paragraph 4?   2

3 What is the tone of paragraph 6 and how does the writer's use of language create this tone?   3

For answers see pages 208–9.

Just before we move on from the idea of tone, a word of advice: if you are asked to identify or name a tone, don't ever just say that it is positive or negative. That's far too vague. You need to say something much more exact. What kind of positive tone is it? Praising? Happy? Encouraging? What kind of negative tone is it? Critical? Despairing? Angry?

Active learning

Earlier in this chapter you learned how to tackle word choice questions. Now answer these. Again, remember you can earn 2 marks together with a deep and insightful comment, or you can pick off the marks by earning them 1+1.

4 How does Lochhead's word choice in paragraph 2 emphasise the challenge of caring for the growing elderly population?   2

5 How does the word choice in paragraph 6 convey the experience of loss?   3

For answers see page 209.

Active learning

Earlier in this chapter you learned how to tackle questions that show your understanding of the ideas and information in the passage. Now answer these:

6 Read paragraphs 7 and 8. Identify any four benefits of the poetry sessions with elderly people.   4

Hint: To make it easy for the marker to see and reward your good work, and to help you keep track that you have done everything the question asked you, set out your answer for this question as a list of bullet points.

7 Read paragraph 9. Identify two ways in which the writer responds to her own increasing age. Use your own words in your answer.   2

For answers see page 210.

Imagery questions

Writers use images to strengthen what they say by putting all sorts of pictures in the reader's mind. Imagery is not the same thing as description. A **description** tells us what something is **like in itself**. An **image** shows that one thing is somehow **like another**. The comparison tells us more about the thing that is being compared. Similes, metaphors and personification are all different sorts of images, though most of the images you will be asked about will be metaphors.

To get us thinking about images and how they add to our understanding, let's think about all the studying and preparation you have to do as a Higher pupil. On any particular night, you might have an English essay to write, a Maths test to study for, some French vocabulary to learn, and a chapter of your Physics textbook to read. If all this were true, you could quite justifiably say:

I have a mountain of homework to do.

How is your homework like a mountain? There's a lot of it. It's a big challenge. It will take a lot of effort on your part. So, if you were to analyse the image of your homework as a mountain, you could do it like this:

Just as a mountain is high and hard to climb, so the amount of homework I have to deal with tonight is enormous and will be really difficult.

Of course, there are ways in which your homework is not like a mountain. You don't need to strap on an oxygen tank before you deal with it. Special clothing and footwear are not required. There's no snow on your French jotter. When you answer imagery questions, you are looking for the **similarities**.

Let's unpick the explanation above. It's a useful way of beginning to analyse an image.

You begin with the **imaginary** thing in the image, saying what it is like:

> **Just as a mountain is high and hard to climb …**

then you explain how this relates to the real thing that the writer is trying to get you to understand:

> **… so the amount of homework I have to deal with tonight is enormous and will be really difficult.**

This, therefore, is a structure you can use to begin your analysis:

> **Just as … (SAY WHAT THE IMAGINARY THING IS LIKE) … so … (EXPLAIN WHAT THIS TELLS US ABOUT THE REAL THING) …**

All through this chapter, you have been reminded about the difference between developed and undeveloped answers. You know that, in an exam, a detailed or insightful comment can earn you 2 marks, while a more basic comment will earn you just 1 mark. Using the '*Just as … so …*' method to break down the image will earn you the first mark, but if you want that second mark, you need to go further. You need to get to the heart of the idea that the image is suggesting.

Active learning

First, read this short passage:

> I've had many teachers in my life, but the greatest of them all was poverty. Poverty was the crucible that formed me. Throughout those cashless years, I learned self-discipline. I could not control how much money my parents had, or how much I had for myself as I set out in the world, but I could control my desires, and my spending. There was no room for self-indulgence. Such penury also moulded my beliefs, and my politics: I became profoundly aware of how my parents' income bore no relation to either their ability, or to their willingness to work. They were victims of a system that did not value what they did.

Now look at the worked example below. When you read the answer, you'll see comments in red to help you understand the marker's thought process.

Q Analyse how the writer uses imagery to convey the impact poverty had on her.

A Just as 'teachers' educate us, so poverty taught the writer something. **(1 mark here for basic analysis of the image.)** We see that the writer learned many valuable life lessons from the period she spent experiencing family and personal poverty. **(2nd mark for fuller analysis of what the image suggests.)**

There are two more images in the mini passage above: 'crucible' and 'moulded'. Using the same question as above, analyse these images, trying to earn the full 2 marks for a detailed, insightful answer.

For answers see page 210.

Active learning

Two particular images are very commonly used. You will hear them all the time in conversation, and see them constantly in the media.

- People dealing with serious illness are often said to be involved in a *'battle'*.
- Participants in many competitive television programmes describe their progress through the contest as a *'journey'*.

First, using the *'Just as … so …'* method, analyse each of these common images.

Then, work with a partner. Try to come up with two new and more original images to use for dealing with illness or competing in a television contest.

Finally, give your new images to another pair to analyse using *'Just as … so …'*. If they can do this, you have probably come up with good, and therefore very welcome, images.

We are going to take the chance here to focus specifically on imagery, but do remember that in the exam this will be referred to alongside another technique, or a question will ask more generally about *language*, in which case it is up to you to decide which features merit your analysis.

Read this article about a rather unusual bar:

Dry bars — are we sobering up?

1   'Alcohol is omnipresent,' says Catherine Salway, handing me something called a Beetroot Coco-tini. 'You can't even go to the cinema now without considering having a glass of wine. But I thought: "There's a way to cut through that, and do the opposite."'

2   Salway is 40, and the founder of a new 'gastrobar' called Redemption, located at the foot of the Trellick Tower on Golborne Road, west London. The decor is stripped-down and chic: bare brick walls, neon signs and furniture that a neighbouring social enterprise has made out of other people's

junk. Sight unseen, you'd think you were in a reasonably typical urban hostelry.

3   But that's not quite true. The food here is 'pretty much' vegan, but what really sets the place apart is a completely alcohol-free drinks menu. The basic idea, Salway tells me, is to offer people a chance to 'spoil yourself without spoiling yourself', and provide a sanctuary of sober calm in the midst of a booze-dominated culture. As she sees it, moreover, her business is on the crest of a wave — as evidenced by a handful of similar projects in other British towns and cities, and statistics that suggest our national dependence on the bottle may at last be starting to wane, not least among people under 30.

Catherine Salway in her dry pub, Redemption

4   Until 2011, Salway was the chief brand director for the Virgin Group. She was also drinking a lot, a habit that developed when she first arrived in London in the giddily hedonistic mid-90s. By now, though, an existential hangover had kicked in: 'I was overweight, drinking too much, pretty miserable. And I thought: "I could just sit here grinding away, doing corporate jobs, or do something meaningful."'

5   The idea for Redemption came to her when she was holidaying in a yogic retreat in Goa ('very clichéd,' she smirks). No booze was available — which, she was surprised to find, gave everyone she was with a pronounced feeling of liberation. 'It was only by alcohol not being present at all that we were freed from it,' she says.

6   And so, via an initial 'residency' at a venue in Hackney followed by the opening of permanent premises here in September 2013, a new business came into being. With backing from two individual investors and over £50,000 of her own money already staked, Salway says she wants to open

up two more branches of Redemption in London. In time, she would like to expand abroad.

7   'Loads of people have told me I'm going to fail: particularly big property moguls from London, and traditional investors — mainly men over 50,' she says. 'A lot of people said to me: "You're mad — London runs on alcohol. It's fuelled by alcohol." And I said: "Well, not everybody, and not all the time."'

8   For all the collective angst about Britain's drinking habits, our consumption of booze does seem to be changing. According to the Office for National Statistics, the share of people who report having a drink in the previous seven days has been falling for at least eight years: 72% of men and 57% of women did so in 2005, but by 2013, the respective figures had fallen to 64% and 52%, and the amount of alcohol consumed by people on their 'heaviest' day had also come down.

9   As Salway explains, it's generational differences that suggest something really is up. According to NHS data, in 1998, 71% of 16 to 26-year-olds said they'd had a drink in the week they were questioned about their habits — but by 2010, that figure had fallen by around a third, to 48%. 'People in their early 20s and teenage years are growing up with parents who get lashed all the time, and that's uncool,' she says. 'I've also heard that there's a lot of displacement through use of technology. Kids aren't going out to get drunk because they've got so much to stimulate them.'

10   On the night I visit Redemption, among the customers are a trio of twentysomethings, slurping apple mojitos around a long table. Jennifer Moule, 28, and Alicia Brown, 27, are both secondary school teachers; 28-year-old Yassine Senghor manages a club, and is therefore well aware of what a contrast to the prevailing model of socialising this place represents. 'The fact that there's no booze makes everything easier,' says Moule, who is splitting her time between chatting, and marking essays on *To Kill a Mockingbird* and *The Crucible*. 'You're not distracted: the evening won't turn into something else.'

11   I mention the idea that their generation is less boozy than its predecessors, hoping for some proud statements of 21st-century puritanism. But no. 'I had a bottle of Malbec last night with my boyfriend,' says Moule. 'Well, he had a glass, anyway.'

12   'But that's what makes this place perfect,' says Brown. 'If we were anywhere else, we'd order a bottle, not just glasses.'

Adapted from an article in the *Guardian*
by John Harris, 21 March 2014

Paragraph 3 contains three images:

1 '*a sanctuary*'

2 '*the crest of a wave*'

3 '*a handful of similar projects*'

Using the '*Just as … so …*' method to help you, explain what each image means and analyse its effect.   **2 marks for each**

4 Read paragraph 4. How does Catherine Salway's use of imagery convey her feelings about her former career?   2

5 Read paragraph 7. How is imagery used to suggest the importance of alcohol as part of London life?   2

For answers see page 211.

You also learned how to answer questions that allow you to show your understanding of a writer's overall ideas and argument. Now answer these:

6 Read paragraphs 8 and 9. **Using your own words as far as possible,** list the evidence that suggests that '*our consumption of booze does seem to be changing*'.   4

Hint: Bullet point your answer.

7 Read paragraphs 10 and 11. In what way is the group of customers described both a **good** and a **bad** example of the trend towards lower consumption of alcohol as discussed in the article?   2

For answers see page 212.

Sentence structure questions

Sentence structure is how a sentence is made and built up. Very often, pupils get structure questions wrong because they don't actually answer the question. Many pupils end up rehashing the content of a sentence when they should be examining its structure.

Structure is not the same as content. The structure of the bag you take to school might be canvas, stitched together and then attached with leather straps and metal buckles; its content might include books, pens, a packet of crisps and your phone.

A number of smaller techniques contribute to sentence structure:

- **Length:** Look at whether a sentence is noticeably long, or noticeably short, especially if its length contrasts with the length of other sentences nearby.
- **Listing:** What is being listed and what does this list suggest?
- **Repetition:** What is being repeated and what does this repetition suggest?
- **Parenthesis:** This can be created with a pair of commas, a pair of brackets, or a pair of dashes. What is the extra information inside the parenthesis about and what is the effect of this?
- **Word order:** Have any words been put in a position in the sentence that particularly creates emphasis?
- **Colons or semicolons:** What do these divide the sentence into? What do colons introduce?
- **Type of sentence:** is it
    - a statement?
    - an instruction?
    - a minor sentence?
    - a question?

    Has the writer used this particular type of sentence to have a particular effect upon the reader? What is this effect, and how is it created?

Look at this extract from the article you've already read about older people and poetry:

> The issue of funding often aggravates the complicated feelings — resentment, among others, let's face it — that 'the elderly' trigger. The people you meet in care homes when some combination of duty, family ties, honouring old friendship takes you there, come, of course, from an incredibly diverse range of backgrounds. They are retired doctors and nurses and teachers who once taught you, and joiners and butchers and builders and former soldiers; folk that never got a start and were 'on benefits' all their lives; parents, neighbours, widowers and divorcees; folk that 'fought drink', or were made redundant at 50. They were fly-men, head-hunters, bank clerks and church-goers and socialists and atheists and pacifists and harmless biddies and bonny-fechters, folk who followed their team and total chancers and ballroom dancers … They were big readers or avid cinema-goers or opera enthusiasts or rock fans or jazzers or into am-dram. They were artists or writers or musicians themselves.

Here are two possible sentence structure questions on this extract, along with suitable answers.

Q1 What is the effect of the use of repetition in this paragraph? **2**

A1 The writer repeatedly uses *'They were'* at the start of sentences. This creates the impression that the residents of care homes have lived a huge variety of different and interesting lives and have contributed to society in many ways.

Q2 Show how the structure of the first sentence allows the writer to communicate with her readers. **2**

A2 The writer uses parenthesis *'— resentment, among others, let's face it —'* to speak directly to the reader. This address to the reader is emphasised by the use of *'let's'* within the parenthesis, which draws the writer and readers together.

As we saw earlier with questions on word choice, tone and imagery, in the exam sentence structure will usually be mentioned alongside other techniques. You may get a question that begins:

By referring to both word choice and sentence structure, analyse …

or you may get a question that puts the onus on you to work out what is worth examining:

Analyse how the writer's use of language …

and it will be up to you to realise that there is some significant aspect of sentence structure you could examine and answer on.

Now read this article about private tutoring:

The new boom in home tuition

1   'Earn £800 a week tutoring in Kazakhstan,' read one email I received earlier this year. Another began, 'Do you fancy going to the Bahamas for three months?' Summers in St Tropez, Hong Kong and Tuscany were also up for grabs.

2   Some may dismiss these emails as spam. In fact, they are a few of the 'international opportunities' offered by Bright Young Things, a British agency specialising in 'private bespoke tuition'. Such assignments require at least four hours of work a day — teaching English, for example, or preparing children as young as five for entrance exams to a British private school.

3   Private tutoring is that rare thing: a booming British industry, in demand at home and abroad. The online education resource EdPlace estimates, not entirely convincingly, that British parents spend as much as £6bn a year on private

lessons for their children. A recent Ipsos Mori poll for the Sutton Trust found that 24% of all young people in the UK have received private tuition at some point; in London, the figure rises to 40%.

4   Across the country, and especially in the capital, agencies have sprouted in the hope of benefiting from this boom. Some have prospered. But more significantly, tutoring has become a career — and for young people working in the arts, it is increasingly a second career, supplementing their creative endeavours.

5   As a young journalist who has just started working freelance, I recently joined these ranks. Last month I attended a training day alongside postgraduate students, former teachers and recent graduates at a loose end — as well as young writers, actors and journalists.

6   At a time of high unemployment, hiring freezes and unpaid internships, it's not hard to see the appeal of a job paying between £25 and £40 an hour (and even more at some high-end agencies). For me, tutoring promises to be a far more dependable source of income than writing, for which it will leave plenty of time. It is also livelier and less solitary — and, unlike many forms of casual labour, intellectually stimulating.

7   For young adults in the creative industries, tutoring has become a long-term means of supporting their other work. 'Virtually all of my friends who are working creatively in the arts tutor,' says Edward Kiely, a comedian who has been tutoring for almost two years. He tutors between 17 and 19 hours a week, which is enough to support his writing and performing. 'I never thought that there'd be enough out there for it to be a full source of income,' he says.

8   Tutoring has become a kind of inadvertent private subsidy for the arts. Until recently, an aspiring novelist might have signed on or worked as a copywriter, and a drama school graduate might have turned to temping or waitressing. Now, if they have a good degree, they have an option that offers higher wages for fewer hours.

9   If the hourly rates are tutoring's main attraction, the independence and flexibility it allows are also important. Although agencies play a key role in finding clients and processing payments, tutors are essentially self-employed. For Jackson Gordon, a songwriter, his work as a musician

is entrepreneurial — 'you are your own boss'. To work in a conventional office job alongside that 'is such a weird clash of values'. With tutoring, hours can be negotiated: 'Once you've built a relationship with your families, they're usually up for tutoring on a week-to-week basis,' says Henry Eliot, a writer who also edits a magazine about London. For musicians or actors who might have to travel for a concert or attend an audition, such flexibility makes it easy to keep two careers going.

10   Some tutors have concerns over the levels of pressure their students — many of them still at primary school — are under, stoked by a combination of their parents and their schoolmates. And although some tutees attend state schools, many tutors I spoke to expressed misgivings about work that tends to aid already privileged, wealthy people. 'You're further enhancing the educational capital of people who already have the cards stacked in their favour,' says Kiely.

11   The Sutton Trust estimates that 31% of students from better-off families have had some private tuition, compared to 15% from less well-off families. Not-for-profit organisations such as the Manchester-based Tutor Trust offer free tuition to students from poorer backgrounds. The Trust trains its tutors, who work a free hour for every six they are paid, and connects them with disadvantaged schools around Manchester.

12   Despite their reservations, most of my interviewees said they enjoy tutoring and are grateful for the opportunities it has given them. The alternatives, for Davis, would have been ushering and bar work, 'which would have been damaging to my career' because they require more time for less money.

13   Others would give up teaching if they could afford to, but accept they might have to wait a while. For myself, as a freelance journalist just starting out, it's hard to imagine being able to manage without an additional source of income.

Adapted from an article in the *Guardian* by
Daniel H. Cohen, 26 October 2013

You are going to try some sentence structure questions on this passage. Again, remember you can earn 2 marks together with a deep and insightful comment, or you can pick off the marks by earning them 1+1.

1 How does the sentence structure in paragraph 1 engage the reader? 2

2 What is the effect of the author's use of parenthesis in the second sentence of paragraph 3 (*'The online education resource … for their children.'*)? 2

3 How does the sentence structure of paragraph 5 convey the popularity of tutoring as a career? 2

4 How does the sentence structure of paragraph 6 emphasise the challenges of the graduate job market? 2

For answers see page 213.

Questions about conclusions

You may meet a question about conclusions. In the Reading for Understanding, Analysis and Evaluation exam paper, such questions may be worded like this:

> **Explain the effectiveness of the final paragraph as a conclusion to the writer's argument.** 2

They can also come up in the Scottish set text section of the Critical Reading exam paper — usually in questions about poetry, where the whole text can be printed in the exam paper. Such a question might look like this:

> **By referring to ideas and/or language, evaluate the effectiveness of the final stanza as a conclusion to the poem.** 2

We're going to deal with this type of question here, in the chapter on the Reading for Understanding, Analysis and Evaluation exam; it is up to you to remember that you can also apply this knowledge to Scottish set text questions.

Active learning

Work with a partner. **Don't look** at the bottom of the page. (Cover it up if you think you will feel tempted.) List as many answers as you can for the following questions:

1 What is a writer trying to do with his or her conclusion?

2 What are some of the features you might expect to find in a well-written conclusion?

When you've had some time to think and make notes, share your answers with the rest of the class. Add to your own lists as you hear other people's answers.

Now you can look at the suggested answers at the bottom of the page. Are there any there that you didn't think of? Add them to your lists.

The most important thing to remember about this kind of question is that you are being asked about effective **conclusions**. When pupils get these questions wrong, it is very often because they write about something that makes the writer's work effective but not about what makes it effective **as a conclusion**, as a way of finishing off and wrapping up a piece of writing. If you are not dealing with the idea of conclusion, you are not answering the question and you cannot earn the marks.

You won't go wrong if, in your answer, you quote or refer to something in the conclusion and then show how it refers back to something — either an idea or the language — from earlier in the passage.

Go back to pages 111–4 and re-read the passage about how the internet constantly tries to catch and hold our attention.

Now look at this worked example question:

Q By referring to ideas and/or language, explain the effectiveness of any **two** aspects of the final paragraph as a conclusion to the article.   **4**

A The final paragraph mentions Facebook and its founder Mark Zuckerberg. This refers back to the writer's earlier mention of Facebook in paragraph 1, bringing the passage full circle.
In the final sentences the writer suggests we might 'all be a bit happier' if we made fewer visits to Facebook, tying in with an idea explored throughout the passage, that our time on the internet is making us feel depressed.
By concluding with this idea of spending less time on Facebook, the writer offers readers a challenge for them to act upon, and by holding out the prospect of possible happiness, he offers readers a vision of a better life.

1 Possible answers include: to sum up; to have a (final) impact on the reader; to be memorable; to be convincing; to make the reader think, etc.

2 Possible answers include: deliberate reference back to ideas from earlier in the text; deliberate reference back to language from earlier in the text; rhetorical question; short, impactful sentence, etc.

Read the following article about how people behave on planes:

Recline and fall

Flying is nightmarish, but we've all got our little life-hacks that we use to make it bearable. Maybe you bring a neck pillow, splash out on noise-cancelling headphones, or import some melatonin to get over jetlag. My favourite tip is this: on a long-

5 haul flight, I wait until the food is served, and then reach over to the tray of the person on my right, and take their dessert. The sugary goodness really improves my trip, and the thrill of taking something that isn't mine is great. A lot of people get angry when I do this, but they're just being unreasonable; if

10 they really care about dessert, they should just reach over and take one from the tray of the person on their right.

Sure, there's always some poor sod who's on the far side of the plane who can't steal anyone's cake — and some lucky guy who's over on the other side and gets two — but if airlines

15 didn't want me to do it, why did they make the seats so close together in the first place?

I kid, of course. Your sugar is safe around me — unless, that is, you recline your seat, grinding my knees, just so you can be 10 degrees closer to the horizontal for a flight in which you're

20 going to try to sleep for 20 minutes, and then give up and watch films you didn't bother to see in the cinema first time around. If you do that, I will take your food, march to the exit row, and throw it out the door, in the hope that you'll chase after it and have the full 36,000 feet to realise your error.

25 Reclining a seat is a zero-sum game. Any possible improvement in comfort you get comes at the expense of the person whose space you are stealing. And since planes have some seats that can't recline — those against the bulkhead, or in front of the exit row — there will always be losers who

30 can't even recline their own seats to restore the equilibrium.

It's one of those minor sociopathies of modern life, like playing music on your phone's loudspeakers or leaving the keyboard clicks on when you type out a text on the tube. But unlike those crimes that any right-thinking person agrees demand

35 retribution, seat-reclining is seen as a tolerable, even acceptable thing to do. One friend, a tall man with joint issues, had to politely ask the woman in front to return her seat to the upright position because she had, ever so slightly, dislocated his knee. Instead, she shouted at him until the flight attendant intervened.

40 'But how can you sleep on the plane if you don't recline your seat?' I am asked. Be honest: you can't sleep on the plane whether or not you recline your seat. Moving the headrest of your chair 30cm into your fellow traveller's personal space does not magically transform your ticket into a first-class seat
45 with a lie-flat bed: it just messes up their trip.

That's particularly true if they're a weirdo like me, who sleeps best on planes slumped forward onto the tray table — a position not physically possible if the seat in front is reclined, and one that feels actively dangerous to be doing while the
50 seat reclines. If I die travelling, it won't be because of a terror attack, it will be because someone forcefully shoved their chair back while I was sleeping and broke my neck.

'If airlines didn't want you to recline your seat, then why did they put a button on the armrest that lets you do just that?'
55 my foes cry. Look, I'll put aside the fact that you're basing your standards of human behaviour on what an airline thinks is acceptable — the only corporations that would prefer it if they could just strip all their customers naked in the departure terminal, surprise them with chloroform, and ship them
60 stacked in coffins to their destination — and admit that there are plenty of situations in which you can recline your seat.

Maybe there's no one behind you. Maybe there's a child behind you. Maybe there's reincarnated Hitler behind you. In those situations, recline away. But if you are sat in front of a
65 full-sized adult human being, then look them in the eye and ask yourself if you're willing to take something from them just because you can. And if you are, maybe just steal a cookie from their tray while they're not looking.

Adapted from an article in the *Guardian* by Alex Hern, 26 June 2018

Active learning

Answer this conclusion question:

1 By referring to ideas and/or language, evaluate the effectiveness of the final paragraph as a conclusion to the article. 2

And, because this particular passage gives such a good opportunity, try this question, which is actually about how the passage begins:

2 Read lines 1–10. Identify two ways in which the writer attempts to engage the reader's interest in the opening paragraph. 2

For answers see page 214.

It is not easy to give more practice in conclusion questions here; you would have to read a whole new passage in order to try just one question. You will have an opportunity to answer a conclusion question when you reach the practice exam papers at the end of this chapter.

Until then, remember to:

- Look out for these questions **both** in the Reading for U, A and E exam **and** in the poetry set text section of the Critical Reading exam.
- Make sure that you answer about what makes the writing **effective as a conclusion**, not just as a piece of writing.

You have now learned about some of the key question types in Higher Reading for Understanding, Analysis and Evaluation. You have learned about showing your understanding of the writer's ideas, and about word choice, imagery, tone, sentence structure and conclusion questions. Soon you will get a chance to practise all of this in a specimen Higher paper.

Before that though, here is a different way of using what you've learned. To improve your grasp of Reading for Understanding, Analysis and Evaluation, you are going to create questions about a new passage. These questions will then be given to someone else to answer, and you will eventually mark their answers.

First, read the passage:

Homemade used to mean simple, healthy fare. But thanks to food blogs and TV, cooking from scratch has become competitive. Welcome to the hell that is haute homemade.

I have had enough. I will not plate up. There, I have said it. Plating up has infiltrated the contemporary lexicon. The term once innocently referred to serving food on individual plates, as opposed to letting people serve themselves from serving
5   dishes. Now it means making like you're a Michelin-starred artist and painstakingly arranging individual ingredients on appropriate plates (white and round does not cut it) in such a way as to be visually gratifying. Food must be styled, picture-perfect, plated like a pro.

10   A few weekends ago, I was looking for ideas on what to do with scallops. Friends were coming for supper and I wanted to make an effort. I found a section called Recipes For The Weekend in a glossy magazine. Perfect. But all I could find was Scallops and Ibérico Ham with Parsley Foam. The parsley
15   foam raised alarm bells: it sounded a bit molecular.

Then I saw the photograph. A lozenge of green sputum like a slug descending from a concave structure of ham and a single radicchio leaf. Where the foam meets the meat, a forget-me-not has been placed, like a satin rosebud on an
20   old-fashioned undergarment.

Who, in their right mind, would make this? Who? The recipe, which comes from a Michelin-starred chef, has a cooking time of four hours, plus freezing time. Four hours. Then you've got to plate up. Weigh that up against how long it
25   would take your guests to eat the thing (four minutes, tops) and you have to ask yourself: what's the point?

Home cooking, as a term, has got above itself. Home entertaining is the new going out, and it's hell: time-consuming, stressful, expensive. It's no longer good enough
30   to buy ready-made puff pastry; you've got to make your own. Make your own bread, too. Mix, knead and roll your own pasta, while you're at it. The home cooking that goes on is, in fact, haute cuisine. Homemade means turning back the clock and spending hours in the kitchen, making everything
35   from scratch and turning ingredients into lifestyle-affirming, narcissistic creations.

I came across a food video telling me not 'to unceremoniously plop tonight's dinner onto a plate'. Given that the dinner in question was chicken, veg and mash, it is hard to see why

40 not. I pressed play. Cue some frenetic piano music and the shaming of a 'plopped' dish: a chicken breast, mound of mash, untidy heap of broccoli and messy pile of carrots. The viewer is then talked through 'the art' of plating up. A bit of chicken is laid on a plate, with a bone thrusting skywards

45 and accompanied by nil-by-mouth quantities of veg. Two sprigettes of broccoli, four slices of 'cut-on-the-bias' carrot and one, just one, cauliflower floret are arranged beside the chicken. Where once one might pour some gravy, it's now time to 'pool the sauce and swipe through'. A manicured

50 hand runs the back of a spoon through the rectangle of gravy. No dish is complete without little spots of something unidentifiable and, sure enough, the presenter uses a 'squeezy bottle' to put three Smartie-sized spots between each arrangement of veg.

55 Cutting up a carrot won't do. You've got to puree the buggers and, once you've done that, according to another video, you've got to 'run your spoon straight through it and you end up with this cool kind of a swoosh'.

'I feel like I have to take the day off in order to prepare if

60 friends are coming over,' a friend commented the other day. 'The thing is, I like putting big pots on the table and everyone helping themselves.' While she ploughs her lonely path, the rest of us are doing things that shouldn't be tried at home. I'm talking vinegar balls.

65 These are a must for a 'classic pheasant dish' by the Michelin-starred chef Andy McLeish. His poached and roasted pheasant 'is made more impressive with the addition of sherry vinegar pearls', it says in *Harper's Bazaar*. 'It may take a while to whip this dish up, but it is worth it.' I check the preparation time:

70 three and a half hours. Whip up is not the verb I'd use. The sherry vinegar pearls are part of the plating up. They require agar agar, a chinois, a squeezy bottle, a fine nozzle and not much going on in your life.

If you do master the vinegar ball, you'll be in good shape

75 when it comes to preparing the butter to go with your bread rolls. Bread rolls! Yes, some of us still have gluten-tolerant, non-fasting, friends who eat the stuff. Obviously, you can't slice a bit of Lurpak and squish it into a ramekin. No, you've got to render the butter into individual edible Saturns,

80 smoking it first, moulding it into a ball and lowering a ring of sherry vinegar jelly around it.

Whoever wrote, 'You don't have to be a trained chef to learn the basics of plating', on startcooking.com, is lying.

85 Startcooking.com says that rule number five of plating up is, 'Play with height.' The photograph shows a pile of rice crouching in one corner of a square brown plate, a medley of chicken and veg beside it. Then the height rule is explained: 'It's good to have a bit of height, but don't overdo it or your guests won't know how to proceed! If you have a mound of mashed potatoes (mid-height),
90 you may want to lean your pork chop against it so that it is standing up (high), with a row of snow peas (low) in front.'

The rules for plating up mention 'your centrepieces', and we're no longer talking candles or, heaven forbid, flowers. The centrepiece should be edible, not disposable. Domestic mistress
95 of the universe Martha Stewart tells us how 'to create an hors d'oeuvre centerpiece that recalls a vegetable patch'. Instead of putting some raw carrots on a plate, a battalion of raw veg is divided up in a planter. Are we children, that everything needs to look like a plaything? Are we scared of food?

Adapted from an article by Genevieve Fox in the *Guardian*, 14 December 2013

Active learning

First, find a partner.

Then assemble the resources that will help you. As well as looking back through this chapter of the book, it may also be useful to have some past papers from recent Higher exams as a guide to question wording and layout.

Next, let your teacher divide up the class.

- Half the pairs in the room should follow instructions **1 to 4**.
- The other pairs should follow instructions **5 to 8**.

Now work with your partner to make up questions on this passage, following the instructions given. Make sure that for each question you:

- tell pupils where to look in the passage
- word the question clearly and unambiguously
- indicate how many marks are available
- create a mark scheme for yourself which should tie in with the number of marks you've said are available.

Here are the instructions.

1 Make up a tone question about line 1 ('*I have had … have said it.*').

2 Make up a word choice question about lines 16–20 ('*Then I saw … old-fashioned undergarment.*').

3 Make up a question about lines 21–26 ('*Who, in their right mind … what's the point?*'). Your question should require pupils to use their own words in showing their understanding of the writer's argument.

4 Make up a question about lines 27–36 ('*Home cooking, as a term … narcissistic creations.*'). Your question should require pupils to use their own words in showing how the writer develops her ideas.

5 Make up a word choice question about lines 43–48 ('*A bit of chicken … arranged beside the chicken.*').

6 Make up an imagery question about lines 62–64 ('*While she ploughs … vinegar balls.*').

7 Make up a sentence structure question about lines 74–81 ('*If you do master … jelly around it.*').

8 Make up a question about the writer's use of contrast in lines 74–81 ('*If you do master … jelly around it.*').

When you have finished, swap your questions with a pair who worked on the other set. Answer each other's questions, then swap them back and mark each other's answers.

For suggested answers see pages 214–5.

The comparison question

At the start of this chapter you were told that the Reading for Understanding, Analysis and Evaluation exam would consist of two non-fiction passages. So far though, we have only looked at one passage at a time. The question types you have been learning about, and the questions you have tackled, have all been designed to prepare you for Passage 1 of that exam.

It's time now to learn about Passage 2, and the final question.

Passage 2 will be shorter — usually around 600–700 words compared to the 800–900 of Passage 1. It will be followed by just one question. This question will be worth 5 marks, and will get you to make a comparison between the ideas and content of two passages.

You have 90 minutes altogether in the exam, which is quite a generous amount of time. Try dividing it up like this:

- Use the first hour to read Passage 1 carefully, and to answer the questions on it.
- Use the remaining half hour for Passage 2 and the comparison task.

The examiners want you to have the ability to follow, and summarise, the key ideas running throughout the passages. They also want you to be able to see the connections between ideas, and to be able to take a step back and look at texts more widely, as opposed to the very detailed scrutiny that some of the other questions demand. So, the final question on the exam paper will give you a lot to think about.

Picture yourself in the exam. You've been there for an hour, and you've just finished answering the questions on Passage 1. You now know that passage and its contents really well. You have read the whole passage through at least once at the start, and have probably read most of it over and over again in short sections as you answered the questions.

It's time for Passage 2.

Above the passage you'll find an instruction, something like this:

Read the passage below and attempt question 8. While reading, you may wish to make notes on the main ideas and/or highlight key points in the passage.

Next you will see a short introduction to the content of the passage, something like this:

In the second passage below, the writer discusses his own experience of tutoring.

And then you'll see the passage. This next piece of advice is going to sound rather odd, but it's important, which is why it's set out to grab your attention:

DON'T READ THE PASSAGE YET!

Why not? Because you don't know yet what the final question in the exam is, and if you don't know that then you don't know how you should read that second passage, or what you should be looking out for as you read it.

So, skip down to the bottom of the page to find the question. Let's assume that in this case it looks like this:

8   Both writers discuss the private tuition industry. Identify **three** key areas on which they **agree** about this industry. You should support the points you make by referring to important ideas in the passages.
    You may answer this question in continuous prose or in a series of developed bullet points.   **5**

Now you know what you must do, and what you can or might do, to answer this question.

You must:

- know Passage 1 really well already
- read Passage 2 very carefully
- identify the areas on which the two writers agree
- refer in detail to both passages to give evidence supporting these areas of agreement.

You can, or might:

- make notes as you read Passage 2
- underline parts of Passage 2
- highlight sections of Passage 2
- go back and underline, highlight or make notes about Passage 1 as well
- answer in continuous prose, if you want to, *OR* answer in a series of bullet points, if you'd rather do it that way.

Active learning

You're about to see a Passage 2 that follows on from the tutoring passage you have just been working on.

First, as you saw explained above, remember to skip to the end and read the question **before** you read the passage, so that you know what you are reading for.

Then, read the passage, as the instruction says.

Read the passage below and attempt question 8. While reading, you may wish to make notes on the main ideas and/ or highlight key points in the passage.

In the second passage below, the writer discusses his own experience of tutoring.

1   Working as a private tutor nowadays is a bit like being a confiseur for Marie Antoinette: no matter how much you spin the sugar into a confection about feeding society, you're really just making life sweeter for the rich. And I should know, having taught a predominantly wealthy elite for over a decade.

2   Five years into the most thorough economic malaise since the Great Depression, and amid more cuts than you'd find on a straight-to-DVD movie, it should come as scant wonder that one of the few boom industries is private education. In the strata of the recession-proof uber-rich, the private tutor can often appear as simply the next human accessory, summoned before the court to perform.

3   Yet in a society plagued by the disease of aspiration, it's no longer just about the very rich. Salaried and striving parents are queuing up to fuel the boom in a market valued in excess of £6bn a year, hyperventilating that their kids are being left behind as an already unequal form of education plunges into something that would make the feudal system look like the dictatorship of the proletariat.

4   Amid terror tales of two-year-olds receiving elocution tutorials, and salacious reports of super tutors creaming £1,000 per hour, the method for ensuring your child makes it with the likes of Old Etonians David Cameron, the Archbishop of Canterbury and Bear Grylls appears simple: start 'em young and pawn your granny to do so.

5   I began tutoring with no formal teaching qualification, just a respectable degree from one of the world's top universities and a knack for working with a child without leaving either one of us in shreds. Soon I was called to the sort of west London streets I thought had been dismantled once Mary Poppins had finished filming. The class of degree was less important than the whispered name of the university. I repeatedly watched parents hypnotised by the dubious dream of some sort of intellectual osmosis, passing accomplishment like a cold, from tutor to pupil.

6   What made the process endurable was being called on every so often by a normal family, for whom tutoring was an expensive and rare gift that succeeded in helping an already able child fulfil their potential. Sometimes I worked for the council, or on a donation-only basis, or for free. Helping those who were living proof that money does not happiness make, the ones struggling to cope with their parents' divorce, excluded and facing depression, made tutoring feel, if not as moral as curing cancer, then at least something marginally less dirty than selling arms to Bahrain.

7   Of course, one-to-one tuition is an amazing process. The problem is that under the current system, already polarised between the wafer-thin few and the frantic, competing many, children already excessively advantaged are being further preferred. In many cases, the next step for such kids is to have the tutor turn up and sit the paper for them.

8   Invariably it's the parents who could do with an education. I'm thinking of the media mogul who, in addition to his five-storey Mayfair house and Oxfordshire mansion, kept a château

in the Loire valley, closed up throughout the year, save for the two weeks in the summer when it was needed. Recently I was offered any financial incentive I cared to mention to continue working for the sons of a convicted billionaire murderer.

9   The malaise with private tutoring is not the absence of regulation. The agencies I've worked for have been tightly run with all tutors CRB checked, and for every passing private-school graduate who fancies earning some cash between gap years, there are scores of tutors from local comps; intelligent, kind, and warm-blooded enough to understand how to be interested in someone's emotional wellbeing for longer than the duration of a gin and tonic.

10 No, the real problem is that we continue to panic buy into a system so fatally unequal and personally exhausting and then wonder why there remains an issue with the lessons our kids are learning.

Adapted from a piece in the *Guardian*,
3 May 2013

Question on both passages

8   Look at both passages.
Both writers discuss the private tuition industry.
Identify **three** key areas on which they **agree** about this industry.
You should support the points you make by referring to important ideas in the passages.
You may answer this question in continuous prose or in a series of developed bullet points.   5

Active learning

In the exam you can, as we've seen, write on, highlight, or underline parts of your exam paper. You can do this on Passage 2 and also on Passage 1 as you track down the shared ideas.

However, your teacher won't want you writing on this book, so you may need to read this passage or both passages again.

When you're ready, note down three areas the writers agree on. Here's one to get you started:

> Both writers agree that private tuition can be well paid.

Write this one down in your notebook, and add at least two more you have spotted by yourself.

Next, compare your list with a partner's. How many more can you each add?

Once you've identified the key areas on which the two writers agree, you are ready to support these areas by making detailed reference to both passages. The best way to set this out is by stating the comparison, and then quoting or referring underneath to support this.

> Both writers agree that private tuition can be well paid.
>
> > Daniel H. Cohen refers to an email he received offering him £800 a week to tutor in Kazakhstan. He goes on to say that tutors can earn 'between £25 and £40 an hour' and says that the pay can be 'even more at some high-end agencies'.
> >
> > The second writer refers to 'salacious stories of super tutors creaming £1000 per hour'.
>
> The (sometimes very) large sums involved show that working as a tutor can be lucrative.
>
> **Good answer!**

Do you remember the exam paper saying you could answer this question in 'a series of developed bullet points'? The pupil above has written one 'developed bullet point' by going through these three steps:

1 He has found, and given, one area of agreement between the writers.
2 He has thoroughly evidenced this area of agreement by quoting from each passage.
3 He has tied this together with a closing comment or explanation.

In fact, this developed bullet point is very like the **Point, Evidence, Explain** structure you will also use in your critical essays, and in some paragraphs of your discursive writing for the portfolio.

Suppose instead he had written this. It's not wrong, but it's not as good.

> Both writers agree that private tuition can be well paid.
>
> Daniel H. Cohen refers to an email he received offering him £800 a week to tutor in Kazakhstan.
>
> The second writer refers to some tutors earning '£1000 per hour'.
>
> **A decent start, now develop this.**

Active learning

Go back to the list you made of the areas on which the two writers agreed. Working with the passages beside you, so that you can gather in the evidence you need, create a **developed** bullet point for each area of agreement.

When you have finished, your teacher might ask you to hand them in for marking, or you could swap with another pupil and mark each other's.

Although this question is worth 5 marks, that does not mean you have to find five areas of agreement. Think again about the differences between the fully developed example of a bullet point that you saw above and the not wrong, but not nearly so good one. The mark scheme that the examiners follow says that if you can write about three areas of agreement, and do so with detailed and insightful use of evidence, not just quoting but also supporting those quotations with explanations, then you can earn 5 marks for this question.

This example question asked you to look at the points on which the two writers were in agreement. The question in your exam might not be quite like this. It might, for example, ask you to discuss the key areas on which two authors disagree. As always, the most important advice is:

ANSWER WHAT THE QUESTION ASKS!

Active learning

You have now learned about questions on word choice, tone, imagery, sentence structure and conclusions. You've learned how important it is to use your own words, and have answered questions that let you show your understanding of writers' ideas and arguments. You have also learned how to do the 5-mark comparison question.

You will now see a two-passage Reading for Understanding, Analysis and Evaluation task.

All the way through this chapter you have been reminded that although you were learning about some question styles (such as word choice, sentence structure, tone or imagery) separately, they would probably be mentioned together in the exam. Questions 2, 3 and 5c on page 152 are examples of this type. Try this approach. Once you have decided which feature or language you are going to answer on, use headings to organise and clarify your answer. If you've found two different techniques or language features to write about, use two headings.

This task should take you 90 minutes. As you answer, remember you can earn 2 marks together with a deep and insightful comment, or you can pick off the marks by earning them 1+1. And always:

ANSWER WHAT THE QUESTION ASKS!

When you have finished, hand your work in to your teacher for marking.

The following two passages focus on sexism and gender in film.

Passage 1

Read the passage below and then attempt questions 1 to 7.

The first passage, taken from the *Guardian* newspaper, considers one way of rating films.

1   You expect movie ratings to tell you whether a film contains nudity, sex, profanity or violence. Now cinemas in Sweden are introducing a new rating to highlight gender bias, or rather the absence of it.

2   To get an A rating, a movie must pass the so-called Bechdel test, which means it must have at least two named female characters who talk to each other about something other than a man.

3   'The entire *Lord of the Rings* trilogy, all *Star Wars* movies, *The Social Network*, *Pulp Fiction* and all but one of the *Harry Potter* movies fail this test,' said Ellen Tejle, the director of Bio Rio, an art-house cinema in Stockholm's trendy Södermalm district.

4   Bio Rio is one of four Swedish cinemas that launched the new rating last month to draw attention to how few movies pass the Bechdel test. Most filmgoers have reacted positively to the initiative. 'For some people it has been an eye-opener,' said Tejle.

5   Beliefs about women's roles in society are influenced by the fact that movie watchers rarely see 'a female superhero or a female professor or person who makes it through exciting challenges and masters them', Tejle said, noting that the rating doesn't say anything about the quality of the film. 'The goal is to see more female stories and perspectives on cinema screens,' she added.

6   The state-funded Swedish Film Institute supports the initiative, which is starting to catch on. Scandinavian cable television channel Viasat Film says it will start using the ratings in its film reviews and has scheduled an A-rated 'Super Sunday', when it will show only films that pass the test, such as *The Hunger Games*, *The Iron Lady* and *Savages*.

7   The Bechdel test got its name from American cartoonist Alison Bechdel, who introduced the concept in 1985. It has been discussed among feminists and film critics since then, but Tejle hopes the A-rating system will help spread awareness among moviegoers about how women are portrayed in films.

8   In Bio Rio's wood-panelled lobby, students Nikolaj Gula and Vincent Fremont acknowledged that most of their favourite films probably would not get an A rating. 'I guess it does make sense, but to me it would not influence the way I watch films because I'm not so aware about these questions,' said Fremont, 29.

9   The A rating is the latest Swedish move to promote gender equality by addressing how women are portrayed in the public sphere. Sweden's advertising ombudsman watches out for sexism in that industry and reprimands companies seen as reinforcing gender stereotypes, for example, by including

skimpily clad women in their adverts for no apparent reason. Since 2010, the Equalisters project has been trying to boost the number of women appearing as expert commentators in Swedish media through a Facebook page with 44,000 followers. The project has recently expanded to Finland, Norway and Italy.

10   For some, though, Sweden's focus on gender equality has gone too far. 'If they want different kind of movies they should produce some themselves and not just point fingers at other people,' said Tanja Bergkvist, a physicist who writes a blog about Sweden's 'gender madness'.

11   The A rating has also been criticised as a blunt tool that does not reveal whether a movie is gender-balanced. 'There are far too many films that pass the Bechdel test that don't help at all in making society more equal or better, and lots of films that don't pass the test but are fantastic at those things,' said Swedish film critic Hynek Pallas.

12   Pallas also criticised the state-funded Swedish Film Institute — the biggest financier of Swedish film — for vocally supporting the project, saying a state institution should not 'send out signals about what one should or shouldn't include in a movie'.

13   Research in the US supports the notion that women are under-represented on the screen and that little has changed in the past 60 years. Of the top 100 US films in 2011, women accounted for 33% of all characters and only 11% of the protagonists, according to a study by the San Diego-based Centre for the Study of Women in Television and Film.

14   Another study, by the Annenberg Public Policy Centre at the University of Pennsylvania, showed that the ratio of male to female characters in movies has remained at about two to one for at least six decades. That study, which examined 855 top box-office films from 1950–2006, showed female characters were twice as likely to be seen in explicit sexual scenes as males, while male characters were more likely to be seen as violent.

15   'Apparently Hollywood thinks that films with male characters will do better at the box office. It is also the case that most of the aspects of movie-making — writing, production, direction, and so on — are dominated by men, and so it is not a surprise that the stories we see are those that tend to revolve around men,' Amy Bleakley, the study's lead author, said in an email.

Adapted from an article in the *Guardian*,
November 2013

Passage 2

Read the passage below and attempt question 8. While reading, you may wish to make notes on the main ideas and/or highlight key points in the passage.

In the second passage, the writer considers how quite unexpected films can be judged unsatisfying by the Bechdel test.

1   With its excellent health care, superb state-sponsored child-minding provision, and greener-than-Kermit environmental policies, Sweden is practically the canary in the coalmine for putting politically correct policies into practice. It therefore comes as no surprise that cinemas in Stockholm are the first in the world to make gender representation a factor in an unofficial ratings system, pledging to give an A rating to films that pass the Bechdel test. So should feminists and other folk of a liberal-minded persuasion around the world be throwing their copies of *The Second Sex* in the air with joy, and blessing the Swedes' hand-knitted socks?

2   The Bechdel test was invented in the mid-1980s when Alison Bechdel's comic strip *Dykes to Watch Out For* featured a character who refused to watch a movie that didn't have at least two women who talk to each other about something besides a man. It's a notion rather beautiful in its stringent simplicity, which is why it's stuck around, come to be taken so seriously, and even applied to forms of media other than film. Bechdel actually introduced it in wry light-hearted fashion, via two women debating in the street what to go see at the cinema. The punchline was that the only film that the character who proposed the theory saw as qualifying was Ridley Scott's *Alien*, which was already five or six years old at the time the strip was published.

3   Today, if sticking to the letter of the Bechdel test, there wouldn't be much more at regular multiplexes for the characters to choose from, especially given the dominance now of effects-driven, male-demographic-skewed blockbusters. Ellen Tejle, the director of one of the four cinemas in Stockholm to adopt the Bechdel-driven rating system, said that the campaign has been aimed at opening viewers' eyes to how rarely they see 'a female superhero or a female professor or person who makes it through exciting challenges and masters them,' and that 'the goal is to see more female stories and perspectives on cinema screens.'

4   Well, good for her and the other theatre managers, and good for the Swedish Film Institute for supporting the initiative if this means getting audiences to think more about how

feminine perspectives and relationships are missing from so many movies. I'd like it more if they were highlighting the shocking paucity of female directors working today, down, according to a 2012 report, to only 5% of active directors in Hollywood, a 2% reduction on 2010, but you can't win 'em all.

5   However, I'm not so sure if I feel so supportive of television channel Viasat Film. Their idea of promoting Tejle and Co's Bechdel test-initiative is to have a 'Super Sunday', showing surefire-ratings earner *The Hunger Games* (fair enough), the loathsome Margaret Thatcher biopic whitewash *The Iron Lady*, and Oliver Stone's violent drug dealer drama *Savages*, not exactly a woman-centric film even if it does technically pass the Bechdel test. Maybe any publicity is good publicity — but really? Is that the best they could do?

6   Judging by the comments beneath the original article in the *Guardian*, this kind of affirmative-action programming still has the power to get people's knickers in a serious twist, provoking howls of fury about the 'nanny state' (the Swedish government is not making this a law, guys — it's just a few cinemas creating publicity) and how flawed the test is if it 'fails' films like the *Lord of the Rings* cycle or *The Shawshank Redemption* or, oh God the pity, Clint Eastwood and Jeff Bridges 70s buddy movie, *Thunderbolt and Lightfoot*.

7   Personally, I too have reservations about the validity of Bechdel test, if we're going to take it so seriously, because it would 'fail' some of the best films I've seen this year at festivals like the London film festival. Jonathan Glazer's magnificent *Under the Skin* probably wouldn't come up to snuff, given Scarlett Johansson's character is practically the only woman in it, and yet it's a film deeply concerned with female power and agency that in its sly metaphoric way says way more about gender than, say, *The Iron Lady*. Nicole Holofcener's acclaimed bittersweet examination of a love-triangle, *Enough Said,* might fail on the grounds that the two women in it mostly talk about men. Even the relentlessly slushy but effective *Saving Mr Banks*, which stars Emma Thompson as children's author P. L. Travers locking horns with Tom Hanks' Walt Disney over adapting *Mary Poppins*, would also fail, even though it features one of the stronger female protagonists of the year.

Adapted from an article on the *Guardian* film blog, November 2013

Attempt ALL questions
Total marks — 30

1 Read paragraphs 1 and 2. According to the writer, in what way have Swedish cinemas gone beyond filmgoers' usual expectations of movie ratings? Use your own words in your answer. **2**

2 Read paragraph 3. By referring to at least two examples, analyse how the writer's language emphasises the gender bias of most films. **4**

3 Read paragraph 5. By referring to at least two features of language, analyse how this paragraph conveys the current depiction of women in film. **4**

4 Read paragraphs 6 to 8. What evidence is there that moves to highlight gender bias in film are 'catching on'? Use your own words in your answer. **2**

5 Read paragraphs 9 to 11.
  a Identify two further instances of Sweden's desire to promote gender equality. Use your own words in your answer. **2**
  b Explain the function of the sentence, 'For some, though, Sweden's focus on gender equality has gone too far' in the development of the writer's argument. **2**
  c By referring to at least two examples, analyse how the writer's use of language in paragraphs 10 and 11 emphasises the opinions of those opposed to the use of the Bechdel test. **4**

6 Read paragraphs 13 and 14. Identify any two details given in these paragraphs that support the claim in the first sentence of paragraph 13. Use your own words in your answer. **2**

7 Read paragraph 15. Evaluate the final paragraph's effectiveness as a conclusion to the passage as a whole. **3**

Question on both passages

8 Look at both passages.
Both writers consider the application of the Bechdel test to films. Identify the key areas on which they agree, and those on which they disagree. You should support the points you make by referring to ideas in both passages.

You may answer this question in continuous prose or in a series of developed bullet points. **5**

For answers see pages 216–21.

You may have noticed that some of the types of questions you have learned about in this chapter did not appear in this practice task. The examiners always ask the questions they feel passages deserve, and not every sort of question will come up every time. However, you still need to know how to answer every question type, because you don't know when they will come up.

Now try this second Reading for Understanding, Analysis and Evaluation task.

The following two passages explore how the length of the working week affects employees.

Passage 1

Read the passage below and then attempt questions 1 to 8.

1   When a new group of interns recently arrived at Barclays in New York, they discovered a memo in their inboxes. It was from their supervisor at the bank, and headed: 'Welcome to the jungle.' The message continued: 'I recommend bringing a pillow to the office. It makes sleeping under your desk a lot more comfortable … The internship really is a nine-week commitment at the desk … An intern asked for a weekend off for a family reunion — he was told he could go. He was also asked to hand in his BlackBerry and pack up his desk.'

2   Although the (unauthorised) memo was meant as a joke, no one laughed when it was leaked to the media.

3   Following 30 years of deregulation, the nine-to-five feels like a relic of a bygone era. Jobs are endlessly stressed and increasingly precarious. Overwork has become the norm in many companies — something expected and even admired. Everything we do outside the office — no matter how rewarding — is quietly denigrated. Relaxation, hobbies, raising children or reading a book are dismissed as laziness. That's how powerful the mythology of work is.

4   Technology was supposed to liberate us from much of the daily slog, but has often made things worse: in 2002, fewer than 10% of employees checked their work email outside of office hours. Today, with the help of tablets and smartphones, it is 50%, often before we get out of bed.

5   Some observers have suggested that workers today are never 'turned off'. Like our mobile phones, we only go on standby at the end of the day, as we crawl into bed exhausted.

6   You might almost think this frenetic activity was directly linked to our biological preservation and that we would all starve without it. As if writing stupid emails all day in a cramped office was akin to hunting-and-gathering of a previous age … Thankfully, a sea change is taking place. The costs of overwork can no longer be ignored. Long-term stress, anxiety and prolonged inactivity have been exposed as potential killers.

7   Researchers at Columbia University Medical Center recently used activity trackers to monitor 8,000 workers over the age of 45. The findings were striking. The average period of inactivity during each waking day was 12.3 hours. Employees who were sedentary for more than 13 hours a day were twice as likely to die prematurely as those who were inactive for 11.5 hours. The authors concluded that sitting in an office for long periods has a similar effect to smoking and ought to come with a health warning.

8   When researchers at University College London looked at 85,000 workers, mainly middle-aged men and women, they found a correlation between overwork and cardiovascular problems, especially an irregular heartbeat or atrial fibrillation, which increases the chances of a stroke five-fold.

9   Labour unions are increasingly raising concerns about excessive work, too, especially its impact on relationships and physical and mental health. Take the case of the IG Metall union in Germany. Last week, 15,000 workers (who manufacture car parts for firms such as Porsche) called a strike, demanding a 28-hour work week with unchanged pay and conditions. It's not about indolence, they say, but self-protection: they don't want to die before their time. Science is on their side: research from the Australian National University recently found that working anything over 39 hours a week is a risk to wellbeing.

10   Is there a healthy and acceptable level of work? According to US researcher Alex Soojung-Kim Pang, most modern employees are productive for about four hours a day: the rest is padding and huge amounts of worry. Pang argues that the workday could easily be scaled back without undermining standards of living or prosperity.

11   Other studies back up this observation. The Swedish government, for example, funded an experiment where retirement home nurses worked six-hour days and still received an eight-hour salary. The result? Less sick leave, less stress, and a jump in productivity.

12   All this is encouraging as far as it goes. But almost all of these studies focus on the problem from a numerical point of view — the amount of time spent working each day, year-in and year-out. We need to go further and begin to look at the *conditions* of paid employment. If a job is wretched and overly stressful, even a few hours of it can be an existential nightmare. Someone who relishes working on their car at the weekend, for example, might find the same thing intolerable in a large factory, even for a short period. All the freedom, creativity and craft are sucked out of the activity. It becomes an externally imposed chore rather than a moment of release.

13   Why is this important?

14   Because there is a danger that merely reducing working hours will not change much, when it comes to health, if jobs are intrinsically disenfranchising. In order to make jobs more conducive to our mental and physiological welfare, much less work is definitely essential. So too are jobs of a better kind, where hierarchies are less authoritarian and tasks are more varied and meaningful.

15   Capitalism doesn't have a great track record for creating jobs such as these, unfortunately. More than a third of British workers think their jobs are meaningless, according to a survey by YouGov. And if morale is that low, it doesn't matter how many gym vouchers, mindfulness programmes and baskets of organic fruit employers throw at them. Even the most committed employee will feel that something is fundamentally missing. A life.

Adapted from an article in the *Guardian* by Peter Fleming, January 2018

Passage 2
Read the passage below and attempt question 9. While reading, you may wish to make notes on the main ideas and/ or highlight key points in the passage.

The second passage discusses what happened when one company made a change to the working week.

1   On the first long weekend of her employer's experiment with a four-day working week, Kirsten Taylor freaked out a little bit. Like a housework hurricane, she got through mounds of

clothes-washing, weeded the garden, cleaned the windows and mowed the lawn.

2 'I actually found that day really hard. I ran myself ragged,' laughs Taylor, who is a solo mother. 'I hadn't yet programmed that routine into my life. I thought: I don't know when the next one of these is coming, I better get everything done. I don't think I did it well, but heck it was a productive day!'

3 Taylor is one of 200 employees at New Zealand company Perpetual Guardian, which is halfway through a six-week long trial which could have profound implications for the future of labour. Staff are working four days a week but getting paid for five.

4 New Zealanders work an average of 1,752 hours a year, making them close to average compared with their OECD peers. Germans spend the least amount of time working annually, closely followed by Denmark, Norway and the Netherlands, while Mexicans, Koreans and Costa Ricans clock the most. Luxembourg is the most productive country in the world, despite its workers toiling away for an average of only 29 hours per week.

5 Christine Brotherton, head of people and capability for Perpetual Guardian, said many employees brought a similar level of focus to making the most of the extra day off as they would apply to their work. 'People have been thinking quite hard about that day off and how best to use it. Some people come back to work and are incredibly energised. They have been training for marathons, going to the dentist, getting their car serviced, or doing the shopping for their elderly parents. All the stuff that has been put on the back burner, but either helps themselves or their family. Life administration. But some people haven't quite realised that if we have three days off, the four at the office have to be very productive, and we need to address that,' she adds.

6 For the last two years a Swedish care home trialled a six-hour workday, with mixed results. Benefits included a 10% drop in sick leave and higher job satisfaction, but overall increased costs by 20%.

7 Perpetual Guardian's CEO, Andrew Barnes, a Briton, says the experiment is generating interesting data.

8 According to Barnes, some employees have found the reduced time to complete their work stressful. 'People were really positive going in, then a bit negative, then positive again,' he

says. 'In general terms, people are more positive because they are suddenly able to do things that they otherwise couldn't do.'

9   Supporters of reduced working hours have been cheering on the trial. 'I don't feel the pressure for it to succeed, but I think my staff do. People are telling me: we have to make this work for New Zealand,' says Barnes. 'From my point of view, it's very difficult as an owner of a business to see any way that this is not positive for me at the moment.'

10   But he expressed disappointment at the lack of interest in the trial shown by the New Zealand government, despite its potential implications for addressing issues from work/ life balance and the gender pay gap to the health and mental wellbeing of workers.

11   Having survived her day of housework, Kirsten Taylor has now settled into the new routine. She loves spending more time with her son, saving money on childcare and getting through her to-do list. Her personality and work style suit the arrangement perfectly, she says.

12   While her colleagues still socialise during the workday, the office space is quieter and more concentrated, and 'water-cooler chats' are briefer. 'I am feeling significantly better equipped when I begin the work week now,' she says. 'The trial was definitely more pressurised than I would ever have expected. But I don't know anyone who wants to return to the old routine.'

Adapted from an article in the *Guardian* by Eleanor Ainge Roy, January 2018

Attempt ALL questions

Total marks — 30

1 Read paragraph 1.
   Analyse **two** ways in which the writer attempts to engage the reader's interest in the opening paragraph.   2

2 Read paragraph 3.
   By referring to both word choice and sentence structure, analyse how the writer conveys the nature of modern working life.   4

3 Read paragraph 4.
   Explain any two ways in which we now know that we were wrong to think technology would '*liberate us from … the daily slog*'. Use your own words in your answer.   2

4   Read paragraph 6.
    By referring to both tone and sentence structure, analyse how
    the writer emphasises that '*this frenetic activity*' is not good for
    workers.   **4**

5   Read paragraphs 10 and 11.
    Explain three ways in which a shorter working week could be
    beneficial to employers and employees. Use your own words in
    your answer.   **3**

6   Read paragraph 12.
    By referring to at least two examples, analyse how the writer
    uses language to convey his argument about '*the conditions
    of paid employment*'.   **4**

7   Read paragraph 14.
    Explain what kind of jobs the writer believes would be '*conducive
    to our … welfare*'. Use your own words in your answer.   **2**

8   Read paragraph 15.
    By referring to at least two examples, analyse how the writer uses
    language to convey the difficulty of improving of working life.   **4**

Question on both passages

9   Look at both passages.
    Both writers discuss how working life affects employees.
    Identify three areas on which they agree. You should support the
    points you make by referring to important ideas in both passages.
    You may answer this question in continuous prose or in a series of
    developed bullet points.   **5**

For answers see pages 222–7.

You will need lots of practice in this task before your exam. This book
can only help you begin that process. You've seen some examples of
what the questions in this exam might be like. Now it's up to you to
get as much practice as possible. There are past papers that you can find
online, or buy, or that your teacher will have in school. And remember,
always:

ANSWER WHAT THE QUESTION ASKS!

CHAPTER 4 Critical Reading: The Scottish Text

Critical reading involves being able to demonstrate your understanding of texts you have studied in class.

You will be tested on this by sitting an exam (sometimes called the Question Paper) in May of your Higher year.

The exam is broken down into two parts: the Scottish text and the critical essay.

These will be dealt with in this chapter and the next one, starting here with the Scottish text, which is Section 1 of the exam paper.

The entire exam is only **1 hour and 30 minutes** long. That's not long for everything you have to do, so you need to be thoroughly prepared before you go into the exam. You also need to know your texts very well. You need practice in exam technique. This chapter will help you to do both these things.

How to use this chapter

The chapter will begin by teaching you in detail about two Scottish poems. Then you will learn about the Scottish text questions. Your work on this will be based on the two poems in this book.

 Warning

The poems you will explore were on the list of Scottish texts at the time when this book was being written. BUT, this list may change from time to time. Before you launch into learning everything there is to know about these poems, get your teacher to check if they are still on the list. You might need to study different poems for your exam.

Two poems by Norman MacCaig

The Scottish text options include prose (both short stories and novels) as well as poems. There are also several plays on the Scottish text list. It just isn't possible in a book of this size to cover all the potential texts. So, in this book, we're going to look at poems because these are the shortest types of text, and the easiest therefore to fit in. Poems are also ideal for this book because the Scottish text question asks you to compare or link one part of a writer's work to one or more other parts of their work. By looking at two poems, we can make this sort of comparison.

The poems are both by a writer called Norman MacCaig.

MacCaig was born in Edinburgh in 1910 and went to school and university in the city. He worked as a primary school teacher and was a pacifist, spending time in prison during the Second World War because of these beliefs.

Norman MacCaig

His writing was published from the 1950s onwards. His poems are often set in two of the places that were most important to him: Edinburgh, where he lived, and the West Highlands, the place his mother's family originally came from and which he visited throughout his life.

He liked his poetry to be clear. His poems tend to be short and he claimed not to spend long writing each one: he once said they took 'two fags' — the length of time it took him to smoke two cigarettes — to write. This doesn't mean he didn't concentrate on his poetry. He was widely published, spent time with other Scottish poets of the period and won awards and honours for his work. Later in life, he held posts at Edinburgh and Stirling universities because of his poetry.

Some of his later poems, written after friends and family members passed away, are sad and moving. He lived a long life, dying in 1996.

There are six MacCaig poems on the set text list. The two that we will study have been chosen because of their similarities, which will help later when we look at the Scottish set text question. They are both set in New York.

Both poems will be printed in this book, but you need to have copies for yourself, on paper. This way you can underline, highlight and make notes as you work, so that you are engaging and interacting with the poems.

'Brooklyn Cop'

Getting in

The first poem is called 'Brooklyn Cop'. Before you read it, think about these questions:

1   What do you think a Brooklyn cop would look like?
2   How do you think this person would behave?
3   What would be important to this person?

Share your answers with the rest of the class before you carry on.

Meeting the text

You are about to read the poem. Remember, it's a good idea to have a copy of it on paper so you can annotate it. As you read, work out how well the character, as described in the poem, fits the ideas that your class just shared.

Brooklyn Cop

Built like a gorilla but less timid,
thick-fleshed, steak-coloured, with two
hieroglyphs in his face that mean
trouble, he walks the sidewalk and the
thin tissue over violence. This morning   5
when he said, 'See you, babe' to his wife,
he hoped it, he truly hoped it.
He is a gorilla
to whom 'Hiya, honey' is no cliché.

Should the tissue tear, should he plunge through   10
into violence, what clubbings, what
gunshots between Phoebe's Whamburger
and Louie's Place.

Who would be him, gorilla with a nightstick,
whose home is a place   15
he might, this time, never get back to?

And who would be who have to be
his victims?

Thinking through

Now discuss your first impressions of the poem, and the character, using the questions you saw before.

1 What does this person look like?
2 How does this person behave?
3 What is important to this person?

So, how well does the poem match your earlier assumptions?

Let's get to work

As we study this poem, we'll look especially at how MacCaig's techniques allow him to build up a picture of the cop, and how he uses that picture to explore ideas about human nature. We'll work through the poem step by step, with teaching and commentary. Throughout the work, **key techniques** will be picked out in **red** and there will be short questions for you to answer.

The title

In the biography above, you read that MacCaig's life and his poetry were closely connected to two places, Edinburgh and the north-west of Scotland. The two poems we'll study here are unusual therefore because these poems, both written in April 1966, are very obviously set somewhere very different.

MacCaig's **word choice** of 'Brooklyn' tells us this immediately. We are far from home, which can be exciting but equally can be strange or uncomfortable. The **word choice** of 'Cop', which is an **American slang** term, underlines this. The fact that he tells us specifically that the cop is from 'Brooklyn', not just America or New York, suggests an area that, at the time the poem was written, had a tough reputation. It implies violence and threat. By using the **slang** word 'Cop' rather than a more formal word like 'officer' or 'policeman', MacCaig is of course using a suitable Americanism, but he may also be hinting that this character does not deserve our respect.

Overall, the **title** should work to bring to mind a particular stereotype, one we might know from films or television. Your answers to the **Getting in** questions that you worked on before you read the poem probably fitted that stereotype.

Stanza 1

The first stanza gives us a picture of the cop that fits that stereotype. He comes across like a stock character, rather than an individual. The poem begins with a **simile**, '*Built like a gorilla*', which is also a **cliché**; an unoriginal phrase.

Q1 What does the **simile** tell us about the cop?

Q2 What effect does MacCaig get from using a **simile** that is also a **cliché**?

MacCaig gets some **humour** from this first line, as we don't tend to think of gorillas as '*timid*'. But when we think about it more carefully, this apparently funny line again suggests violence.

Line 2 doesn't just tell us about the cop's build and appearance. The use of '*fleshed*' and '*steak*' suggests bodies are just meat.

Q3 What does this imply about how the cop treats people?

Line 3 contains a **metaphor**.

Q4 What is a '*hieroglyph*'?

Q5 What are the '*two hieroglyphs*' on the cop's face?

Most of us don't know how to read hieroglyphs, which requires specialist knowledge. They are foreign symbols and hard to understand, so MacCaig reads these for us, telling us what to think, that they '*mean trouble*'.

Now we know what the cop looks like, we find out what he does as he pounds his beat.

Q6 What real thing does the cop walk?

Q7 What **metaphorical** idea does the cop walk?

The expression '*thin tissue*' tells us how little separates the cop from violence. Tissue tears incredibly easily; it's not something you can walk on. There is also a **contrast** here between the real, hard '*sidewalk*' and the fragile, **metaphorical** '*tissue*'.

The poet uses another **cliché** in line 6.

Q8 Quote the **cliché**.

This might imply that there's a lack of real human emotion or relationship here. But MacCaig uses a couple of techniques in line 7 that challenge this and that make the cop seem human and vulnerable.

Q9 Which example of **word choice** does this? How does it have this effect?

Q10 Explain how **repetition** in this line also humanises the cop.

He's a different man when he's at home. We realise for the first time that he may be afraid of the violence around him, and that he knows he could die during his day's work.

But, just as we catch this glimpse, the earlier stereotype returns even more strongly.

Q11 Which earlier **simile** has now become a **metaphor**?

Q12 What is the effect of this?

And if, as line 9 says, '"*Hiya, honey" is no cliché*' to the cop, he again seems to lack real humanity, especially in his interactions with any women he meets during his day's work.

Stanza 2

So far, MacCaig has mostly given us a realistic picture. In this second half of the poem, he moves more into conjecture, into making assumptions about the cop's life and behaviour.

Q13 Which **repeated** word in this stanza tells us we're being shown a hypothetical picture?

We return again to the **metaphor** of the '*tissue*' that is the only barrier between the cop and violence.

Q14 Which **sound effect technique** does the poet use to draw our attention to how fragile this is?

We're asked to consider what could happen '*should he plunge through*' this barrier. The **word choice** of '*he*' suggests that it could easily be the cop himself who initiates the violence, and that other, perhaps innocent, people could get hurt.

Q15 What does the **word choice** of '*plunge*' suggest about the cop's violence?

The violent **word choice** of '*clubbings*' and '*gunshots*' again suggests that the cop would be to blame for this; he is the one who goes out each day armed with a firearm and a '*nightstick*'.

MacCaig's **repetition** of 'what' makes us notice how excessive and over the top this aggression is. He seems to attack without much thought or question. We could be kind and think this is because he wants to get home safe to his 'babe', but perhaps he's just a thug.

Interestingly, MacCaig's **word choice** for the name of the fast food joint, 'Whamburger', suggests both speed and violence, telling us about the neighbourhood he patrols.

Try reading the stanza out loud. It's one long sentence, but it's **not properly grammatical**. To have it be good English, we'd need to insert a few words, making it say something like '… *what clubbings, what gunshots **there would be** between Phoebe's Whamburger and Louie's Place.*' The stanza does function, but it's incomplete, like the cop who is able to do his job but seems to have some of his humanity missing.

Stanza 3

Again, this is a one-sentence stanza. It's also a **rhetorical question**, which has an effect on us as we read it.

Q16 What does this question make us feel?

The gorilla **metaphor** is used yet again to dehumanise the cop, and we are told the animal has '*a nightstick*'. Surely, suggests the poet, it can't be a good idea to arm such a powerful brute? In Britain we'd call this weapon a truncheon. MacCaig's **word choice** reminds us of the poem's American setting but also tells us the cop can be out working in the dangerous dark, at a time when he'd rather be at home.

By putting '*this time*' in **parenthesis** in line 16, the poet emphasises the risks the cop faces; tonight could be the night when he never does get safely back home. So, once more, we feel at least a little sympathy for this potentially aggressive character, as he could be injured or die just for going out to work. There's a deeper idea here too: the cop might never get back '*home*' to any kind of true humanity; he might be too far lost in hostility and aggression.

Stanza 4

The poem ends with another **rhetorical question**. Try reading it out loud. It's really hard to get your tongue around. As in stanza 2, its **grammar is impaired** and unclear. This makes us read it carefully as we try to work out what the writer means.

Q17 What does MacCaig mean here? Put the stanza into your own words to show you understand it.

Though there have been times in the poem where we might sympathise with the cop, it doesn't end that way. The final word is '*victims*', which suggests the cop deliberately causes harm. Did you notice that the stanzas got shorter and shorter as the poem went on? This **last line** is also the shortest in the poem: it all narrows down to one point of focus, that the cop can be an attacker, which is quite a bleak conclusion.

The message of the poem

As the title makes clear, the poem is a portrait of one character. But that character is nameless and is identified by his job and location. We have seen already how this makes him a stereotype.

So, we might think MacCaig is using this poem to suggest that American cops can be brutal. That's true on occasion, of course, and you will be aware of news reports about acts of US police violence.

But if we think that's the whole message, we are letting ourselves off the hook. The cop is a person, a human being, and we are people too. He's the only person in the whole poem, and he's **not specifically named**, which means he can stand for any or all of us; he can represent humanity. And he lives in one of the most advanced, most highly developed, richest and most successful countries in the world.

Q18 What is MacCaig's message in this poem?

Technique revision

Now that you've worked your way through the material about 'Brooklyn Cop', you should know the poem, and its techniques, very well. Here's a revision task.

Later in this chapter, when we look at critical essay writing, you'll learn how to use the **PEE** structure to build paragraphs in your essays. This stands for making a **Point** about something the writer is doing or a technique the writer uses; giving **Evidence** (preferably by quoting) from the text; and finally **Explaining** the **Effect** on the reader.

Active learning

Take a large piece of paper. Mark it up into a grid like the one below. For every technique, fill in a quotation from the poem and explain the effect it has on the reader. Some boxes have been filled in for you.

Point — a technique	Evidence — quotation	Explanation of effect
Title	*Brooklyn Cop*	Brings to mind a stereotype the reader knows from films and TV
Word choice	*Brooklyn*	Gives us the American setting, and suggest a tough area: threat and violence

You can carry on the rest of the table yourself. You'll need a whole sheet of paper, maybe two, as you need to add the following techniques:

- American slang
- simile
- humour
- contrast

- alliteration
- parenthesis
- not giving the cop a name
- short last line.

Give **each** of the following examples of word choice a separate row in your table: *cop; fleshed + steak; tissue; truly; he; plunge; clubbings + gunshots; Whamburger; nightstick; victims.*

Deal separately with **four** different uses of repetition: *gorilla; hoped it; should; what.*

Deal separately with **three** different metaphors: *hieroglyph; gorilla; tissue.*

Deal separately with **two** different clichés.

Deal separately with **two** different examples of incomplete grammar.

Deal separately with **two** different examples of rhetorical questions.

You'll find another of these revision exercises at the end of the work on the next MacCaig poem in this book. The task won't be explained so fully again; you'll just get a list of the techniques to revise, but you can look back to this page to remind you what to do.

It's time now to go on to our second MacCaig poem.

Hotel Room, 12th Floor

 Getting in

Before you read the next poem, think about these questions:

1 Have you ever stayed in a hotel? If so, what did you like about it? What did you dislike?
2 How many buildings or landmarks in New York can you name?
3 Have you ever visited New York?
   a If you have, what did you like and dislike about the city?
   b If you haven't been there, would you like to? Why, or why not?

Share your answers with the rest of the class before you carry on.

 Meeting the text

You are about to read another MacCaig poem set in New York. Again, it's a good idea if you have a copy of it on paper, so you can annotate the poem. As you read it for the first time, work out the answers to these questions.

1 Which two different times of day are referred to?
2 How does the speaker feel about being in New York?

Hotel Room, 12th Floor

This morning I watched from here
a helicopter skirting like a damaged insect
the Empire State Building, that
jumbo size dentist's drill, and landing
on the roof of the PanAm skyscraper.   5
But now midnight has come in
from foreign places. Its uncivilised darkness
is shot at by a million lit windows, all
ups and acrosses

But midnight is not   10
so easily defeated. I lie in bed, between
a radio and a television set, and hear
the wildest of warwhoops continually ululating through
the glittering canyons and gulches —
police cars and ambulances racing   15
to the broken bones, the harsh screaming
from coldwater flats, the blood
glazed on sidewalks.

The frontier is never
somewhere else. And no stockades   20
can keep the midnight out.

 Thinking through

Share your answers to the **Meeting the text** questions you were given at the start of the poem with the rest of the class.

 Let's get to work

As we study this poem, we'll look especially at how MacCaig's techniques create a picture of the city, and how he uses that picture to explore ideas about human nature. We'll work through the poem step by step, with teaching and commentary. Once again, **key techniques** will be picked out in **red** and there will be short questions for you to answer. Once you have studied this poem, you'll be able to compare it to 'Brooklyn Cop', which we looked at earlier.

The title

As in the previous poem, the title has a lot to tell us.

The **word choice** of '*Hotel Room*' lets us know the speaker is away from home, and that he is transient, just passing through; nobody settles for long in a hotel. '*12th Floor*' puts him high up. At the time of writing, in 1966, this would also have been a clue about how very far from home the speaker must be. No British hotel building would then have been so tall, and readers would have imagined an American skyscraper even before the poem namechecked two of these.

This high position means MacCaig is disconnected from other people. It gives him a vantage point, a place from which to make judgements about us and our human nature.

Stanza 1: lines 1 to 5

The poem's first words are '*This morning*'. The **word choice** here tells us that what he saw had a powerful impact on him, as if he had to write about it almost immediately. But it's something he only saw; he '*watched*' rather than taking part. So the idea of disconnection that we already found in the title is here too.

The poet describes a helicopter '*skirting*' the Empire State Building.

Q1 How does this **word choice** make the helicopter similar to the speaker?

Think about what kind of aircraft that is. Ordinary people don't fly around in helicopters. A helicopter might be used by the rich to fly above the poor; or by the authorities to watch over the people; or by the military to control or attack. Helicopters suggest power, status and wealth; and the speaker, shut in his hotel room, is cut off from all of this.

MacCaig says the helicopter is '*Like a damaged insect*'.

Q2 What figure of speech is this?

Think about the connotations of '*insect*'. Many of us don't like insects. Many of us find them creepy or scary. You might encounter them on unhygienic, dead, decaying things. And the helicopter is even worse than this, because it's like a '*damaged*' insect: something nasty made even more grotesque.

MacCaig isn't saying the helicopter itself is damaged: it wouldn't be flying around the New York skyline if it was. He's saying that even a functional helicopter is like a damaged, unpleasant beastie. There is something wrong with our modern technology, and there's something wrong with us if we are impressed by it.

Q3 What **metaphor** does MacCaig use to describe the Empire State Building?

Q4 Looking at the photograph to help you, explain why this is a suitable metaphor.

Q5 What are the connotations of '*jumbo*'?

Q6 What are the connotations of '*dentist's drill*'?

The '*PanAm skyscraper*' was built for one of America's most successful airlines. We've already considered how ordinary people don't use helicopters, but in 1966 when the poem was written, most ordinary people would not have been able to afford a flight by plane either.

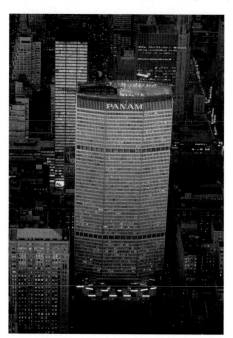

These two buildings therefore **symbolise** qualities like wealth and status, but in the poem an insect, which might be found on a dung heap, flies around one to land on the other. MacCaig may be criticising us for spending money on big-name, iconic projects like these, but ignoring the needs of the poor.

Both images we've seen so far, the insect and the dentist's drill, are disagreeable, repulsive. The poet seems unimpressed by human economic power or technical achievement.

(By the way, if it feels like we have analysed every single word of the poem so far, that tells you what a brilliant writer MacCaig was. Everything here has a purpose; nothing is wasted.)

Stanza 1: lines 6 to 10

This poem, not so far a riot of laughs, becomes **literally and metaphorically** darker; the use of '*But*' signals a **turning point** from light to dark. It is '*now*' midnight. In poetry, light is nearly always a metaphor for something good, but the daylight of '*this morning*' does not even survive to the end of the first stanza. The darkness is stronger.

MacCaig uses this change from daylight to '*darkness*' to examine what happens when our modern accomplishments are removed, and the darker, '*uncivilised*' side of human nature comes out. As readers, we are stuck in that midnight moment with MacCaig: his use of '*now*' creates **immediacy**, a sense that this is happening now, and makes us experience it with him.

Q7 What are the connotations of '*midnight*'?

We are told that midnight '*has come in*,' as if it has turned up uninvited.

Q8 What technique does MacCaig deploy by using this verb?
Q9 What are the connotations of '*foreign*'?
Q10 What are the connotations of '*shot*'?

Despite what that use of '*shot*' here suggests, it is at least the light from the windows — remember that light is always a positive idea in poetry — shooting at the darkness. We could argue, therefore, that stanza 1 ends on a hopeful note: there are '*a million*' of those lit-up windows, which sounds like a lot to fight against the darkness.

Stanza 2

However, the light doesn't win. MacCaig tells us that '*midnight is not/ so easily defeated*,' and the **placement** of '*not*' at the end of the line emphasises the negativity here, and the fact that darkness has won this conflict.

MacCaig tells us he is lying '*in bed, between/a radio and a television set*'. His use of '*between*' suggests he is somehow trapped or constricted. This is a poem about visiting New York, one of the most vibrant cities on Earth, and yet he never seems to leave his hotel room, where he is surrounded by lifeless objects. A '*radio and a television set*' might imply communication, but the speaker is alone, and is in contact with no one.

His use of '*hear*' in line 12 reminds us of '*watched*' in line 1. Now that it's dark, he can't see what's outside. Things are always more frightening and noises more scary in the dark, when we can't see what is actually happening.

MacCaig uses a **sound effect** to draw our attention to what he can hear.

Q11 Which **sound effect technique** does he use in line 13?

Q12 Which three real and actual noises does he hear in the rest of this stanza?

Q13 Use a dictionary to find out what '*ululating*' in this line means.

The writer is using this word as a **metaphor** for the sound of emergency sirens. It's also the first step in an **extended metaphor** that runs through the rest of the poem.

At this point we need a reminder that the poem was written in 1966, when attitudes and ideas were very different to what they are today. MacCaig is drawing on his readers' ideas of what was then called 'the Wild West' and of images that they would know from 'Western' movies.

We know that people lived in what is now the USA long before settlers began arriving from Europe in the seventeenth century. We would call these 'native peoples' or 'native Americans'. MacCaig's readers would have called them 'Red Indians' and regarded them as warwhooping savages. In the 1960s, readers would have looked back around a hundred years to a period when settlers were moving west across North America, taking control of land and driving away or killing native peoples. Though we'd now see this as brutality that led to human death, as well as the killing of millions of animals and the destruction of environments, to MacCaig's readers, and especially to 1960s Americans, this was 'when the west was won'.

Now that we understand that mindset, we can unpick the extended metaphor.

Q14 What real feature of New York City life is described here as ululating '*warwhoops*'?

Q15 What real feature of New York City life is described here as '*canyons and gulches*'? (**Hint:** There's a clue in '*glittering*'.)

Moviegoers, used to watching Westerns, would think of these '*canyons and gulches*' as narrow, dangerous places where settlers' wagon trains might be ambushed on their way across the west.

This extended metaphor of the historic Wild West allows MacCaig to say something about the present. He's writing in the present tense, so readers can't look back and say that violence is a thing of the past. In fact, this reference to a violent past is used to say that America's supposedly civilised present isn't that wonderful. Twentieth-century American riches and success were built upon that violent history. Human nature, says MacCaig, is violent and evil to the core and that doesn't change.

We see him **list** the results of that violent nature at the end of the stanza.

Q16 What three results of violence does the poet **list**?

He **repeats** the word '*the*'. As this is an impersonal word, it implies that anyone can be a victim. He also describes the screaming as '*harsh*'. A scream can't be anything but harsh, so this is an example of **tautology**, saying the same thing twice in different ways, and it emphasises the unpleasant sound.

'*Coldwater*' simply means what it says, that in a city where the rich can live in skyscrapers and fly around in helicopters, some people are so poor that they live in flats that don't even have hot running water. MacCaig is definitely showing us the stark contrast between the rich and poor who live side by side in New York. By using this word in the part of the poem that deals with violence, he may also be saying that if you treat people brutally, they are more likely to behave like brutes and descend into violence. The result is nasty: if blood is '*glazed on* [the] *sidewalks*' then there's so much that the pavement looks positively slick and shiny, like a piece of glazed pottery.

Stanza 3

In the final, very brief, stanza, MacCaig returns to the **extended metaphor** of the Wild West. The '*frontier*' was the edge of the supposedly civilised world, which kept moving further and further west during the nineteenth century as more of America was settled by European immigrants. To New York's nineteenth-century residents looking west, or to its twentieth-century residents looking back in time, the frontier would have been a frightening prospect, something they were glad to be far away from. MacCaig does not allow them this comfort, telling them the frontier '*is never/somewhere else*'.

Q17 You already saw one example of MacCaig's use of **placement** in line 11. Explain how he now makes a similar use of placement in the quotation above.

There is no solution to the problem of human nature, because '*no stockades/can keep the midnight out*'.

Q18 Use a dictionary to find the meaning of '*stockades*'. How does this add to the extended metaphor the poet has been using?

The use of negative word choice in '*never*' and '*no*' emphasises that bleakness. We can't '*keep the midnight out*' or the '*frontier*' back, because these things aren't somewhere else far away; they are inside each of us, and are part of our very nature. As with 'Brooklyn Cop', the conclusion, and the poet's message, is bleak. (If you are studying the other MacCaig poems on the Scottish set text list, you should also be able to see a connection here to his ideas in the poem called 'Basking Shark'.)

Technique revision

Now that you've worked your way through all the work on 'Hotel Room, 12th Floor', you should know the poem very well. It's time to revise your knowledge of MacCaig's techniques.

Active learning

You're going to carry out the same exercise that you did at the end of the 'Brooklyn Cop' work. (Look back to it now if you need to be reminded more fully of the instructions.) Take a large piece of paper and mark it up into a **PEE** grid. For every technique, fill in a quotation from the poem and explain the effect it has on the reader. For a grid about 'Hotel Room, 12th Floor' you need to work with the following techniques:

- something both literal and metaphorical
- simile
- symbol
- immediacy
- personification
- turning point

- alliteration
- extended metaphor
- list
- repetition
- negative word choice
- tautology.

Give **each** of the following examples of word choice a separate row in your table: *Hotel Room; 12th Floor; this morning; watched; skirting; helicopter; insect; damaged; jumbo; dentist's drill; midnight; foreign; shot; between; a radio and a television set; hear; canyons and gulches; coldwater; glazed; never + no.*

Deal separately with the placement of *not* and of *never*.

Deal separately with **two** metaphors: *dentist's drill* and *ululating*.

That's the end of our work on these two poems. They work well together. Each shows the impact that a trip to New York had on MacCaig, and how his response to the challenges of that city in the 1960s led to a wider exploration of human nature.

There are four other MacCaig poems on the Higher list. You will need to study them **all** if you hope to use them for the Scottish set text question.

Remember, your teacher should double check if these poems are still on the set list at the time when you are using this book!

If Norman MacCaig has been taken off the Scottish text list by the time you take this course, you could still study 'Brooklyn Cop' and 'Hotel Room, 12th Floor' as texts for the critical essay. If you do that, your Scottish set texts will need to come from a different genre, not poetry but either prose or drama.

The Scottish set text questions

Now that we have spent time looking at two of the set Scottish poems, you can learn about how to tackle this part of the exam. (Remember, the Scottish set text questions are in the first section of your Critical Reading exam paper, and you also have to go on and write a critical essay during the same 90-minute exam. We'll deal with that in the next chapter.)

What you will be assessed on

In the set text section of the exam you will read an extract — or in the case of poetry, usually a whole poem — from a Scottish text you have previously studied in school, and will then answer some questions.

There will be several questions focusing on the poem or extract itself. These questions will usually be worth 2, 3 or 4 marks. There will be a total of 10 marks' worth of these questions.

The last question will be a far bigger one, worth 10 marks. It will test your broader knowledge of the rest of a novel or play, or of other short stories or poems by the same writer.

Active learning

You're going to try some questions on the first MacCaig poem you studied. Your teacher may want you to work on your own, or perhaps with a partner or in a group. Start by turning back to 'Brooklyn Cop' and reading it again. Then try each question. If you are working with someone else, do make sure you still write down your answers as you would in an exam.

You already learned in the chapter on Reading for Understanding, Analysis and Evaluation that you get no marks at Higher level for quoting. It's the same here. Unlike at National 5, you get nothing for quoting; all your marks come from explanation and analysis. Remember, you can get 2 marks at once for a detailed and insightful answer, but it's also perfectly all right to earn your marks 1+1.

1 Look at lines 1–9. By referring to **at least two examples**, analyse how the poet's use of language conveys an unsettling impression of the cop.   4

2 Look at lines 10–13. By referring to **at least two examples**, analyse how the poet uses language to convey the central concern(s). 4

3 Look at lines 14–18. Evaluate the effectiveness of these lines as a conclusion to the poem. You should deal with ideas and/or language. 2

Give your answers to your teacher to mark.

For answers see pages 229–30.

Before we go on to look at the final, 10-mark question, the one that gets you to place this poem in the wider context of MacCaig's other work, here's something for you to think about:

Active learning

Work with a partner or in a small group. Get a large sheet of paper and give it the heading *Similarities*. Compare the two poems and use the sheet to create a record or poster of your discoveries. The first two have been done for you.

SIMILARITIES

- both set in New York

- both deal with the theme of violence

Carry on finding more answers in your group. If you push yourself to think of the content of the poems, their themes and ideas, the techniques MacCaig uses, and also the ways in which he uses these techniques, you should be able to get at least ten similarities.

That task was designed to get you comparing the two poems we've looked at, as this is what you will be expected to do in the last question on your set Scottish text.

The final, 10-mark question

As we saw already, the last question will be a far bigger one, worth 10 marks. This is another way in which Higher English is more exacting than National 5, where this final question was worth just 8 marks. This question will get you comparing the extract, or the poem, to the rest of the work you've studied. For example:

- If your Scottish text is a play or novel, and the extract focused on one character, you might be asked to look at that character over the course of the text.

- If your Scottish text is a play or novel, and the extract focused on a particular theme, you might be asked how that theme is explored and developed in the rest of the text.
- If you have studied poetry, the final question may ask you how something the writer does in the poem printed in the exam paper, such as exploring a particular theme or idea, or using a particular technique, compares to other poetry you have studied by the same writer.

These are just some of the possibilities for that last question. As always, the best advice is:

ANSWER WHAT THE QUESTION ASKS!

There is a very specific method and structure for answering this 10-mark question. You should have already learned and used this method at National 5 for the 8-mark set text question; this is just a slightly evolved way of doing the same thing.

The SQA marker will read your answer with this structure in mind, so you must learn to use it. The method may seem a little odd at first, but once you get the hang of it you will have a reliable method for picking up a lot of marks all in one go.

Here is a possible 10-mark question for 'Brooklyn Cop'.

- By referring closely to this poem, and at least one other by MacCaig, show how he uses his observations of reality to explore wider issues. **10**

There are three steps to answering the 10-mark question:

1 Identify elements of **commonality**. **2**
2 Deal with the poem (or extract from a longer text) **printed in the exam**. **2**
3 Deal with **another poem or poems**, or **another area** of a longer work studied. **6**

We'll deal with these one step at a time, with worked examples to let you see what is meant.

Step 1 is to identify elements of **commonality**. How does this poem (or this extract) have something in common with another poem or poems, or with another area of the same longer text?

There is a big clue for you here in the question. It asks you about 'reality' and about 'wider issues'. That does mean you won't get marks just for saying that MacCaig deals with reality in his poetry. That's already in the question. The keyword in the question is '*how*'. You need to tell the marker **how** MacCaig does this throughout his work and **what** kind of issues this allows him to explore. The markers want you to show a general understanding of key shared elements in the writer's work. So, you might write something like this:

Commonality

MacCaig, in his poetry, observes real people and places in a way that allows him to explore the violence that is a key, dark aspect of human nature.

The commonality example above works for the two poems we've studied, 'Brooklyn Cop' and 'Hotel Room, 12th Floor', but remember that you can refer in your answer to more than one other poem. If you have studied all six of the MacCaig poems on the set text list, your commonality point might read like this instead:

Commonality

MacCaig, in his poetry, observes real people and places in a way that allows him to explore wider issues such as the darkness of human nature, and our relationships both with nature and with our own history and heritage.

Step 2 is to deal with the poem (or extract from a longer text) **printed in the exam**. You can get 2 marks here for a detailed and insightful comment, or 1+1 for two simpler comments. So, you might write something like this:

This poem

MacCaig writes that the cop walks a 'thin tissue over violence'. This metaphor tells us that the barrier between civilised behaviour and violence is thin and very easily ruptured like tissue paper. Humans can easily give way to violence.

He also writes 'what clubbings, what gunshots'. The repetition of 'what' suggests that human nature can be excessively violent, in a manner that is over the top.

Active learning

There are other ways a pupil could earn 2 marks for this stage in the 10-mark question. Try to find at least two other ways of tackling this stage of the overall answer. When you write your response, use a heading, as in the example answer.

Step 3 of answering the 10-mark question is to deal with **another poem or poems** by the same writer, or to deal with **another area** of a longer work such as a play or novel if that is what you have studied. You can earn your 6 remaining marks by earning 2 marks for a detailed, insightful comment, or 1 for a simpler comment. Keep going until you think you have done enough to earn 6 marks in total. Remember, you already identified a commonality between 'Brooklyn Cop' and 'Hotel Room, 12th Floor', so you might write something like this:

'Hotel Room, 12th Floor'

In this poem, MacCaig suggests the violence that is a key aspect of human nature by his use of the word 'warwhoops'. This implies that people actually enjoy, and gain a thrill from, going into conflict with each other, as 'whoops' suggests joy and excitement.

Active learning

There are other ways a pupil could earn the marks for this stage in the 10-mark question. Complete this answer, keeping going until you think you have enough for 6 marks in total.

Now you know how the pattern works:

- 2 marks for commonality
- 2 for the poem or extract
- 6 for another poem, or another area or areas of a longer text.

You need to learn that pattern and be able to apply it to the 10-mark questions you meet in future. But that's all you need to do. There's no need to try to turn this into a kind of mini essay.

Active learning

You're now going to try some questions on the second MacCaig poem you studied, 'Hotel Room, 12th Floor'.

This time you should definitely work on your own. Start by turning back to the poem and reading it again. Then try each question, writing down your answers as you would in an exam. Again remember, all your marks come from explanation and analysis, not from quoting, and you can get 2 marks for a detailed and insightful comment or you can earn your marks 1+1 with simpler comments.

1 Read lines 1–9. By referring to **at least two examples**, analyse how the poet's use of language creates a sense of menace.   4

2 Read lines 10–18. By referring to **at least two examples**, analyse how the poet uses imagery to convey an atmosphere of violence.   4

3 Read lines 19–21. Evaluate the effectiveness of these lines in conveying the poet's message. You should deal with ideas and language.   2

4 By referring to this poem and at least one other, discuss how MacCaig uses imagery to develop his ideas.   10

Once you have finished, give your work to your teacher to mark.

For answers see pages 230–2.

That brings us to the end of our work on the Scottish set text question. Remember that you will need much more practice than this. Past papers and other material that your teacher may have will all help you with this.

CHAPTER 5 Critical Reading: The Critical Essay

You know already that Critical Reading involves being able to demonstrate your understanding of texts you have studied in class. You will be tested on this by sitting an exam (sometimes called the Question Paper) in May of your Higher year.

The exam is broken down into two parts: the Scottish text and the critical essay. The Scottish text, which is section 1 of this exam paper, has been covered in Chapter 4 of this book. This chapter will deal with the critical essay, section 2 of the same exam.

The entire exam is only **1 hour and 30 minutes** long. That's not long for everything you have to do, so you need to be thoroughly prepared before you go into the exam. You also need to know your texts very well. You need practice in exam technique.

You've written critical essays before, for your National 5 exam. You should already understand what you are being asked to do. Remember:

- A critical essay is **not** a chance for you to write everything you know about a text.
- It is **not** a chance to explain your favourite things about a text.
- It is **not** a chance to tell the marker about the bits you understand best, or find easiest to explain.
- It is **not** an invitation to write a commentary on the whole text from start to end.

A Higher critical essay is a kind of test. It tests your ability to **select** from your knowledge of a text, and to use that selected knowledge to meet the demands of a **specific** task or question.

What you will be assessed on

In this part of the exam you will be given a choice of questions. These questions will be divided into six sections. Each section contains questions about a different genre. These are:

- drama
- prose fiction
- prose non-fiction
- poetry
- film and television drama
- language.

There will be **three** questions for each genre. These questions will not name any specific texts. Instead, they will be quite broad and general questions that are likely to suit many texts from that genre.

Remember, the genre you choose to write about in your essay cannot be the same one you choose for your Scottish set text question: if your chosen Scottish writer is Norman MacCaig, your critical essay cannot be about poetry; if your Scottish set text is *Men Should Weep*, you cannot write your essay about drama; if your set text is *The Cone Gatherers*, your essay cannot be about prose fiction.

You will have about 45 minutes to write the essay, and it will be marked out of 20 marks.

The examiners will be looking at **four** different areas of your essay-writing skill: **knowledge and understanding**, **analysis**, **evaluation** and **technical accuracy**.

- **Knowledge and understanding** means how well you can show that you understand and know the text you have studied. It also includes how well you use evidence from the text to write an essay that clearly answers the question you have been asked.
- **Analysis** means being able to examine and explain the way the writer writes: the language features and techniques he or she uses and the effects created by these.
- **Evaluation** means having a personal response to and a personal opinion about what you have read. This response will be shaped to fit the particular essay question you choose.
- **Technical accuracy** is how clearly you put across your ideas. This includes your spelling, grammar, sentence structure, paragraphing and punctuation. It also means that your essay will be clearly understandable at first reading.

As you work through this chapter you will learn to produce essays that display all these skills.

How to use this chapter

The next few pages will teach you how to do this. As we have studied two MacCaig poems, we will make quite a lot of references to poetry essays and will use examples from his writing, but the techniques you will learn will help you to write about any kind of text that you have studied this year. Remember, if you have already written about MacCaig in the set text section of the exam, you cannot write your essay on his work. Whichever texts you have studied in class, you will need to know them deeply and thoroughly, so you can pick the right details from that knowledge to use in the exam.

Choosing an essay

At the top of the essay section of the exam you'll find a general instruction like this:

> **Attempt ONE question from the following genres — Drama, Prose Fiction, Prose Non-Fiction, Poetry, Film and Television Drama, or Language.**
>
> **Your answer must be on a different genre from that chosen in Section 1.**
>
> **You should spend approximately 45 minutes on this Section.**

Pay attention to this. You **must** make sure you don't write on either the same text or the same genre as you do in the Scottish text section of the exam. (You can write about a text that is printed, in whole or in extract form, in the exam paper, as long as it's **not** the one you answered on in that earlier Scottish text section and is **not** from the same genre as the one you covered earlier.)

In the first few minutes of your exam you need to weigh up your choices quickly but carefully, so that you can do your best work overall and earn as many marks as possible.

How will you choose the best question? To begin to work this out, we need to look at the way the individual questions are worded.

All the essays tasks follow the same pattern. They are set out in two paragraphs. For example:

> **Choose a poem which makes effective use of imagery and/or sound to convey central concern(s).**
>
> **With reference to appropriate techniques, discuss how the poet's use of imagery and/or sound contributes to the presentation of the poem's central concern(s).**

To choose which essay to write, you're going to look at just the **first paragraph** of the essay task.

As soon as you see these words, you need to run through a quick mental checklist. Let's assume you go into the exam having studied Norman MacCaig. You can ask yourself:

Have I studied any poems?

To which the answer would be:

Yes.

So, you **might** be able to write this essay. Now it's time to focus in even tighter on that first paragraph and look at **what kind of poem** the examiners want you to write about. So now you need to ask yourself:

Do any of the poems I've studied use imagery and/or sound?

This essay question turns out to be quite a good one, because you get two quite positive answers:

Both 'Brooklyn Cop' and 'Hotel Room, 12th Floor' use imagery and sound techniques.

It's time to narrow down your choice. To help you do this, take another look at the words in the **second paragraph** of the task. This paragraph is where the examiners tell you how they actually want you to tackle the essay. The words of the second paragraph give you instructions that you must follow. If you don't obey these instructions in paragraph 2 of the task, you aren't answering the essay question and you will not meet the standard for a Higher essay.

For this essay, these words in paragraph 2 are important:

… how the poet's use of imagery and/or sound contributes to the presentation of the poem's central concern(s).

Now you can narrow down your options by asking yourself:

Does one of these poems make more use of imagery and sound techniques than the other?

If you look back at the poems, you will see that both 'Brooklyn Cop' and 'Hotel Room, 12th Floor' use similes, (extended) metaphors and alliteration. So either poem works very well for this question.

At this stage you could decide to write your critical essay on one of these MacCaig poems, or you could carry on looking through the exam paper until you find a different essay that appeals to you even more and fits your possible essay texts even better.

The good news is that finding an essay question is not meant to be difficult. The examiners try very hard to make the questions quite open and general. In any set of three questions about a particular genre of writing, it should nearly always be possible for you to find at least one task that fits a text you have studied in that genre.

Before we leave the idea of choosing your essay, remember, if MacCaig is the only author you've studied for Scottish set text, you can't do your critical essay on him too. And remember, your essay question must come from a different genre than your Scottish set text.

Writing your introduction

The first paragraph you write in the essay will be your introduction. Whenever you write a critical essay, the same three things should appear in the opening sentence:

- the title of the text you read
- the name of the author
- a clear indication of what you will be writing about.

As we've already seen, the first paragraph of the essay task helps you to choose which task you are going to do. Once you have chosen an essay to tackle, that same first paragraph of the task instructions is also useful for something else. It helps you to write the introduction to your essay. To do this, you are going to **recycle** many of the words from that paragraph.

Let's assume that you have chosen to do the essay task we looked at in detail earlier, and that you are going to write about 'Hotel Room, 12th Floor'. Here's the first paragraph from the essay task we saw earlier on. Look at the words printed in bold type.

> **Choose a poem which makes effective use of imagery and/or sound to convey central concern(s).**

You can recycle some of those words in the first sentence of your essay. The words you recycle will help you to give a clear indication of what you will be writing about. You still need to add the title and author to these to have a complete first sentence, which would end up looking like this:

One poem which uses both imagery and sound effectively is 'Hotel Room, 12th Floor' by Norman MacCaig.

If you feel like being a bit more stylish, you could try an opening like this:

Norman MacCaig, in 'Hotel Room, 12th Floor', uses both imagery and sound effectively to convey his central concerns.

Look at these opening paragraphs from two other questions that fit the MacCaig poems we've been working with:

● Choose a poem which deals with an issue of importance to human experience.
● Choose a poem in which the poet effectively creates a character or persona.

First, turn each one of the suitable openings into a basic opening sentence of an essay. The first example above will help you.

Now look at the example opening paragraphs again and use them to help you write more stylish opening sentences for these essays.

After the opening sentence, it's a good idea to continue your introduction by writing a **short** summary of your text. Any teacher can choose to teach his or her class any texts that they enjoy, and that they think their class will like. This means that you may end up writing your critical essay about a text that the exam marker has never read, or maybe even never heard of. Writing a **short** summary will give the marker a little bit of context and background, making it easier for him or her to understand comments you make about that text in your essay.

Warning

Take care! You'll have noticed two bold type reminders that you should be writing a **short** summary. The summary itself does not earn you any marks. It just helps you and the exam marker to get your heads clear. You must not waste precious exam time by waffling.

To let you see what I mean by a **short** summary, here's one for 'Brooklyn Cop':

In this poem, the poet creates a vivid picture of the eponymous cop, doing so in a way that allows him to explore the violence within the character and within humanity.

That summary is just 31 words long. It should be easily possible to summarise most texts in fewer than 50 words.

Do you know the word *eponymous* as used in the summary? It means named or referred to in the title. The cop is eponymous because he is the cop in the title of the poem. Black Panther is the eponymous Marvel character. Romeo and Juliet are the eponymous lovers. If you can use that word appropriately in your essays, you'll sound clever and make a good impression on the examiner. And if you've used it once already in an essay and you don't want to repeat yourself, the word *titular* means the same thing, so you could write about the titular cop or the titular superhero or the titular tragic couple.

Active learning

First, complete these two tasks.

1 Write a brief summary of 'Hotel Room, 12th Floor'.

2 If you have studied other literature or media texts in your Higher course so far, write a brief summary for each of them.

Now swap your summaries with another pupil.

Read and mark each other's work. Try to make each other's summaries as brief, clear and efficient as possible.

The main body of your essay

Once you've written the introduction and summary, it's time for the main body of your essay. This main body will be made up of several paragraphs — four or five will be enough.

We've already looked very carefully at the fact that the first paragraph of the essay instructions tells you what sort of text to write about. The second paragraph of the essay instructions tells you **what you are actually going to do** in your essay. Remember, if you don't do what that second paragraph tells you to do then you aren't answering the question and you will never meet the standard for a Higher essay. Look at this essay question:

> **Choose a poem in which the poet effectively creates a character or persona.**
>
> **Discuss, with reference to appropriate techniques, how the poet's effective creation of the character or persona enhances your appreciation of the poem as a whole.**

If you look at this instruction carefully, you will see that as you write this essay you have two things to think about:

1 the poet's **creation** of the character
2 how this **enhances your appreciation of the poem as a whole**

and that as you deal with these two things, you must make appropriate references to the way the writer uses techniques.

Almost all of the critical essay questions you will find in the exam are worded like this; they give you something particular to examine, and then ask you how this affects your understanding, or your appreciation, of the text as a whole.

Your school probably keeps piles of past papers from Higher Critical Reading exams. Ask your teacher to bring copies of past papers for the most recent two or three years, so that you get a good sense of what the exam is likely to be like for you and your class.

Look at the essay questions: you'll find these at the back of the big, fat exam booklet. You might concentrate on looking at poetry questions, as we are using MacCaig as our example or, if you have been studying another text for your critical essay, you could look at the questions each year that fit that genre.

For each question:

- notice what the precise focus of the question is
- look for the bit of the question that asks you to relate that to the text as a whole.

You should see a strong pattern in way the essay questions are worded.

Remember, the important thing you must always do is read the question to find out clearly and exactly what you have to do and what you have to write about.

ALWAYS ANSWER WHAT THE QUESTION ASKS!

So, now that you know what you are supposed to do, how are you going to do it? Let's look again at that essay task that we decided would be good for 'Hotel Room, 12th Floor'. Here's the question in full:

Choose a poem which makes effective use of imagery and/or sound to convey the central concern(s).

With reference to appropriate techniques, discuss how the poet's use of imagery and/or sound contributes to the presentation of the poem's central concern(s).

A good way to tackle this essay is to start by **reminding yourself** which images and sound effects are important in 'Hotel Room, 12th Floor'. If you are planning this essay in an exam, you could make yourself a very quick, bullet-pointed reminder list like this:

- metaphor – 'dentist's drill'
- metaphor – 'ululating'
- simile – 'damaged insect'
- extended metaphor – Wild West
- alliteration – 'wildest of warwhoops'.

If you wrote one paragraph for each of these, you'd have five paragraphs in the main body of your essay. As you write these paragraphs:

- every one of the main body paragraphs must help you to do what your chosen task tells you to do
- every one of the main body paragraphs must use evidence from the text.

Active learning

Here's an example of a paragraph which does the two things mentioned above. Read it carefully and decide:

1 Which words in the paragraph show that the pupil is trying to stick to the chosen task?

2 Which words in the paragraph show the pupil is using evidence from the text?

One effective image is MacCaig's description of

'the Empire State Building, that

jumbo size dentist's drill'

Firstly, this is effective in conveying a sense of what this skyscraper looks like: the building does taper to a sharp point, much in the manner of a dentist's drill. However, the image also has a far deeper effect. Most people are afraid of having their teeth drilled so, by using this comparison, MacCaig brings to mind ideas of fear and pain. The Empire State Building, one of the world's architectural wonders, is reimagined as something unpleasant and distressing. This ties in with one of the central concerns of the poem, that the modern and supposedly civilised city is actually a frightening place, where people get hurt.

Did you manage to answer the questions?

For answers see page 232.

Did you notice how this pupil set out the quotation? It is indented — moved away a little from the left-hand side of the page — to make it stand out. But you don't need to skip a line above or below the quotation. You are not starting a new paragraph: the quotation is part of the paragraph. The pupil also used quotation marks ' ' around the quoted words.

Let's focus a bit more carefully on the paragraphs in the main body of your essay. There are two things you can do in these paragraphs so that they will be well written and will help you to achieve the task you've chosen:

1 Begin the paragraph with a **topic sentence**.
2 Use the **PEE structure**.

Topic sentences

Topic sentences are called this for two reasons:

1 they tie in with the topic of your essay
2 they let the reader understand the topic of the paragraph you're on.

Using a topic sentence at the start of the paragraph sets you off in the right direction.

Active learning

You're going to see again the full wording of four essay tasks. You'll also see a list of sentences. Each one is a topic sentence from one of the essays. Can you decide which essay each topic sentence belongs to?

Here are the essay tasks:

1 Choose a poem which deals with an issue of importance to human experience.

  With reference to appropriate techniques, explain how the issue is presented and discuss how it enhances your appreciation of the poem.

2 Choose a poem in which the poet effectively creates a character or persona.

  Discuss, with reference to appropriate techniques, how the poet's effective creation of the character or persona enhances your appreciation of the poem as a whole.

3 Choose a film or television drama in which the opening sequence is particularly effective in engaging the audience's interest.

  With reference to appropriate techniques, discuss how the film- or programme-makers succeed in engaging the audience's interest.

4 Choose a novel or a short story in which there is a central character to whom you react with mixed feelings.

  With reference to appropriate techniques, briefly explain why you react to the character in this way, and discuss how this reaction adds to your appreciation of the novel as a whole.

Here are the topic sentences. Can you match each one to the right essay task? It doesn't matter if you don't know the text the topic sentence is about; you are just looking at how well it ties in with the essay question.

a The character of the cop is also made clear through his habit of speaking in clichés.

b One way in which Spark makes us have mixed feelings towards Miss Brodie is by at times showing her to be a truly inspiring teacher.

c MacCaig also deals with the issue of violence through his use of astute word choice.

d One way in which the opening engages the audience's attention is by Edgar Wright's clever use of the billboards and signs that Baby passes as he walks through the city.

Did you notice that two of the topic sentences begin with, 'One way in which …' and then use the name of the author or director? This is a perfectly satisfactory way to start a paragraph, and it will help you be clear for the marker and keep things clear in your head.

However, you should also have noticed that two of the topic sentences were more individual and more distinctive. Just as you saw on page 185, when we were learning about writing essay introductions, there's a basic way to do this, but there is also a more stylish way. Once you feel you've mastered the basics, you should be looking for ways to impress the marker with your style and flair.

The PEE Structure

You already met a version of the **PEE structure** in the chapter about the writing portfolio, where it was used as a way of organising paragraphs in discursive essays. You can also use PEE as a way of structuring critical essay paragraphs.

- **P** — tells you to make a **Point** about the writer's technique. In other words, mention something you can see the writer deliberately doing.
- **E** — tells you to give **Evidence**: this will nearly always be by quoting from the text, though it may sometimes be easier to give evidence by referring to something in the text.
- **E** — tells you to **Explain** the **Effect** of this, to show what the writer is doing to us, the readers.

The **P** part of this is also the topic sentence of the paragraph, so there's a bit of an overlap between the idea of using a topic sentence and the idea of following the PEE structure.

Active learning

Copy the following paragraph into your notebook. It's deliberately about a poem you are unlikely to study for Higher, so that you really have to think about how the pupil is organising the paragraph. Once you've copied it out, do these three things:

1 Underline the **P** part with a straight line.

2 Underline the **E for Evidence** part with a wiggly or jagged line.

3 Draw a box round the **E for Explanation** part.

One way in which Morgan makes his ideas memorable is by saying the same thing in three ways at once. He tells us that when faced with the guitar, the baby, and the chihuahua:

'Monsters of the year

go blank, are scattered back,

can't bear this march of three.'

If the 'monsters' go 'blank' then they must have no ideas and nothing to say for themselves. If they are 'scattered' then they are separated and no longer any kind of force. If they 'can't bear' then they are powerless compared to the three who 'march' in an organised and powerful way. These three ways of telling us that the 'monsters' can no longer cope impress on the reader how powerful the three gifts are.

Did you notice the three parts of the PEE structure? And did you notice that the explanation element of this included a mention of 'the reader'? The techniques writers use are effective because of who they affect: they affect us, the readers. Your personal response to and engagement with the text — your evaluation of it — should permeate your whole essay. You should also have spotted that the pupil is writing in **present tense**. You should do this whenever you write about what you have read.

Active learning

Read the essay extract again. Circle all the verbs that show that the pupil is writing in present tense.

Writing about techniques

On the exam paper, above each set of essay tasks, you will see a paragraph of advice. The wording of this paragraph follows a pattern.

Active learning

To get you to spot the pattern of this paragraph in the essay instructions, you're going to see the advice for two different types of essay. The first one is for poetry essays; the second one is for prose fiction essays. Read the two paragraphs and then answer the two questions below.

Answers to questions on **poetry** should refer to the text and to such relevant features as: word choice, tone, imagery, structure, content, rhythm, rhyme, theme, sound, ideas …

Answers to questions on **prose fiction** should refer to the text and such relevant features as: characterisation, setting, language, key incident(s), climax, turning point, plot, structure, narrative technique, theme, ideas, description …

1 Which words are always used at the **start** of the advice above the essay tasks?

2 What do you always see at the **end** of the advice above the essay tasks? What do you think this means?

What this paragraph of advice does is just remind you to write about some of the techniques the author uses, or some of the things that made that text worth studying in the first place. Remember that **a technique is anything a writer deliberately chooses to do**. While some techniques have particular names, like those listed in the paragraphs above, anything a writer does on purpose to have an effect on the reader is a technique.

It doesn't even actually matter which techniques and features you write about. You don't have to write about the ones named in the paragraph, because the three dots at the end of that paragraph allow you to write about whichever techniques and features you believe are important for the text and task you have chosen. What does matter is that you should deal with the writer's techniques, because the question has told you to do so, and because the markers will be looking for this in your essay.

For example, suppose you were writing an essay on 'Brooklyn Cop'. Depending on which essay you chose, you could pick any of the following techniques and features that we looked at as we studied the poem, none of which are on the list in the box in the exam paper:

repetition	cliché	incomplete grammar
rhetorical questions	American slang	humour
contrast	parenthesis	title
not giving the cop a name	short last line	

You can also write about the technique of word choice, which **is** named in the advice box above the poetry questions on the exam paper, as well as about various kinds of imagery and about the sound technique of alliteration.

The way that you write about techniques is all tied in with that useful **PEE structure**. The **P** part, remember, is where you make a **Point** to introduce the technique. The first **E** part has you quoting **Evidence** of that technique being used by the author. When you get to the second **E** part of the structure you are **Explaining** how the writer creates an **Effect** on the reader; how he or she achieves what he or she set out to do to us.

There are words and phrases you can use to show that you are dealing with the writer's techniques.

The following words and phrases describe **what the writer does** or **what part of the text does**. They will help you to show that you are **analysing** the author's work.

has connotations of	suggests	shows	hints
creates	mirrors	establishes	underlines
reinforces	emphasises	highlights	
foreshadows	exemplifies	explains	
demonstrates	echoes	reveals	

The following words and phrases describe **how the reader feels** or **how the text affects us** as we read. They will help you to show that you are **evaluating** the author's work and the way that it has an effect upon us.

thought-provoking	inspiring	horrifying
hard-hitting	stimulating	pivotal moment
key idea(s)	fast-paced	effective
gripping	skilful(ly)	perceptive
moving	profound	striking
important	intelligent	thoughtful

Active learning

Work in a group. Read the wording of this essay task, which you have met before and which you know is suitable for getting you to write about 'Brooklyn Cop':

Choose a poem which makes effective use of imagery and/or sound to convey central concern(s).

With reference to appropriate techniques, discuss how the poet's use of imagery and/or sound contributes to the presentation of the poem's central concern(s).

First, think of at least three images or sound techniques MacCaig uses in this poem.

Then, compare your own group's answers with those from the rest of the class.

Next, agree on the best answers for building paragraphs for the essay. You need to end up with as many good ideas as the number of groups in the class.

Now, work just with your own group again. Take one of the paragraph ideas your class agreed on and write it up into a paragraph for this essay. Remember to:

- use quotations from the text and indent the words that you quote
- make sure you start with a topic sentence and that this topic sentence works as the **P** part of the **PEE** structure in your paragraph
- use some of the keywords and phrases from the boxes above.

Last, read your paragraphs aloud in class or give them to your teacher for marking.

The conclusion

After your introduction, summary and main body, you need to finish off your essay with a conclusion. The conclusion ought to do two things:

1   sum up and round off what you have written
2   give your response to the text as a reader.

Summing up just means reminding the examiner what you have written about. It should be only one sentence long and could sound something like this:

> Clearly, MacCaig's use of imagery and sound allows him to address concerns about human nature and the violence within us all.

Giving your response to the text takes a little more thought. Earlier in your school career, your personal responses were probably a bit like this:

> I liked the poem because he paints a good picture of the cop. I would recommend it to other pupils to read.

You have to do something a little more complicated at Higher level. Firstly, your response shouldn't feel 'tacked-on' to the end. It should instead be the culmination of all those little touches of personal response and engagement that have run through the whole of what you've written so far. Also, your reader's response, just like everything else in your essay, should fit your chosen task and text.

This task was about how MacCaig uses imagery and sound to convey his central concerns. Your response should say something about how well you think he does this. You could say whether you think his ideas come across clearly. Here's one example of how a pupil tackled it — you're going to see her whole final paragraph.

Clearly, MacCaig's use of imagery and sound allows him to address concerns about human nature and the violence within us all. The figure of the nameless cop becomes a universal one, standing for all humanity. MacCaig's imagery, especially the repeated 'gorilla' image, shows how inhuman, how vicious and how violent human nature truly is, and forces us as readers to question and challenge our own behaviour and attitudes.

So, that's it. You know how to write a critical essay. If you've worked through this chapter, you found out step by step how you can tackle this part of the exam. Before you go into the exam, your teacher will give you lots of chances to practise essay writing in class.

Active learning

You're going to see the whole of the wording for an essay task that suits at least one of the MacCaig poems.

First of all, above the essay choices for poetry, the exam paper has this wording:

Answers to questions on **poetry** should refer to the text and to such relevant features as: word choice, tone, imagery, structure, content, rhythm, theme, sound, ideas …

Then, you see this essay task:

Choose a poem in which the ending is important in highlighting central concerns.

With reference to appropriate techniques, explain how the ending highlights central concerns and discuss how it enhances your appreciation of the poem as a whole.

Now, using all the advice from this chapter and everything you have learned, write this essay. Remember, you need to have:

- an introduction
- a short summary
- about four or five well-constructed main body paragraphs

Hint: Spend a few minutes jotting down ideas for the four or five body paragraphs of your essay.

- a conclusion in which you summarise the essay and include a reader response.

Check over your essay and then hand it in to your teacher for marking. Don't just check your content, look at your language too: your spelling, grammar, paragraphing, punctuation and expression.

Essay writing in the exam

During the Higher course you will get lots of chances to write essays about the texts you study. At first your teacher may support you in some of the following ways:

- giving you a plan to follow
- making a plan with the class
- letting you plan in groups or pairs
- letting you use your texts and notes while you write the essay
- giving you as long as you need to finish the essay
- letting you take the essay home to finish it.

However, by the time you get to the exam you need to be able to quickly choose, plan and write your essay, all in 45 minutes. Three things will help you with this.

First, remember, the questions are planned to be open and general. The examiners aren't trying to catch you out; they're trying to offer you a variety of opportunities to show off what you have learned.

Second, you need to know your texts really well before you go into the exam, and you need to know all your notes and materials about those texts. That way you can pick out the right material to use to answer the essay question you have chosen.

Think of it like this. There's probably all sorts of different equipment in your kitchen. If you know what you're going to cook, and you know what you're about to do, you can pick out the right items. Baking cupcakes needs very different utensils to making a lasagne.

Similarly, the information you use to write an essay about how the author makes you feel sympathy for a character might not be the same information you would use to write an essay about how the writer deals with a particular theme or issue or one about how the writer uses a particular technique.

Third, you need to make a quick plan in the exam before you write your essay. It can be a list of the four or five key ideas you want to base your main body paragraphs on, or a mind map or spider plan with a leg for each main body paragraph. However you do it, you need to know what you are going to say to answer the question.

Sometimes, pupils go into the exam and panic. No matter how scared you are, don't be tempted to write about the Film and Television Drama option if you haven't been taught that in class. Even if you are Scotland's biggest *Doctor Who* fan, don't write about what you haven't been trained to write about. The same applies to the language section. There might well be a question in there about teenage slang, and you may be a slangy teenager, but don't try to write about it if you haven't been taught to do so.

Another danger in the exam is that you might write the essay you want to write, and not the one the examiners want. It's really important to learn essay **skills** — and that's what this whole chapter has been about — but there's no point trying to learn a particular essay off by heart, even if it's one you got a good mark for in class. You can only write about what the examiners want on that day.

CHAPTER 6 Revision for the Higher Exam

If you've worked your way through this book, and through the Higher English course, then you have been well prepared. You have been given lots of knowledge and have been taught skills and strategies.

You can also be confident that some of your marks are already in place. Remember, your portfolio earns you up to 30 of the 100 marks available.

Can you remember how many marks each part of the exam is worth?

- Reading for Understanding, Analysis and Evaluation
- Scottish text
- Critical essay

The answers are upside down at the bottom of the page. Don't look until you've tried to remember for yourself!

Preparing you for an exam is your teacher's job; passing it is up to you. Having a marvellous teacher, or a useful textbook, might help you understand something when you first hear it or read it, but you'll need to revise and strengthen that understanding in your own time. This short chapter will give you some ideas about how to do this.

Once you reach the Easter holidays — and any exam leave your school gives you — you will have a sizeable chunk of time for revision and preparation.

Look at your exam timetable; your school may give you one, or you can create one for yourself using the SQA website. Think about these things:

- How many exams are you doing?
- Which dates are they on?
- Do you have any exams that come very close together?
- Do you have any long gaps between exams?

Now draw up a revision timetable. Divide each day into chunks. Plan to revise for at least three different subjects each day. Build in time for meals, sleep, exercise, friends and doing things you enjoy. These things matter too, and stressed people who go without them find exams harder, not easier.

TIME	MONDAY	TUESDAY	WEDNESDAY
08:00 – 09:00	English	Coffee with friends	Maths
09:00 – 10:00	English	English	Maths
10:00 – 10:20	B	R E A	K
10:20 – 11:20	Maths	History	English
11:20 – 12:20	Maths	History	English
12:20 – 01:00	L	U N C	H
01:00 – 02:00	Biology	Spanish	Biology
02:00 – 03:00	Biology	Spanish	Biology
03:00 – 04:00	Gym session	Maths	Cinema

Now that you've planned to spend some time revising, what are you actually going to do?

Well, what you're certainly NOT going to do is just sit and read over your notes. If you do that, your mind will quickly glaze over, because you're not giving it anything new. Your brain will decide it's seen all this before and doesn't need to pay attention.

You need to revise actively. You need something to do. The rest of this short chapter will give you some ideas.

First of all, for all parts of the exam, you can do **past papers**. You can download these and their answer schemes for free from the SQA website, and you can also buy books of these. Your teacher may also be able to give you past papers that you haven't already used in school. You can also buy books of specially written **practice papers** to work through.

If you are using a past or practice paper, make your experience as much like the exam as possible. Find a room where you can be on your own with no distractions: no phone, music or TV. Work at a table. Set an alarm for the amount of time you'll have in the exam and work for exactly that long. Once you've finished, take a well-deserved half-hour break.

Even if your teacher has not asked you to do a particular past paper, he or she might be willing to mark it for you. It's a good idea to check with your teacher first and, if you do want them to mark something extra like this for you, provide copies of both the task itself and the mark scheme. Make sure you give them a few days to do it in and thank them for doing this.

There are also good materials, including revision quizzes and tests, on the BBC Bitesize website.

Active revision for the Reading for Understanding, Analysis and Evaluation exam

In this exam, you will have 90 minutes to earn up to 30 marks. There will be two non-fiction passages to read, both pieces of writing that you've never seen before. You will read the first passage then answer questions on it. There are usually 7 or 8 questions about that first passage and they can be worth 2, 3 or 4 marks each. Then you will read the second passage and answer a 5-mark question that gets you to somehow compare the work of the two writers.

Here are some active ways you can revise for this exam paper:

- You could work again through the chapter of this book that deals with the RUAE exam. Read the teaching materials, try the questions when they come up and check your answers against those in Chapter 7.
- You could find an article from a good-quality newspaper and rewrite it — or parts of it — in your own words. This will help you practise your paraphrasing skills.
- You could find an article from a good-quality newspaper and make a bullet-pointed list of the writer's key ideas about his or her subject. This will help you check your understanding and practise your summarising skills.
- You could find an article from a good-quality newspaper and annotate it, circling significant word choice and underlining uses of imagery. This will help you practise identifying relevant language features, as you have to do in some of the questions.
- You could find an article from a good-quality newspaper and practise making up questions based on it, then swap these with a friend to answer each other's questions. This again will help you practise looking for language features and will make you more aware of how questions are worded.

 How many more active revision strategies can you think of?

Active revision for the Scottish set text

This is the first of the two tasks in the exam paper called Critical Reading. You will see part of a Scottish set text that you have studied thoroughly in class: either one poem from a list of six or an extract from a longer work such as a play, short story or novel. There are usually about four questions. The last question is always worth 10 marks; the other questions add up to 10 marks and are worth 2, 3 or 4 marks each. You should spend about 45 minutes on this and can earn up to 20 marks.

Here are some active ways you can revise for this exam paper:

- If your set texts are poems, print out a new copy of each one. Then, from memory, annotate the poem with notes of everything you can remember about it. Next, compare this with the notes and information you have in your folder. Using a different colour to show you what you didn't remember, add any other notes you've missed to your new copy of the poem.

- Re-read your set text(s). As you read, make a list of key quotations you think you should know. You need about 10 to 12 of these for prose or drama texts. If your set texts are poems, try to have one quotation for each theme and one for each key technique that the writer uses.

- Now take your quotations and a pile of little cards or sheets of paper. Write the first three or four words of each quotation on the front of each card and the rest on the back. Carry the cards around with you. When you have an odd moment, test yourself. Look at the few words on the front of each card. Can you complete the quotation?

- Have a look at a selection of past papers. Concentrate especially on the first few questions, the ones based on the poem or extract printed in the exam. What sorts of questions tend to come up for your text? Make a note of typical questions. Plan how you would answer these.

- If your set text is a group of poems, pick a poem you don't have a past paper for. Can you make up some questions based on it? This will help you practise looking for language features and will make you more aware of how questions are worded.

- Have a look at a selection of past papers. This time, concentrate especially on the final, 10-mark question. What sorts of questions tend to come up for your text? Make a note of typical questions. Plan how you would answer these.

- Now look back at page 176 when you learned the method for answering the 10-mark question. You need to revise this method just as much as revising the set text itself. Remind yourself how this method works.

- Now try answering those 10-mark questions.

How many more active revision strategies can you think of?

Active revision for the critical essay

This is the second of the two tasks in the exam paper called Critical Reading. You will see a number of quite broad, general, essay questions. They will be organised under headings naming different genres: drama, prose fiction, prose non-fiction, poetry, film and television drama, and language. You will choose one essay question, making sure it comes from a different genre than the Scottish set text you just answered about, and will write an essay about a text that you have studied in class. You should spend about 45 minutes on this and can earn up to 20 marks.

Here are some active ways you can revise for this exam paper. Some of them are the same as, or similar to, strategies suggested above for the Scottish set text, as both tasks involve your knowledge and understanding of texts you've studied in class.

- If your critical essay texts are poems, print out a new copy of each one. Then, from memory, annotate the poem with notes of everything you can remember about it. Next, compare this with the notes and information you have in your folder. Using a different colour to show what you didn't remember, add any other notes you've missed to your new copy of the poem.
- If one of your critical essay texts is a film or a TV drama, watch that media text again in full. If your teacher has also taught you about certain key scenes or sequences, watch those shorter extracts again several times over.
- Re-read your essay text(s). As you read, make a list of key quotations you think you should know. You need about 10 to 12 of these for prose or drama texts. If your essay texts are poems, try to have one quotation for each theme and one for each key technique that the writer uses.
- Now take your quotations and a pile of little cards or sheets of paper. Write the first three or four words of each quotation on the front of each card and the rest on the back. Carry the cards around with you. When you have an odd moment, test yourself. Look at the few words on the front of each card. Can you complete the quotation?
- If your critical essay text is a play or a novel, find out if there is a film or TV version of it you can watch. There may even be a live stage production of your chosen play being put on near where you live. **Remember**, these texts may be cut, adapted or changed quite a lot when they are filmed, and you must make sure that in the exam you write about the original author's text you studied. But watching a filmed or performed version of your essay text can really bring it to life and freshen it up for you.

- Have a look at a selection of past papers. What sorts of questions tend to come up? Make a note of typical questions that would fit your essay text(s).
- Now take each of these typical question types and make a plan for an essay that would answer that question. You could look back at the section of Chapter 5 that dealt with critical essay skills. Your plans should include four or five ideas for paragraphs that would fit and help you to answer the essay question.

 How many more active revision strategies can you think of?

The night before your exam, check what time it starts. Make sure you've got everything you need, including two or three black or dark blue pens to write with, and pack your bag. Set your alarm and get a good night's sleep.

Next morning, no matter how nervous you feel, have a good breakfast. You don't want to feel ravenous halfway through working out where two writers agree on a particular topic! Get to school at least 15 minutes before the start of the exam and make sure you know where you should be sitting.

ANSWERS

Chapter 2

Answers to questions about register on page 85

A mise en scène, representation, institutional factors — film/media studies
B jurisprudence, precedent, duty of care — law
C enjambment, assonance, rhyme scheme — poetry
D bond, hedge fund, annuity — finance
E grind, carving, wipe out, 360 — snowboarding
F fold, sauté, ballotine — cookery

Chapter 3

Answers to understanding questions on page 108

1 Read paragraph 1. According to the writer, what is the difference between the original meaning of *nostalgia* and what we now understand this word to mean?　　2

Expected answer(s)	Additional guidance
Candidates should show an understanding of the original meaning of the term and of its current understood meaning. 1 mark for each point from the **Additional guidance** column. Candidates must attempt to use their own words. No marks for straight lifts from the passage. (Marks awarded 1+1.)	Possible answers include: • original meaning: gloss of *'a yearning for … a specific time and place'* • current understanding: gloss of *'in a general, sentimental way'*.

2 Read paragraph 3. Explain the two different ways in which the use of modern technology may have affected our feelings of nostalgia.　　2

Expected answer(s)	Additional guidance
Candidates should show an understanding of the two different ways in which technology may affect nostalgia. 1 mark for each point from the **Additional guidance** column. Candidates must attempt to use their own words. No marks for straight lifts from the passage. (Marks awarded 1+1.)	Possible answers include: • It makes us feel closer (to home/to those we miss): gloss of *'the illusion of closeness'*. • It upsets us by reminding us of what we are missing: gloss of *'sadden the caller by reminding them sharply of what they have left behind'*.

3 Read paragraph 6. How does the remainder of the paragraph
develop the idea that there is '*a poor brake on the migratory urge*'? **2**

Expected answer(s)	Additional guidance
Candidates should provide evidence from the paragraph to show an understanding that many people plan to migrate or are open to the idea of migration. 1 mark for each point from the **Additional guidance** column. Candidates must attempt to use their own words. No marks for straight lifts from the passage, though markers should not expect very precise paraphrase of statistical information. (Marks awarded 1+1.)	Possible answers include: • gloss of '*630 million adults or 14% of the world's population would move abroad permanently if they had the chance*' e.g. more than 600 million/around a seventh • gloss of '*another 1.1 billion would move temporarily for better-paid work*' e.g. over a billion.

Answers to word choice questions on page 115

1 Read paragraph 1. By referring to at least two examples, explain
how the writer's word choice conveys the strength of competition
between web companies for users' attention. **4**

Expected answer(s)	Additional guidance
Candidates should analyse how the writer's word choice conveys the competition between web companies. 2 marks may be awarded for detailed/insightful comment plus quotation/reference. 1 mark for more basic comment plus quotation/reference. 0 marks for quotation/reference alone. (Marks may be awarded 2+2, 2+1+1 or 1+1+1+1.)	Possible answers include: • '*better*' suggests trying to out-do each other • '*rivals*' suggests they are in competition • '*however*' suggests they will do anything to attract users' clicks • '*doesn't care*' suggests all means of attracting user attention are allowable • '*survive*' suggests almost vicious, to-the-death competition between web companies • '*hyper-competitive*' suggests exaggerated, over-the-top rivalry.

2 Read paragraph 2. By referring to at least two examples, explain how
the writer's word choice in the rest of the paragraph supports his
statement that '*this war for your attention isn't confined only to Facebook
or Twitter or Pinterest, or to the purveyors of celebrity gossip or porn.*' **4**

Expected answer(s)	Additional guidance
Candidates should analyse how the writer's word choice supports his statement. 2 marks may be awarded for detailed/insightful comment plus quotation/reference. 1 mark for more basic comment plus quotation/reference. 0 marks for quotation/reference alone. (Marks may be awarded 2+2, 2+1+1 or 1+1+1+1.)	Possible answers include: • '*higher-minded*' suggests better quality/more intelligent/more serious publications also want users' attention • '*institutions*' suggests important/established/serious bodies also want users' attention • '*even*' suggests level of surprise that such bodies are competing for user attention • '*never mind*' suggests it is not just the web companies we expect, but also other more unexpected ones, that compete for user attention.

3 Read the first sentence of paragraph 4. ('*There's a slightly depressing view … in the brain.*') How does the writer's word choice suggest the disappointing nature of the rewards the web offers? **2**

Expected answer(s)	Additional guidance
Candidates should analyse how the writer's word choice implies the disappointing nature of the reward. 2 marks may be awarded for detailed/insightful comment plus quotation/reference. 1 mark for more basic comment plus quotation/reference. 0 marks for quotation/reference alone. (Marks may be awarded 2 or 1+1.)	Implied by: • *'just'* suggests minimal/a little but no more • *'pigeons'* suggests users are treated as less than human • *'a squirt'* suggests very small amount of pleasure/ reward • *'so-called'* suggests questionable whether users do indeed feel good/rewarded.

4 Read paragraph 6. How does Bogost's word choice convey his concern about the game he created? **2**

Expected answer(s)	Additional guidance
Candidates should analyse how Bogost's word choice conveys his concern. 2 marks may be awarded for detailed/insightful comment plus quotation/reference. 1 mark for more basic comment plus quotation/reference. 0 marks for quotation/reference alone. (Marks may be awarded 2 or 1+1.)	Implied by: • *'concerned'* suggests worry • *'disturbed'* suggests worry • *'compulsively (attached)'* suggests worry that users have become addicted/unable to quit.

Answers to understanding questions on page 115

5 Read paragraphs 3 and 4. How do the examples given by the writer in paragraph 4 develop the idea of '*variable schedules of reward*' as introduced in paragraph 3? **2**

Expected answer(s)	Additional guidance
Candidates should provide evidence from the paragraph to show an understanding of the idea of variable reward. 1 mark for each point from the **Additional guidance** column. Candidates must attempt to use their own words. No marks for straight lifts from the passage. (Marks awarded 1+1.)	Possible answers include: • gloss of *'when you click refresh on your email/check your phone/visit Facebook/open Twitter'* • gloss of *'you might or might not find an update of the sort you'd been hoping for'*.

6 Read paragraph 5. How can the Cow Clicker game be understood to be both '*the funniest*' and '*the most horrifying*' example of the compulsion to click? **2**

Expected answer(s)	Additional guidance
Candidates should provide evidence from the paragraph to show an understanding of both sides of the description. 1 mark for each point from the **Additional guidance** column. Candidates must attempt to use their own words. No marks for straight lifts from the passage, but markers should not expect very precise paraphrase of statistical information. (Marks awarded 1+1.)	Possible answers include: • funniest: gloss of '*you click on a cow and that's it*'/ reference to simplicity/banality of game/reference to silliness of clicking on animated cow to make it moo/ reference to only getting response every 6 hours • most horrifying: reference to people being willing to wait 6 hours/people willing to pay (real or virtual) money to play (more often)/more than 50,000 users/people paying $20 (or more)/'*pointless improvements*'.

Answers to tone questions on page 121

1 How does the writer establish a surprised tone in paragraph 1? **2**

Expected answer(s)	Additional guidance
Candidates should analyse how the writer's use of language establishes the surprised tone. 2 marks may be awarded for detailed/insightful comment plus quotation/reference. 1 mark for more basic comment plus quotation/ reference. 0 marks for quotation/reference alone. (Marks may be awarded 2 or 1+1.)	Possible answers include: • reference to and comment on: '*Hell*' at start of sentence e.g. exclamation/mild expletive to convey surprise • reference to and comment on: '*Me*' at start of sentence e.g. singling herself out to show her surprise that this has happened to her • reference to and comment on: '*Omigod*' at start of sentence e.g. exclamation/mild expletive to convey surprise • reference to and comment on: '*I'm actually*' and/or '*technically*' e.g. use within parenthesis emphasises these words.

2 How does the writer establish a persuasive tone in paragraph 4? **2**

Expected answer(s)	Additional guidance
Candidates should analyse how the writer's use of language establishes the persuasive tone. 2 marks may be awarded for detailed/insightful comment plus quotation/reference. 1 mark for more basic comment plus quotation/ reference. 0 marks for quotation/reference alone. (Marks may be awarded 2 or 1+1.)	Possible answers include: • reference to and comment on: '*we need to*' as urging society to take action • reference to and comment on '*should be*' and/or '*could be*' as offering a vision of a better society • reference to and comment on: '*should be, could be*' e.g. use of these phrases together emphasises real possibility for change in attitude • reference to and comment on writer's use of '*we/ us*' throughout paragraph e.g. draws reader in, creates shared sense of obligation or purpose • use of very short sentence '*To us*' and/or '*To them*' is emphatic/definite, adding to sense of author's certainty and therefore persuasiveness.

3 What is the tone of paragraph 6 and how does the writer's use
of language create this tone? **3**

Expected answer(s)	Additional guidance
Candidates should identify a tone and then analyse how the writer's use of language establishes the tone. 1 mark for successful identification of tone. Thereafter, 2 marks may be awarded for detailed/insightful comment plus quotation/reference. 1 mark for more basic comment plus quotation/reference. 0 marks for quotation/reference alone. (Marks for analysis may be awarded 2 or 1+1.)	Possible answers include: Tone: • surprise. Established by: • reference to and comment on: *'I'm told that'* e.g. author would not have expected this but had to be told by others • reference to and comment on: *'raw wee elegy'* e.g. she would not have expected such a painful poem/such a brief poem/a poem about death to be so popular • reference to and comment on: *'painful'* e.g. surprising that a poem about pain has been popular • reference to and comment on: *'a poem that I might have flinched away from'* e.g. surprising that others have been drawn to a poem the writer herself might have avoided in some situations • reference to and comment on: *'it's not a matter of'* e.g. shows the situation is very different to/opposite of what might have been expected • reference to and comment on: *'(it's proven to be) quite the reverse'* e.g. shows the situation to be the opposite of what might have been expected.

Answers to word choice questions on page 121

4 How does Lochhead's word choice in paragraph 2 emphasise
the challenge of caring for the growing elderly population? **2**

Expected answer(s)	Additional guidance
Candidates should analyse how the writer's word choice emphasises the challenge. 2 marks may be awarded for detailed/insightful comment plus quotation/reference. 1 mark for more basic comment plus quotation/reference. 0 marks for quotation/reference alone. (Marks may be awarded 2 or 1+1.)	Possible answers include: • *'daunting'* suggests care of the elderly is difficult/a lot to face up to/a worry/etc. • *'burden'* suggests care of the elderly is a heavy responsibility.

5 How does the word choice in paragraph 6 convey the experience of loss? **3**

Expected answer(s)	Additional guidance
Candidates should analyse how the writer's word choice conveys the nature of loss. 2 marks may be awarded for detailed/insightful comment plus quotation/reference. 1 mark for more basic comment plus quotation/reference. 0 marks for quotation/reference alone. (Marks may be awarded 2+1 or 1+1+1.)	Possible answers include: • *'universal'* suggests we (will) all experience loss (in the end) • *'painful'* suggests hurt/grief caused by loss • *'intimate'* suggests personal/private/individual experience of loss.

Answers to understanding questions on page 121

6 Read paragraphs 7 and 8. Identify any four benefits of the poetry sessions with elderly people. **4**

Expected answer(s)	Additional guidance
Candidates should show an understanding of the benefits of these sessions. 1 mark for each point from the **Additional guidance** column. Candidates must attempt to use their own words. No marks for straight lifts from the passage. (Marks awarded 1+1.)	Possible answers include: • they take people out of their usual situation; gloss of *'escapism'* • they divert/amuse/pass the time: gloss of *'entertainment'* • they are enjoyable: gloss of *'pleasure'* • they reinvigorate the memory: gloss of *'People who can't remember … learned by heart.'* • they bring back other memories as well as the memory of poetry: gloss of *'And then they remember …'* • they improve emotion: gloss of *'shifts of mood'* • they help people to become involved: gloss of *'engagement'*/reference to man who now joins in.

7 Read paragraph 9. Identify two ways in which the writer responds to her own increasing age. Use your own words in your answer. **2**

Expected answer(s)	Additional guidance
Candidates should show an understanding of two different ways in which the writer responds to her own ageing. 1 mark for each point from the **Additional guidance** column. Candidates must attempt to use their own words. No marks for straight lifts from the passage. (Marks awarded 1+1.)	Possible answers include: • refusal to accept it is happening: gloss of *'Of course I'm not old'/'denial'* or reference to description of (white) hair as *'platinum blonde'* • dressing vibrantly/youthfully: gloss of or reference to description of her shoes • fear/anxiety/trepidation/etc.: gloss of or reference to final sentence of passage.

Answers to imagery questions on pages 123–4

Expected answer(s)	Additional guidance
Candidates should analyse the writer's use of imagery. 2 marks may be awarded for detailed/insightful comment plus quotation/reference. 1 mark for more basic comment plus quotation/reference. 0 marks for quotation/reference alone. (Marks may be awarded 2 or 1+1.)	Possible answers include: • *'crucible'* suggests a testing environment in which the writer's character was formed • *'moulded'* suggests that poverty shaped the writer in a particular, exact way.

Answers to imagery questions on page 127

1	*'a sanctuary'*	2
2	*'the crest of a wave'*	2
3	*'a handful of similar projects'*	2

Expected answer(s)	Additional guidance
Candidates should analyse the writer's use of imagery. 2 marks may be awarded for detailed/insightful comment plus quotation/reference. 1 mark for more basic comment plus quotation/reference. 0 marks for quotation/reference alone. (Marks may be awarded 2 or 1+1.)	Possible answers include: • *'a sanctuary'* suggests a place of safety, refuge or calm/an escape from booze culture/protects drinkers from booze culture • *'the crest of a wave'* suggests Redemption is first but others are following/suggests momentum or power of dry bar movement/suggests unstoppable or inevitable change • *'a handful'* suggests so far very few pubs like Redemption.

4　Read paragraph 4. How does Catherine Salway's use of imagery convey her feelings about her former career?　　2

Expected answer(s)	Additional guidance
Candidates should first identify an appropriate image and then analyse the writer's use of imagery. 2 marks may be awarded for detailed/insightful comment plus quotation/reference. 1 mark for more basic comment plus quotation/reference. 0 marks for quotation/reference alone.	Possible answers include: • *'grinding'* suggests dull/relentless/repetitive/unrewarding.

5　Read paragraph 7. How is imagery used to suggest the importance of alcohol as part of London life?　　2

Expected answer(s)	Additional guidance
Candidates should first identify an appropriate image and then analyse the writer's use of imagery. 2 marks may be awarded for detailed/insightful comment plus quotation/reference. 1 mark for more basic comment plus quotation/reference. 0 marks for quotation/reference alone.	Possible answers include: • *'fuelled'* suggests seen as necessary to keep London life going/just as a car is kept going by fuel, so London is kept going by alcohol.

Answers to understanding questions on page 127

6   Read paragraphs 8 and 9. **Using your own words as far as possible**, list the evidence that suggests that '*our consumption of booze does seem to be changing*'.   **4**

Expected answer(s)	Additional guidance
Candidates should identify and cite evidence that alcohol consumption is changing. 1 mark for each point from the **Additional guidance** column. Candidates must attempt to use their own words. No marks for straight lifts from the passage, but markers should not be overly punitive if candidates cite statistical information. (Marks awarded 1+1+1+1.)	Possible answers include: • reported consumption dropping: gloss of '*the share of people who report having a drink in the previous seven days has been falling*' • this fall is now well-established: gloss of '*has been falling for at least eight years*' • consumption is falling for both genders: gloss of or ref to percentages cited as drinking in last 7 days • volume consumed at any one time also falling: gloss of '*the amount of alcohol consumed by people on their "heaviest" day had also come down*' • younger people reducing their alcohol consumption most of all • younger people replacing drink with other pursuits: gloss of '*displacement (through use of technology)*'/'*so much to stimulate them*'.

7   Read paragraphs 10 and 11. In what way is the group of customers described both a **good** and a **bad** example of the trend towards lower consumption of alcohol as discussed in the article?   **2**

Expected answer(s)	Additional guidance
Candidates should show an understanding both of how the customers embody the supposed trend towards reduced drink, and how they do not. 1 mark for each point from the **Additional guidance** column. For full marks, candidates must have an answer from both the 'good' and 'bad' sides. Candidates must attempt to use their own words. No marks for straight lifts from the passage. (Marks awarded 1+1.)	Possible answers include: Good example: • they are drinking non-alcoholic drinks • one is still sober enough to do her marking • if they were anywhere else they would order a whole bottle, here they drink by the glass • they believe the lack of booze '*makes everything easier*'. Bad example: • Moule drank with her boyfriend the night before • implication that she drank considerably more than her boyfriend: '*Well, he had a glass, anyway.*'

Answers to sentence structure questions on page 132

1 How does the sentence structure in paragraph 1 engage the reader?　　**2**

Expected answer(s)	Additional guidance
Candidates should analyse how the writer's sentence structure engages the reader. 2 marks may be awarded for detailed/insightful comment plus quotation/reference. 1 mark for more basic comment plus quotation/reference. 0 marks for quotation/reference alone. (Marks may be awarded 2 or 1+1.)	Possible answers include: ● use of question (*'Do you fancy …'*) intrigues reader/ makes reader think they would like to earn this much money ● repeated structure of offers (*'one … another …'*) is engaging/inviting/offers sense of possibility.

2 What is the effect of the author's use of parenthesis in the second sentence of paragraph 3 (*'The online education resource … for their children.'*)?　　**2**

Expected answer(s)	Additional guidance
Candidates should analyse the effect of the use of parenthesis. 2 marks may be awarded for detailed/insightful comment plus quotation/reference. 1 mark for more basic comment plus quotation/reference. 0 marks for quotation/reference alone. (Marks may be awarded 2 or 1+1.)	Possible answers include: ● *'not entirely convincingly'* allows him to cast doubt on size/value of tuition industry ● *'not entirely convincingly'* allows him to cast doubt on reliability of EdPlace as a source/authority ● use of *'not'* challenges the statistics which follow this parenthesis ● use of *'entirely'* undermines *'convincingly'*, casting doubt on EdPlace's estimate.

3 How does the sentence structure of paragraph 5 convey the popularity of tutoring as a career?　　**2**

Expected answer(s)	Additional guidance
Candidates should analyse how the writer's sentence structure conveys the popularity of this career. 2 marks may be awarded for detailed/insightful comment plus quotation/reference. 1 mark for more basic comment plus quotation/reference. 0 marks for quotation/reference alone. (Marks may be awarded 2 or 1+1.)	Possible answers include: ● use of listing/use of two lists suggests tutoring is popular with a wide variety/large number of people ● first list suggests tutoring is popular with a wide variety/large number of those who are well-educated ● second list suggests tutoring popular with a wide variety/large number of creative/cultured people.

4 How does the sentence structure of paragraph 6 emphasise the challenges of the graduate job market?　　**2**

Expected answer(s)	Additional guidance
Candidates should analyse how the sentence structure emphasises the challenges. 2 marks may be awarded for detailed/insightful comment plus quotation/reference. 1 mark for more basic comment plus quotation/reference. 0 marks for quotation/reference alone.	Possible answers include: ● use of list (*'high unemployment, hiring freezes and unpaid internships'*) emphasises lack of opportunity/ lack of reward by showing number and variety of challenges/by showing how many factors prevent graduates getting stable jobs.

Answers to conclusion and opening questions on page 136

1 By referring to ideas and/or language, evaluate the effectiveness of the final paragraph as a conclusion to the article. **2**

Expected answer(s)	Additional guidance
Candidates should evaluate the effectiveness of the final paragraph as a conclusion. 2 marks may be awarded for detailed/insightful comment plus quotation/reference. 1 mark for more basic comment plus quotation/reference. 0 marks for quotation/reference alone. (Marks may be awarded 2 or 1+1.)	Possible answers include: • reference to stealing another passenger's food, as mentioned in paragraph 1, brings passage full circle • reference to stealing another passenger's food, as mentioned in paragraph 1, returns to/reinforces idea of hostile behaviour on planes • reference to 'reincarnated Hitler' as a reason for reclining one's seat emphasises writer's main point of how little excuse there is for reclining one's seat • use of three 'maybe'/repetition of 'maybe' emphasises writer's main point of how little excuse there is for reclining one's seat • reference to such a common figure as 'a full-sized adult human being' emphasises writer's main point of how little excuse there is for reclining one's seat • reference to taking something from another passenger 'just because you can' emphasizes petty/wrongful nature of reclining one's seat.

2 Read lines 1–10. Identify two ways in which the writer attempts to engage the reader's interest in the opening paragraph. **2**

Expected answer(s)	Additional guidance
Candidates should identify two ways in which the writer attempts to engage the reader's interest. 1 mark for each point from the **Additional guidance** column. For full marks there should be comments on at least two examples. (Marks awarded 1+1.)	Possible answers include: • idea of 'nightmarish' invites readers sympathy/recognition • word choice of 'nightmarish' is emotive/extreme and engages reader's interest • use of 'we've' invites reader's involvement • use of 'my favourite tip' creates sense of writer sharing information/advice (and therefore building relationship with reader) • humorous tone created by (obviously outrageous/exaggerated) example of stealing other passengers' food.

Possible answers for task (pages 139–40) based on *Haute Homemade* passage on pages 137–9

This task involves pupils making up, rather than answering, questions. The following are suggestions; other responses are possible.

1 Make up a **tone** question about line 1 ('*I have had … have said it.*').

Questions created by pupils might require others to identify the tone of these lines and to explain how this tone is established.

2　Make up a **word choice** question about lines 16–20 (*'Then I saw … old-fashioned undergarment.'*).

Questions developed by pupils might focus on how the writer's word choice gives a negative impression of the dish, and on how this impression is created through use of word choice.

3　Make up a question about lines 21–26 (*'Who, in their right mind … what's the point?'*). Your question should require pupils to use their own words in showing their **understanding** of the writer's argument.

Questions created by pupils might require others to comment on the length of time taken to cook the dish, the freezing time also required, the need to plate up, the brief time in which the dish will be eaten, the overall pointlessness, therefore, of such effort.

4　Make up a question about lines 27–36 (*'Home cooking, as a term … narcissistic creations.'*). Your question should require pupils to use their own words in showing how the writer **develops her ideas**.

Questions developed by pupils might refer to the writer's idea that *'Home cooking … has got above itself,'* and might then require others to explain at least two ways this idea is developed in the given lines.

5　Make up a **word choice** question about lines 43–48 (*'A bit of chicken … arranged beside the chicken.'*).

Questions developed by pupils might focus on how the writer's word choice gives a poor or unappealing impression of the dish, and also on how this impression is created through use of word choice.

6　Make up an **imagery** question about lines 62–64 (*'While she ploughs … vinegar balls.'*).

Questions developed by pupils might require others to identify and analyse the ploughing image as one implying difficulty/effort/etc.

7　Make up a **sentence structure** question about lines 74–81 (*'If you do master … jelly around it.'*).

Questions developed by pupils might require others to identify features of sentence structure and analyse their effect. The answer scheme pupils create might refer to the writer's use of the short sentence, *'Bread rolls!'*; the contrasted, *'Yes,'* and *'No,'* openings to sentences; the list of three processes the butter must go through.

8　Make up a question about the writer's use of **contrast** in lines 74–81 (*'If you do master … jelly around it.'*).

Questions developed by pupils might focus on how the writer's language contrasts two ways of presenting/plating butter.

Answers to Gender in Film questions on page 152

1   Read paragraphs 1 and 2. According to the writer, in what way have Swedish cinemas gone beyond filmgoers' usual expectations of movie ratings? Use your own words in your answer.   **2**

Expected answer(s)	Additional guidance
Candidates should demonstrate an understanding both of what filmgoers normally expect from ratings, and how Swedish cinemas have gone further. For full marks, candidates must identify both normal expectations and Sweden's further use of rating. 2 marks may be awarded for detailed/insightful comment plus quotation/reference. 1 mark for more basic comment plus quotation/reference. 0 marks for quotation/reference alone. (Marks may be awarded 2 or 1+1.)	Possible answers include: • usual expectations: gloss of *'whether a film contains nudity, sex, profanity or violence'* e.g. whether films have the potential to offend/disturb viewers • gone beyond: gloss of *'new rating to highlight gender bias'* ('or rather the absence of it') e.g. a new way of measuring whether films are sexist.

2   Read paragraph 3. By referring to at least two examples, analyse how the writer's use of language emphasises the gender bias of most films.   **4**

Expected answer(s)	Additional guidance
Candidates should analyse how the writer's use of language emphasises the gender bias in film. 2 marks may be awarded for detailed/insightful comment plus quotation/reference. 1 mark for more basic comment plus quotation/reference. 0 marks for quotation/reference alone. (Marks may be awarded 2+2, 2+1+1 or 1+1+1+1.)	Possible answers include: Word choice: • *'entire'* suggests how totally the *Lord of the Rings* trilogy is biased • *'all but one'* suggests near-total bias of *Harry Potter* series. Sentence structure: • listing of names of films/film series shows how very many films are biased • listing of names of films/film series shows extent to which some of the most famous/successful films are biased.

3 Read paragraph 5. By referring to at least two features of language, analyse how this paragraph conveys the current depiction of women in film. **4**

Expected answer(s)	Additional guidance
Candidates should analyse how the language of the paragraph conveys the current depiction of women in film. 2 marks may be awarded for detailed/insightful comment plus quotation/reference. 1 mark for more basic comment plus quotation/reference. 0 marks for quotation/reference alone. (Marks may be awarded 2+2, 2+1+1, 1+1+1+1.)	Possible answers include: • 'rarely' suggests paucity of strong female roles • listing of possible female role types emphasises how many roles/variety of roles generally unavailable to women • repetition of 'female' reinforces rarity of such roles being played by women • reduction in status 'superhero … professor … person …' emphasises how poor are the roles offered to women • '(noting that) the rating doesn't say anything about the quality of the film' suggests that there is a lack of quality film-making centred on female characters, even among films that do pass the Bechdel test.

4 Read paragraphs 6 to 8. What evidence is there that moves to highlight gender bias in film are 'catching on'? Use your own words in your answer. **2**

Expected answer(s)	Additional guidance
Candidates should explain evidence that supports the claim in the given sentence. 2 marks may be awarded for detailed/insightful comment plus quotation/reference. 1 mark for more basic comment plus quotation/reference. 0 marks for quotation/reference alone. (Marks may be awarded 2 or 1+1.)	Possible answers include: • gloss of 'the state-funded Swedish Film Institute supports the initiative' • reference to cable TV channel starting to use the ratings in its reviews • reference to cable TV channel starting to schedule a day to show only films that pass the test. Candidates might also refer to evidence that awareness of gender bias is **not** catching on e.g. reference to the students who say the rating would not influence them as they are unaware of the issues.

5 Read paragraphs 9 to 11.

    a Identify two further instances of Sweden's desire to promote gender equality. Use your own words in your answer. **2**

Expected answer(s)	Additional guidance
Candidates should identify two further instances, beyond the use of the Bechdel test. For full marks, candidates should refer both to the activities of the advertising ombudsman and also to the Equalisters project. 2 marks may be awarded for detailed/insightful comment plus quotation/reference. 1 mark for more basic comment plus quotation/reference. 0 marks for quotation/reference alone. (Marks may be awarded 2 or 1+1.)	Possible answers include: • gloss of *'advertising ombudsman watches out for sexism in that industry'* e.g. the body that oversees advertising is on the alert for gender bias • gloss of *'reprimands companies seen as reinforcing gender stereotypes'* e.g. companies that use/peddle/reinforce stereotypes are warned • reference to/gloss of example of removal of *'skimpily clad women'* from adverts e.g. if female models are presented in very little clothing when this isn't relevant to what is being advertised • reference to Equalisters project • gloss of *'trying to boost the number of women appearing as expert commentators in Swedish media'* e.g. attempt to increase the number of females interviewed/featured for their knowledge/expertise.

    b Explain the function of the sentence, '*For some, though, Sweden's focus on gender equality has gone too far*' in the development of the writer's argument. **2**

Expected answer(s)	Additional guidance
Candidates should show an understanding that this sentence forms a link in the writer's line of thought. 2 marks may be awarded for detailed/insightful comment 1 mark for more basic comment. 0 marks for quotation/reference alone.	Creates a link between the introduction of this new focus on gender in films, and the objections of those who are not in favour of such a move.

c By referring to at least two examples, analyse how the writer's use of language in paragraphs 10 and 11 emphasises the opinions of those opposed to the use of the Bechdel test. **4**

Expected answer(s)	Additional guidance
Candidates should analyse how the language of the paragraphs emphasises opposing opinions. 2 marks may be awarded for detailed/insightful comment plus quotation/reference. 1 mark for more basic comment plus quotation/reference. 0 marks for quotation/reference alone. (Marks may be awarded 2+2, 2+1+1, 1+1+1+1.)	Possible answers include: Word choice: • 'madness' suggests attempts at gender equality have gone too far. Sentence structure: • balanced sentence 'There are far too many films … and lots of films …' used to show issue (of gender in film) is more complex than merely applying the Bechdel test. Tone: • 'they should produce' creates persuasive tone, suggesting obligation to make better/less biased films rather than criticising/restricting those that already exist. Imagery: • 'blunt tool' suggests the Bechdel test is a very imprecise way of examining films' gender bias • 'point fingers' suggests accusation of others (rather than effecting change oneself).

6 Read paragraphs 13 and 14. Identify any two details given in these paragraphs that support the claim in the first sentence of paragraph 13. Use your own words in your answer. **2**

Expected answer(s)	Additional guidance
Candidates should give two details that support the claim in the given sentence. 1 mark for each point from the **Additional guidance** column. 0 marks for quotation/reference alone, but markers should not be overly punitive of candidate's attempts to deal with statistical information. (Marks awarded 1+1.)	Possible answers include: • gloss of 'of the top US films in 2011, women accounted for 33% of characters' e.g. only a third of characters in the most successful films were women • gloss of 'of the top US films in 2011, women accounted for … only 11% of the protagonists' e.g. barely a tenth of main characters were female • gloss of 'ratio of male to female characters in movies has remained at about two to one for at least six decades' e.g. there have been twice as many male characters as female ones for the last 60 years • gloss of 'women were twice as likely to be seen in explicit sexual scenes as males' e.g. women are treated as sexual objects twice as often as men • gloss of 'male characters were more likely to be seen as violent' e.g. men in films are far more frequently presented as being aggressive. Candidates might also refer to the fact that two studies are cited as implying that there is a lot of/a variety of evidence to support the claim.

7   Read paragraph 15. Evaluate the final paragraph's effectiveness
    as a conclusion to the passage as a whole.   **3**

Expected answer(s)	Additional guidance
Candidates should evaluate the final paragraph's effectiveness as a conclusion to the passage as a whole. 2 marks may be awarded for detailed/insightful comment plus quotation/reference. 1 mark for more basic comment plus quotation/ reference. 0 marks for quotation/reference alone, but markers should not be overly punitive of candidate's attempts to deal with statistical information. (Marks may be awarded 2+1 or 1+1+1.)	Possible answers include: • the passage concludes with a statement from lead author of a study already mentioned — brings the so far statistical information cited from the study to life • sums up/offers an explanation for the origin of the gender bias dealt with throughout the passage: *'Apparently Hollywood thinks that films with male characters will do better at the box office'/'most of the aspects of movie-making … are dominated by men'* • concludes by offering reader further/wider/deeper concerns to think about: *'most of the aspects of movie-making … are dominated by men'.*

8   Look at both passages. Both writers consider the application of the
    Bechdel test to films. Identify the key areas on which they agree,
    and those on which they disagree. You should support the points by
    referring to ideas in both passages. You may answer this question in
    continuous prose or in a series of developed bullet points.   **5**

Expected answer(s)	Additional guidance
Candidates can use bullet points in this final question, or write a number of linked statements. Key areas of agreement are shown in the grid.	The following guidelines should be used: 5 marks — identification of three key areas of agreement with detailed/insightful use of supporting evidence. 4 marks — identification of three key areas of agreement with appropriate use of supporting evidence. 3 marks — identification of three key areas of agreement. 2 marks — identification of two key areas of agreement. 1 mark — identification of one key area of agreement. 0 marks — failure to identify any key areas of agreement and/or misunderstanding of the task. **NB** A candidate who identifies only two key areas of agreement may be awarded up to a maximum of 4 marks, as follows: • 2 marks for identification of two key areas of agreement **plus** **either** • a further mark for appropriate use of supporting evidence to a total of 3 marks **or** • a further 2 marks for detailed/insightful use of supporting evidence to a total of 4 marks. A candidate who identifies only one key area of agreement may be awarded up to a maximum of 2 marks, as follows: • 1 mark for identification of one key area of agreement **plus** a further mark for use of supporting evidence to a total of 2 marks.

Areas of agreement	Passage 1	Passage 2
Very few films pass the Bechdel test	List in para 3 of films and film series failing the test	Mention in para 2 that when Bechdel test was first proposed, only Ridley Scott's *Alien* (then 6 years old) would have passed
Passing the Bechdel test is not a guarantee of a film's quality	Para 5 *'the rating doesn't say anything about the quality of the film'*	References in para 5 to *'loathsome/whitewash'* of *The Iron Lady* and/or to *Savages* being *'not exactly a woman-centric film'*
The goal of the current use of the Bechdel test to rate films is to raise awareness among filmgoers	Quotation from Ellen Tejle about female characters and about *'female stories and perspectives'*	Quotation from Ellen Tejle about female characters and about *'female stories and perspectives'*
Areas of disagreement	**Passage 1**	**Passage 2**
The value of *'Super Sunday'*	Mentions Super Sunday in paragraph 6 alongside mention of Swedish Film Institute support, and of how initiative is catching on; overall effect is to imply approval of Super Sunday	Paragraph 5 points out the problematic nature of some of the films to be shown on Super Sunday
Place/level of state involvement	Quotes criticism of Swedish Film Institute for sending out *'signals about what one should or shouldn't include in a movie'*	Condemns in paragraph 6 those who complain about the *'nanny state'*; dismisses/patronises them as *'guys'* and implies they have overreacted; *'knickers in a twist'*

Answers to Working Week questions on pages 157–8

1   Read paragraph 1. Analyse **two** ways in which the writer attempts to engage the reader's interest in the opening paragraph.   **2**

Expected answer(s)	Additional guidance
1 mark for each point from the **Additional guidance** column. For full marks there should be comments on two examples. (Marks awarded 1+1.)	Possible answers: • use of real-life example introduces idea of (employers' expectations of) overwork • use of real-life example seems immediately convincing/gives authority to writer's points • *'jungle'* image/word choice conveys nature of workplace as intense, threatening, impenetrable, dangerous, etc. • reference to *'interns'* makes reader realise how challenging the workplace is if even unpaid workers are treated this way/face these expectations • reference to sacking of intern who requested a weekend off makes reader realise irrationality/extremity of employers' expectations.

2   Read paragraph 3. By referring to both word choice and sentence structure, analyse how the writer conveys the nature of modern working life.   **4**

Expected answer(s)	Additional guidance
For full marks candidates must deal with both word choice and sentence structure, but not necessarily in equal measure. 2 marks may be awarded for detailed/insightful comment plus quotation/reference. 1 mark for more basic comment plus quotation/reference. 0 marks for quotation/reference alone. (Marks may be awarded 2+2, 2+1+1 or 1+1+1+1.)	Possible answers: Word choice: • *'relic'* suggests something precious but rare • *'precarious'* suggests insecure nature of modern employment • *'norm'* suggests it is taken for granted/expected that staff will work too much • *'denigrated'* suggests criticism/lack of value of any activity outside work • *'dismissed'* suggests complete rejection of any activity outside work • *'mythology'* suggests strength of the idea of (over)work e.g. powerfully underpins the workplace/shapes workplace culture/passed on from worker to worker as an accepted idea. Sentence structure: • parenthesis *'no matter how rewarding'* emphasises/isolates the writer's point about value of what we do outside work • list *'relaxation, hobbies, raising children or reading a book'* emphasises the variety/scale of activities that do not fit into working life • dash *'— something expected and even admired'* allows writer to clarify/expand on companies' attitude to overwork • placing of *'That's how powerful'* at start of final sentence allows writer to emphasise/draw attention to/sum up the point he makes in this paragraph.

3 Read paragraph 4. Explain any two ways in which we now know that we were wrong to think technology would '*liberate us from … the daily slog*'. Use your own words in your answer. **2**

Expected answer(s)	Additional guidance
Candidates must attempt to use their own words. No marks for straight lifts from the passage. 2 marks may be awarded for detailed/insightful comment plus quotation/reference. 1 mark for each point from the **Additional guidance** column. For full marks there should be comments on two examples. 0 marks for quotation/reference alone. (Marks awarded 1+1.)	Possible answers: • it has had the opposite effect (*'actually made things worse'*) • we check our devices too frequently/at unwise or unnecessary moments (*'often before we get out of bed'*) • the rate at which we use technology to work beyond the working day has vastly increased (*'in 2002, fewer than 10% … Today … it is 50%'*).

4 Read paragraph 6. By referring to both tone and sentence structure, analyse how the writer emphasises that '*this frenetic activity*' is not good for workers. **4**

Expected answer(s)	Additional guidance
For full marks candidates must deal with both tone and sentence structure, but not necessarily in equal measure. 2 marks may be awarded for detailed/insightful comment plus quotation/reference. 1 mark for more basic comment plus quotation/reference. 0 marks for quotation/reference alone. (Marks may be awarded 2+2, 2+1+1 or 1+1+1+1.)	Possible answers: Tone: • sarcastic tone of '*As if writing stupid emails all day … a previous age*' emphasises futility of effort workers make • relieved tone of '*Thankfully …*' suggests benefit of change away from frenetic activity. Sentence structure: • placing of '*Thankfully*' at start of sentence emphasises benefit of change away from frenetic activity • list '*long-term stress, anxiety and prolonged inactivity*' stresses number/range/variety of threats to health posed by work • placing of '*killers*' at end of sentence emphasises dramatic nature of threat to health posed by work.

5 Read paragraphs 10 and 11. Explain three ways in which a shorter working week could be beneficial to employers and employees. Use your own words in your answer. **3**

Expected answer(s)	Additional guidance
1 mark for each point from the **Additional guidance** column. Candidates must attempt to use their own words. No marks for straight lifts from the passage. (Marks awarded 1+1+1.)	Possible answers: • no harmful impact on outputs (*'most modern employees are productive for about four hours a day'*) • most of what we do at work is unnecessary (*'the rest is padding'*) • no harmful impact on finances (*'the workday could easily be scaled back without undermining standards of living or prosperity'*) • better for workers' physical health (*'less sick leave'*) • better for workers' mental/emotional health (*'less stress'*) • actually improves outputs (*'jump in productivity'*).

6 Read paragraph 12. By referring to at least two examples, analyse how the writer uses language to convey his argument about '*the conditions of paid employment*'. **4**

Expected answer(s)	Additional guidance
2 marks may be awarded for detailed/insightful comment plus quotation/reference. 1 mark for more basic comment plus quotation/reference. 0 marks for quotation/reference alone. (Marks may be awarded 2+2, 2+1+1 or 1+1+1+1.)	Possible answers: • *'as far as it goes'* suggest a deeper or more complex issue, beyond merely the amount of time spent at work • *'But'* suggests a turning point in writer's argument to introduce a broader or deeper idea • *'numerical'* suggests reductive/simplistic/mechanistic approach to a far more complex problem • *'We need to go'* suggests an (almost moral) obligation to examine the subject with more depth/nuance/insight/etc. • *'conditions'* suggests it is the nature of work itself that matters • *'wretched'* suggests misery, intolerable conditions • *'nightmare'* suggests horrific nature of working life • *'sucked out'* suggests total draining/workers left empty by the nature of their employment • *'chore'* suggests drudgery of working life. **NB** Candidates might deal with *'nightmare'* and *'chore'* as either images or as examples of word choice.

7 Read paragraph 14. Explain what kind of jobs the writer believes would be '*conducive to our ... welfare*'. Use your own words in your answer. **2**

Expected answer(s)	Additional guidance
Candidates must attempt to use their own words. No marks for straight lifts from the passage. 2 marks may be awarded for detailed/insightful comment plus quotation/reference. 1 mark for more basic comment plus quotation/reference. (Marks may be awarded 2 or 1+1.)	Possible answers: • jobs which do not make us feel left out/marginalised ('*intrinsically disenfranchising*') • jobs with a less punishing workload ('*much less work*') • higher quality jobs ('*jobs of a better kind*') • jobs where company structures are more open and collaborative ('*where hierarchies are less authoritarian*') • jobs offering different activities ('*tasks are more varied*') • work that feels worthwhile ('*tasks are ... meaningful*').

8 Read paragraph 15. By referring to at least two examples, analyse how the writer uses language to convey the difficulty of improving working life. **4**

Expected answer(s)	Additional guidance
For full marks there should be comments on at least two examples. 2 marks may be awarded for detailed/insightful comment plus quotation/reference. 1 mark for more basic comment plus quotation/reference. 0 marks for quotation/reference alone. (Marks may be awarded 2+2, 2+1+1 or 1+1+1+1.)	Possible answers: • definitive statement '*Capitalism doesn't have a great track record for creating jobs such as these*' emphasises that improvement in working life is unlikely • use of statistic '*more than a third of British workers*' shows prevalence of unhappiness at work, emphasising size/insurmountable nature of the problem • '*meaningless*' and/or '*morale is that low*' suggests futility of much work • '*it doesn't matter*' makes efforts at improving working life seem insignificant/doomed • list '*gym vouchers, mindfulness programmes and baskets of organic fruit*' suggests range and variety of responses, all of which are unsuccessful • '*even*' suggests extent of disaffection for the most committed employees, implying the situation will be still worse for those less committed • '*something is fundamentally missing*' suggests a lack at the very heart of the workplace/in the very nature of work itself/a problem so deeply ingrained that it will be extremely hard to solve • short/minor sentence '*A life.*' has powerful impact as conclusion to the passage, suggesting how vital it is to change the workplace: a matter of life or death.

9 Look at both passages. Both writers discuss how working life affects employees. Identify three areas on which they agree. You should support the points you make by referring to important ideas in both passages. You may answer this question in continuous prose or in a series of developed bullet points.

5

Expected answer(s)	Additional guidance
Candidates can use bullet points in this final question, or write a number of linked statements. Key areas of agreement are shown in the grid.	The following guidelines should be used: 5 marks — identification of three key areas of agreement with detailed/insightful use of supporting evidence. 4 marks — identification of three key areas of agreement with appropriate use of supporting evidence. 3 marks — identification of three key areas of agreement. 2 marks — identification of two key areas of agreement. 1 mark — identification of one key area of agreement. 0 marks — failure to identify any key areas of agreement and/or misunderstanding of the task. **NB** A candidate who identifies only two key areas of agreement may be awarded up to a maximum of 4 marks, as follows: • 2 marks for identification of two key areas of agreement **plus** **either** • a further mark for appropriate use of supporting evidence to a total of 3 marks **or** • a further 2 marks for detailed/insightful use of supporting evidence to a total of 4 marks. A candidate who identifies only one key area of agreement may be awarded up to a maximum of 2 marks, as follows: • 1 mark for identification of one key area of agreement **plus** a further mark for use of supporting evidence to a total of 2 marks.

	Areas of agreement	Passage 1	Passage 2
1	Work affects mental health	Para 3 refers to workers being 'endlessly stressed'	Para 10 addresses the 'mental wellbeing of workers'
2	It has become common to work too much	Para 3 says 'Overwork has become the norm in many companies'	Para 10 mentions issues of 'work/life balance'
3	Endless/frantic action is now the norm for workers	Para 4 refers to 'frenetic activity' Para 5 says 'Workers today are never 'turned off''	Reference in para 1 to Taylor still acting like a 'hurricane' even when given time off Para 2 Taylor says she 'ran myself ragged'
4	Work has a lasting effect on mental health	Para 6 mentions 'long-term stress, anxiety'	Para 10 addresses the 'mental wellbeing of workers'
5	Work affects relationships	Para 9 mentions work's 'impact on relationships'	Para 11 says Taylor spent 'more time with her son' when given an extra day off work
6	Spending more time at work does not increase productivity/Reducing work time does not harm productivity	Para 10 says 'most modern employees are productive for about four hours a day' Para 10 'the workday could be scaled back without undermining standards of living or prosperity'	Reference in para 4 to Luxembourg being most productive despite a short average working week Para 12 'the office space is quieter and more concentrated, and "water-cooler chats" are briefer'
7	Research backs up the effectiveness of a shorter working week	Reference in para 11 to effects of Swedish nursing home experiment: 'less sick leave, less stress and a jump in productivity'	Reference in para 6 to effects of Swedish nursing home experiment: 'a 10% drop in sick leave and higher job satisfaction'

Chapter 4

The following wording appears in the SQA marking instructions for Critical Reading under the heading 'General marking principles'.

Marking should always be positive. This means that, for each candidate response, marks are accumulated for the demonstration of relevant skills, knowledge and understanding: they are not deducted from a maximum on the basis of errors or omissions.

We use the term '*possible answers include*' to allow for the possible variation in candidate responses. Credit should be given according to the accuracy and relevance of the candidate's answers.

- For questions that ask candidates to '*identify*', candidates must present in brief form/name.
- For questions that ask candidates to '*explain*' or ask '*in what way*', candidates must relate cause and effect and/or make relationships between things clear.
- For questions that ask candidates to '*analyse*', candidates must identify features of language/filmic techniques and discuss their relationship with the ideas of the text as a whole. Features of language might include word choice, imagery, tone, sentence structure, punctuation, sound techniques, versification, and so on. Filmic techniques might include mise en scène, lighting, framing, camera movement and sound, and so on.
- For questions that ask candidates to '*evaluate*', candidates must make a judgement on the effect of the language and/or ideas of the text(s).

Answers to 'Brooklyn Cop' questions on pages 175–6

1 Look at lines 1–9. By referring to **at least two examples**, analyse how the poet's use of language conveys an unsettling impression of the cop. **4**

Expected answer(s)	Additional guidance
2 marks awarded for detailed/insightful comment plus quotation/reference. 1 mark for more basic comment plus quotation/reference. 0 marks for quotation/reference alone. (Marks may be awarded 2+2, 2+1+1 or 1+1+1+1.)	Possible answers include: • simile *'built like a gorilla'* suggests threat — animalistic/huge/vicious/powerful • *'but less timid'* suggests even greater threat posed by cop than supposedly more savage animal • *'fleshed'* and/or *'steak'* suggest violent attitude of treating bodies as mere meat • *'hieroglyphs'* metaphor suggests cop cannot be read/understood • *'thin'* suggests very small division between peace and violence • *'tissue'* suggests extreme fragility/ease of breaking the barrier between peacefulness and violence • *'See you, babe'/'Hiya honey'* suggest shallow or clichéd relationships (perhaps especially with women) • change of simile of gorilla to metaphor suggests total identification with inhuman/animalistic threat.

2 Look at lines 10–13. By referring to **at least two examples**, analyse how the poet uses language to convey the central concern(s). **4**

Expected answer(s)	Additional guidance
2 marks awarded for detailed/insightful comment plus quotation/reference. 1 mark for more basic comment plus quotation/reference. 0 marks for quotation/reference alone. (Marks may be awarded 2+2, 2+1+1 or 1+1+1+1.)	Possible answers include: • repetition of *'should'* suggests human potential for violence • repetition of *'what'* suggests excess of/unquestioning nature of violence • alliteration in *'tissue tear'* draws attention to the possibility of violence breaking out • word choice of *'plunge'* suggests violence can be sudden/extreme/hard to stop • word choice of *'clubbings'* and/or *'gunshots'* refers to possible nature of violence • word choice of *'Whamburger'* suggests violence.

3 Look at lines 14–18. Evaluate the effectiveness of these lines as a conclusion to the poem. You should deal with ideas and/or language.

2

Expected answer(s)	Additional guidance
2 marks awarded for detailed/ insightful comment plus quotation/reference. 1 mark for more basic comment plus quotation/reference. 0 marks for quotation/reference alone. (Marks may be awarded 2 or 1+1.)	Possible answers include: • framing of these stanzas as rhetorical question leaves reader with something to think about • rhetorical questions put the reader in the position first of attacker, then victim • return to gorilla metaphor emphasises the idea of cop as inhuman, which has been used twice already in the poem • impaired grammar/inverted word order of final stanza provokes reader to grapple with and consider the poet's meaning, therefore creating impact • final word *'victims'* ends on the idea of violence, a central concern of the poem • single-word last line narrows poem down to this central concern • single-word last line brings poem to bleak conclusion.

Answers to 'Hotel Room, 12th Floor' questions on pages 180

1 Read lines 1–9. By referring to **at least two examples**, analyse how the poet's use of language creates a sense of menace.

4

Expected answer(s)	Additional guidance
2 marks awarded for detailed/insightful comment plus quotation/reference. 1 mark for more basic comment plus quotation/reference. 0 marks for quotation/reference alone. (Marks may be awarded 2+2, 2+1+1 or 1+1+1+1.)	Possible answers include: • reference to *'helicopter'* suggests being watched/scrutinised/controlled/attacked by more powerful figures • *'insect'* simile is unpleasant/refers to something many people fear or find disgusting • *'damaged'* suggests pain/violence • *'damaged'* makes helicopter as insect seem even more unpleasant/grotesque • *'dentist's drill'* metaphor is unpleasant/refers to something many people fear or avoid • *'jumbo'* makes frightening idea of drill bigger and more menacing • *'But'* creates turning point from light to more menacing darkness • word choice of *'darkness'* creates a sense of menace • word choice of *'uncivilised'* suggests breakdown of order; loss of safety • word choice of *'midnight'* has connotations of fear/threat/evil/etc. • word choice of *'has come in'* suggests uninvited/unwanted menace • word choice of *'foreign'* suggests fear of the unknown/unfamiliar • word choice of *'shot'* implies threat of violence.

2 Read lines 10–18. By referring to **at least two examples**, analyse how the poet uses imagery to convey an atmosphere of violence. **4**

Expected answer(s)	Additional guidance
2 marks awarded for detailed/insightful comment plus quotation/reference. 1 mark for more basic comment plus quotation/ reference. 0 marks for quotation/reference alone. (Marks may be awarded 2+2, 2+1+1 or 1+1+1+1.)	Possible answers include: • metaphor of *'ululating'* stands for sound of emergency sirens, but also suggests noisy excitement/delight found in danger/threat/violence • metaphor of *'warwhoops'* stands for sound of emergency sirens, but also suggests noisy excitement/ delight found in danger/threat/violence • metaphor of *'warwhoops'* implies supposed savagery of New Yorkers • metaphor of *'canyons and gulches'* stands for New York streets but also suggests potential for ambush/attack • extended metaphor of Wild West compares modern city to somewhere unknown/uncivilised/dangerous and stops reader thinking violence belongs in the past.

3 Read lines 19–21. Evaluate the effectiveness of these lines in conveying the poet's message. You should deal with ideas and language. **2**

Expected answer(s)	Additional guidance
2 marks awarded for detailed/ insightful comment plus quotation/reference. 1 mark for more basic comment plus quotation/ reference. 0 marks for quotation/reference alone. (Marks may be awarded 2 or 1+1.)	Possible answers include: • return to extended Wild West metaphor through word choice of *'frontier'* allows poet to suggest we are on the edge of civilisation/on the verge of being uncivilised • assertion that *'the frontier/is never somewhere else'* makes point that we are on the edge of civilisation/ on the verge of being uncivilised • assertion that *'no stockades/can keep the midnight out'* states the nearness/inevitability of violence/ threat • negative word choice of *'never'* and *'no'* emphasise poet's bleak point • placement of *'never'* at end of line emphasises bleakness of poet's point.

4   By referring to this poem and at least one other, discuss how
MacCaig uses imagery to develop his ideas.   **10**

Expected answer(s)	Additional guidance
Candidates can use bullet points in this final question, or write a number of linked statements.	Up to 2 marks can be achieved for identifying elements of commonality as identified in the question i.e. how MacCaig uses symbolism to develop central ideas in his poetry.
	A further 2 marks can be achieved for reference to the text given.
	6 additional marks can be awarded for discussion of similar references to at least one other poem by MacCaig.
	<u>In practice this means:</u>
	identification of commonality (2) e.g. MacCaig uses imagery to explore ideas of threat/menace/ violence (1) and in doing so makes us re-evaluate/consider darker aspects of our own nature (1).
	From the poem: 2 marks for detailed/insightful comment plus quotation/reference; 1 mark for more basic comment plus quotation/reference; 0 marks for quotation alone.
	e.g. the image of the helicopter as a *'damaged insect'* is used to question the apparent value of human technology, innovation, (supposed) civilisation/progress (2).
	From at least one other text: as above for up to 6 marks.
	Possible answers include:
	• In 'Brooklyn Cop', *'gorilla'* suggests the inhumanity of the cop. • In 'Brooklyn Cop', *'hieroglyph'* suggests difficulty of reading/understanding the cop. • In 'Brooklyn Cop', *'thin tissue'* suggests very narrow divide between order and chaos/civility and violence.
	NB The above examples all refer to 'Brooklyn Cop', as this is the second poem explored in detail in this book, but if pupils have studied the other four MacCaig poems on the set text list, they will be aware of, and may answer on, many other examples of imagery from these other poems.

Chapter 5

Answers to the question analysing the pupil's essay
paragraph on page 189

The words in the paragraph that show the pupil is trying to stick to the
chosen task are: *'One effective image is MacCaig's description of …'*

The words in the paragraph that show the pupil is using evidence from the
text are: *'the Empire State Building, that/jumbo dentist's drill'*.